Contested
Lands

Contested Lands

ISRAEL–PALESTINE, KASHMIR, BOSNIA, CYPRUS, AND SRI LANKA

Sumantra Bose

Harvard University Press
Cambridge, Massachusetts
London, England

To my students at the LSE

2000–2006

Copyright © 2007 by the President and Fellows of Harvard College

All rights reserved

Printed in the United States of America

First Harvard University Press paperback edition, 2010

Library of Congress Cataloging-in-Publication Data

Bose, Sumantra, 1968–
Contested lands : Israel-Palestine, Kashmir, Bosnia, Cyprus,
and Sri Lanka / Sumantra Bose.
    p.   cm.
Includes bibliographical references and index.
ISBN 978-0-674-02447-2 (cloth : alk. paper)
ISBN 978-0-674-04645-0 (pbk.)
1. Peace—Case studies.   2. Ethnic conflict—Case studies.
3. Conflict management—Case studies.   I. Title.
JZ5538.B67   2007
303.6′6—dc22   2006049604

Contents

Maps

Introduction

This is a book about some of the most contested places on earth. Israel-Palestine, Kashmir, Bosnia, Cyprus, and Sri Lanka are all sites of very recent or ongoing peace processes. These peace processes form the central theme of this book. I aim to illuminate the nature and complexities of each case and to draw broader lessons about how the cause of peace can be advanced in adverse conditions. Some parts of the world enjoy relative political stability today, anchored in ties of regional integration and cross-border cooperation that spill across national sovereignties and frontiers. The European Union, which has helped to gradually transform much of the war-torn European continent of 1945, is an example. But other regions—the South Asian subcontinent, the western Balkans, the eastern Mediterranean, and the Middle East—remain dominated by bitter divisions and perennial conflict. Are they fated to remain so? Or are better futures possible?

The following chapters show that these conflicts—generically alike but with distinct histories and contexts—are intractable but not insoluble. Yet the challenge of stabilizing these unsettled parts of the world is enormous. Bosnia, Cyprus, Kashmir, Sri Lanka, and Israel-Palestine are zones of protracted, intense conflicts where ethnonational groups have come to see their interests and frequently their very existence in zero-sum terms, as incompatible with those of other groups. When rival states or mobilized ethnonational groups claim sovereign power over the same territory, the most intractable type of political dispute is born. Struggles over sovereignty are notoriously difficult to resolve; of all genres of political disagreement, they are the least amenable to solutions reached through negotiation, bargaining, and compromise. This is because they typically yield positions and claims that are unacceptable to the other side(s) in the conflict. The problem is aggravated by the traumatic effect of ethnonational war, as violence gives rise to deep animosities and nearly unbridgeable divides.

That is the predicament of the societies described in this book. An intuitive solution is partition—the separation of hostile peoples into sovereign, or at least autonomous, territorial units. Indeed, giving antagonistic groups either sovereignty or autonomy over their "own" patch of land is an intrinsic part of crafting solutions to conflicts defined by collision between clashing agendas of "national self-determination." In Israel-Palestine, Kashmir, Bosnia, Cyprus, and Sri Lanka, borders forged by war have become, or will have to become, the basis of peace settlements. But making a fetish of such borders is neither practicable nor desirable. Recognition of those borders is an essential part of the compromise, driven by pragmatism, and not an end in itself. It is extremely important to construct an architecture of peace that enables systematic cooperation *across* the borders drawn in blood.

This is important partly because those borders—the Green Lines of Israel-Palestine and Cyprus, the Line of Control in Kashmir, the Inter-Entity Boundary Line in Bosnia, and the border between northeastern Sri Lanka and the rest of the country—are a focal point of contention, where one or more of the parties to the conflict do not agree with the trajectory or even the very legitimacy of those lines as political boundaries. It is also important because in the early twenty-first century, an era defined by globalization and its subphenomenon, regional integration and cooperation, it is simply impossible for communities to live in hermetic segregation from one another in ethnonational ghettos. Soft frontiers and the gradual development of ties of cross-border cooperation are the longer-term anchor for the stability of peace settlements, a vital part of the safety net that must be assured to minorities caught on the "wrong" side of the line, and the path to building a culture of coexistence in the world's most troubled and turbulent lands. The poet Robert Frost famously wrote that "good fences make good neighbors." But he also wrote:

> Before I built a wall I'd ask to know
> What I was walling in or walling out,
> And to whom I was like to give offense.
> Something there is that doesn't love a wall,
> That wants it down.

This book shows that the difficult transition from a state of war to durable peace requires third-party engagement, which may take a variety of forms ranging from low-key facilitation to direct intervention. Without some kind of third-party engagement the bitterness and distrust between the parties in conflict will combine with the vested interests of spoilers hostile to settlement to overwhelm prospects of peace. The identity of the third party (or parties) varies across the cases in this book, from Norway in Sri Lanka to the United Nations in Cyprus and the United States in the Israeli-Palestinian conflict, as does the nature of the third party's role. Yet a strong case emerges for the deployment of American leverage or influence from examples such as Bosnia (where the late-1995 peace agreement that terminated the war was engineered by purposeful American diplomatic intervention backed up by military power), Israel-Palestine, and even Kashmir. To be effective in enabling peace, however, American engagement must be evenhanded between the parties and not biased toward the perceptions, interests, and priorities of one of the belligerents. U.S. policy failed to meet this standard in the Israeli-Palestinian peace process of 1993–2000 and contributed in no small measure to the process's failure.

This book also raises questions about the widely presumed efficacy of "incrementalism"—a strategy of step-by-step progress toward a final settlement that emphasizes gradual "confidence building" between the parties in conflict through a phased, sequenced process that tackles the relatively minor and less-contentious issues first. I do not dismiss incrementalism outright. There is logic to an incremental approach in dealing with protracted and complex disputes, the aim being to steadily de-escalate confrontation and pave the way to a substantive settlement. But incrementalism can go awry, and sometimes haywire, if the gradualist and piecemeal approach leads to the prolongation of a peace process without substantial, tangible progress and becomes a means of postponing direct engagement with the crucial issues of the conflict. The Israeli-Palestinian peace process fell into this trap, and the incremental process currently under way between India and Pakistan is unlikely to produce a resolution to the Kashmir conflict. While it is infeasible that permanent solutions will emerge overnight, momentum is vital to peace processes. A process that drags on at a snail's pace can be a recipe for failure, and the cost of failure may be a disastrous relapse into armed conflict. Time is not necessarily on the side of peace and its supporters. Wasted time, squandered momentum, and a lack of resolve to tackle the core issues of the conflict head-on can provide the enemies of negotiation and peace with a golden opportunity. This is the emerging scenario that threatens Sri Lanka's peace process, which looked very promising in 2002–2003. In at least some situations, embarking on a relatively fast track to a comprehensive settlement, with the understanding that the logistics of *implementation* will of necessity be phased over a period of time, is a worthwhile alternative to the perils of incrementalism. The fast-track strategy ended the Bosnian war in late 1995 and was abortively attempted in Cyprus in 2003–2004.

This book is global in its geographic range, which enables a comparison of conflicts and peace processes and the drawing of broad, comparative lessons for making peace. The key lessons—regarding both the *substance* of viable settlements and the *process* of getting to such settlements—are presented in the conclusion. I believe, however, that it is not possible to develop sound general lessons about how to—and how not to—make peace without a deep and nuanced knowledge of individual conflicts in all their complexity. So the following chapters delve deeply into the history of each dispute and provide a sense of how conflict plays out on the ground, at the local level—and what stakes ride on a peace process for people caught up for years in a vortex of violence. This book will transport the reader to the heartlands of ethnonational war— the Tamil Tigers' strongholds in northern Sri Lanka, the Line of Control in Kashmir, the divided cities of Nicosia in Cyprus and Mostar in Bosnia, to contested Jerusalem and the turbulent Gaza Strip.

The meaning of deep antagonism and the urgency of peace can be appreciated only through such journeys to the locales that refract the broader conflict in an intense microcosm. What happens in these locales has decisive consequences for peace, stability, and prosperity across vast swaths of the world. Each of the disputes and peace processes discussed in this book has ramifications for the near and long-term future of entire world regions, including the major flashpoints of regional conflict in the early twenty-first century in the Middle East and South Asia. The stakes could hardly be higher.

ONE

Sri Lanka

I met Maran in September 2004 in Kilinochchi, a small town in northern Sri Lanka that has since the late 1990s housed the administrative and political headquarters of the Liberation Tigers of Tamil Eelam (LTTE). The LTTE, one of the most fearsome and formidable insurgent movements of recent decades, has since its founding as a small radical group in 1976 been waging a protracted war for "Tamil Eelam," a sovereign Tamil state covering Tamil-populated areas of northern and eastern Sri Lanka. It has an estimated twenty thousand fighters and runs its own administration, police service, judicial system, and other protogovernmental institutions in substantial parts of the north and east that are under its military control. Maran was one of a number of appointments arranged for me with officials of the LTTE, often referred to as simply the Tamil Tigers. He had a corporate-sounding title—managing director of the LTTE's planning and development secretariat, established by the organization to oversee reconstruction in the conflict zones of the north and east following a cease-fire in February 2002 in Sri Lanka's two-decade civil war.

Maran turned out to be a stocky man in his late twenties with piercing eyes and an alert demeanor. As I introduced myself, a look of recognition passed over his face. He then rose from behind his computer and pulled a thick, heavy volume from the book-lined shelves in his office. "I know who you are," he exclaimed. The book was a recently published volume on negotiating and implementing durable settlements to protracted civil wars to which I had contributed a chapter.

Maran spoke elegant idiomatic English and read sophisticated social science literature, yet I discovered during our meeting that he had no formal education beyond high school. He was from Jaffna, the main Tamil city in Sri Lanka, located on the northern tip of the island country on a peninsula of the same name. Born in 1976, the year the LTTE was formed, he belongs to a generation of Tamils whose lives have been determined by civil war with the country's Sinhalese ethnic majority and the armed struggle for an independent nation-state. "I was keen to join the movement from childhood," he told me, "but I waited until I finished high school." He then joined the movement's military forces and was among the thousands of young foot soldiers who in late 1995 unsuccessfully resisted a massive government military offensive to retake the Jaffna Peninsula, which the Tigers had controlled and administered as a de facto separate state since 1990. He was injured in combat, and after the defeat he withdrew with thousands of other LTTE fighters to bases on the mainland of the northern province, south of the lost Jaffna Peninsula. In August 1996 he "played a role" in a major Tiger operation that overwhelmed and eliminated a large, strategic government military garrison in a small town called Mullaithivu, located on the northern mainland's eastern coast. About twelve hundred government soldiers were killed by the Tigers in this attack, but Maran, whose soft-spoken modesty was typical of hard-core Tigers, did not mention this. I came away from the interview feeling that I had met a person of exceptional intelligence and ability.

Three months after this meeting, a calamity of nature, the Asian tsunami, struck Sri Lanka. Almost two-thirds of the island's coast-

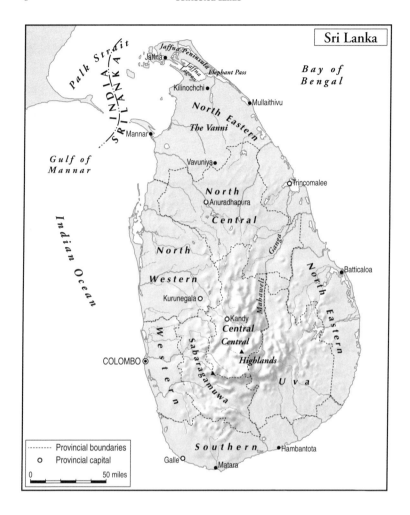

line was devastated, in a vast arc from the Jaffna Peninsula's eastern edges—an area that gave rise to the Tiger movement—to the
heartlands of the ethnic majority's Sinhalese-Buddhist nationalism in the deep south and southwest of the country. At least thirty-
five thousand people perished—among them Sinhalese, Tamils, and
Muslims, Sri Lanka's third-largest ethnic community.

A week after the tragedy, the *Washington Post* reported from "one
of the hardest-hit areas . . . Mullaithivu, once a picturesque fishing

village by rice paddies and thick jungle 175 miles north-east of Colombo, the capital, and an hour's drive from Kilinochchi." The report noted the remarkable efficiency of the rescue and relief effort
launched by the Tigers—"outperforming government operations
in the south"—in Mullaithivu, where the coastline has been under
total LTTE control ever since that successful operation in August
1996 and where the main bases of their naval wing, the Sea Tigers,
are housed. The report mentioned the antecedents and reputation
of the Tigers: "Known for suicide bombers and fanatical teenage
fighters trained to swallow cyanide in the face of capture, the Tigers are regarded as one of the world's most formidable guerrilla
armies, equipped with long-range artillery, surface-to-air missiles
and a small navy of gunboats and supply ships." But in the aftermath of the tsunami "the Tigers have also taken the lead in sheltering refugees, establishing an emergency task force including representatives of international aid organizations and of the central
government, which maintains a low-key administrative presence in
the area." The person "directing the overall effort was E. Maran, 28,
a former guerrilla whose forearm bears an ugly scar from a bullet
wound he suffered fighting government forces in 1995 . . . [and]
who speaks flawless English he learned at a Tiger-run academy."
Several months later in April 2005 Maran was still heading post-
tsunami operations in Mullaithivu, which had by then moved into
the rehabilitation, resettlement and reconstruction stage, as chief of
the area's emergency task force.[1]

The *Washington Post* referred to Maran as a "former" guerrilla. But
has he in fact made an irreversible transition from battle-scarred
warrior to benign aid worker? The answer to that question depends on the fate of Sri Lanka's fragile and troubled peace process.
By mid-2006 the cease-fire agreement of 2002 had virtually unraveled amid a rising spate of killings by both sides in a low-intensity
"dirty war" of attrition, and the peace process, which in 2002–2003

promised to lead to a negotiated settlement to the civil war, had become virtually defunct. Instead of a permanent peace, a formal breakdown of the cease-fire and the resumption of large-scale hostilities loomed.

Between November 1982, when the first LTTE militant fell in combat, and February 2002, when the cease-fire agreement between the GOSL (Government of Sri Lanka) and the LTTE led to a suspension of the armed conflict, the Tigers lost 17,780 members killed in action. Thousands of these fallen fighters are interred in mass cemeteries throughout northern and eastern Sri Lanka. The largest "martyrs' graveyards" contain the remains of between two and three thousand dead and are a place of pilgrimage for many Sri Lankan Tamils. Although a large majority of the LTTE's cadres and war dead are Hindus and a large minority are Christians—consistent with Tamil society's religious composition—most of the Hindu "martyrs" have been buried in these cemeteries alongside their Christian, mainly Roman Catholic, compatriots in accordance with a decision made by the movement's leadership, instead of being cremated in accordance with Hindu religious custom.

According to figures compiled by Robert Pape, an American political scientist, 315 politically motivated suicide attacks were perpetrated by insurgent groups worldwide between 1980 and 2003. Of these, the single largest number attributable to any one organization—76 attacks, or 24 percent—were the handiwork of Sri Lanka's Tamil Tigers (the Palestinian Islamic Resistance Movement, Hamas, was in second place with 54 attacks).[2] Indeed, of the 17,780 combatants who died fighting for the LTTE, 265 were members of the "Black Tigers," the movement's specialized suicide-warfare unit, responsible for executing the 76 suicide attacks. The Black Tigers are honored in the LTTE pantheon as the ultimate warriors and as the cream of its legions of martyrs. The Tigers have not only been the most prolific practitioners of suicidal warfare in the contemporary world. They have also practiced suicidal warfare in novel forms—for example, by blowing up government naval vessels at sea by ramming them with explosives-laden craft manned by "Sea Black Tigers." Black Tigers have also attacked many different kinds of targets, including government military camps in the war zones of the north and east (often as a precursor to "human wave" assaults by hundreds of massed fighters); top government leaders (including two serving presidents and a serving defense minister) in the capital, Colombo, which is located on the country's southwest coast; and both military and economic targets in the capital, such as the Sri Lankan military's command-and-control center, the country's Central Bank, and its only international airport, which is situated immediately north of Colombo. In April 2006 a pregnant woman strapped with explosives infiltrated the Sri Lankan army's headquarters in Colombo and blew herself up in front of the army commander's car. The general was critically wounded but survived, while eight soldiers escorting him were killed. Both men and women—young women make up a large proportion of the LTTE's fighting forces—have conducted Black Tiger attacks.

The first, especially legendary Black Tiger was a young Jaffna Tamil who went by the nom de guerre "Captain Miller." In July 1987 Captain Miller drove a truck bomb into a school building on the northern peninsula that was occupied by the Sri Lankan military—which is overwhelmingly composed of members of the country's Sinhalese-Buddhist majority—killing at least forty soldiers. A statue of the trailblazing Black Tiger marks the site of the blast, and his martyrdom is commemorated annually by local people on its anniversary, 5 July, which is also observed by the LTTE as a day of remembrance for all Black Tiger martyrs. Maran was just eleven when Captain Miller became a household name among Sri Lankan Tamils and a byword for heroism and sacrifice. No wonder the schoolboy made joining "the movement" (*iyakkam* in Tamil) his goal. Indeed, it could be that Maran is himself a Black Tiger, which is an all-volunteer force carefully selected from among those

LTTE members who show the greatest motivation and resolve.[3] The membership of this elite is among the movement's most protected secrets. In the event of the failure of Sri Lanka's peace process and a resumption of large-scale fighting, the poster boy of the Tamil Tigers' tsunami relief program might metamorphose into a different kind of hero.

How did a movement like the Tigers arise and gain such following in Sri Lanka—an island labeled "Serendip" by Arab traders impressed by its aura of tranquility a millennium ago—and among a community, the Sri Lankan Tamils, known until a quarter century ago for pronounced materialistic and bourgeois traits rather than a cult of militancy and martyrdom? And why did such a movement—hundreds of whose fighters have, when faced with capture, died by biting into the potassium cyanide capsules they wear around their necks, and which has the most extreme record of recruiting child soldiers of any conflict outside Africa—climb down from its maximalist stance on "national self-determination" and seek a compromise solution, a rapprochement, with the Sri Lankan state as well as with the international community?[4]

The Making of War

Democracy is conventionally understood as majority rule. Sri Lanka, a British colony from 1796 to 1948, inherited a classically majoritarian political system fashioned on the "Westminster" model. In the first years after independence Sri Lanka, known until 1972 as Ceylon, was considered among the most promising candidates for stable statehood and democratic development of the "new states" emerging from decolonization across Asia and Africa.[5] In contrast to the mainland of the subcontinent, which had been partitioned into two new states, India and Pakistan, in 1947 amidst massive violence, the transfer of power was peaceful and orderly in Sri Lanka.[6] The teardrop-shaped island on the southern tip of the subcontinent also had better standards of socioeconomic development compared to the mainland's mass poverty and chronic underdevelopment. Few, if any, could have predicted Sri Lanka's subsequent fate when it joined the community of states. That fate is a lesson in the consequences of the *concept* of democracy as majority rule—where majorities and minorities are understood to be fluid and shifting—becoming deformed in *practice* to denote the entrenched supremacy of an ethnic, linguistic, and religious majority.

According to the national census of 1981, just before the descent into civil war, ethnic Sinhalese constituted 74 percent of Sri Lanka's total population (which in 2006 is about twenty million). More than 90 percent of Sinhalese are Buddhist, the remainder are Christian. The second-largest community, Sri Lankan Tamils, made up only 13 percent of the population. However, this relatively small minority has a strong territorial concentration. In 1981, 73 percent of all Sri Lankan Tamils lived in the north or east of the country. In the northern province Tamils had an overwhelming 94 percent majority, while in the more multiethnic eastern province they were a 44 percent plurality of the population. In the north and east taken together, Tamils made up 70 percent of the population. These Tamils are approximately 80 percent Hindu in religious faith and 20 percent Christian, mostly Roman Catholics. The northern and eastern Tamils, who have origins in southern India (home to a large Tamil population) but have lived in Sri Lanka for at least a millennium, are distinct from a smaller ethnic Tamil population concentrated in hilly south-central Sri Lanka, who were brought from India by the British during the nineteenth century to work on Ceylon's tea plantations. The term *Tamil* is used in this chapter to denote the more ancient and "indigenous" Sri Lankan Tamils, who live mostly in the north and east and also have a sizable community in Colombo, the national capital.

The cultural differences between the Sinhalese and Tamil communities, while significant, are not as great as often assumed. According to Harvard anthropologist Stanley Tambiah, who is a Tamil from Sri Lanka, "although the major identity components of the Sinhalese are their Sinhalese language and Buddhist religion and of the Tamils their Tamil language and Hindu religion, these populations share many parallel features of traditional caste, kinship, popular religious cults, and customs."[7] And according to Princeton anthropologist Gananath Obeyesekere, who is Sinhalese, although "the first colonizers of Sri Lanka were probably north Indians . . . even the first [Sinhalese] king and his followers married women from south India . . . Thereafter the patterns of royal marriage and mass immigration were wholly from south India, initially from the Tamil country and later, since the thirteenth century, from Kerala."[8] These hybrid origins and cultural similarities notwithstanding, the first British colonial secretary of Ceylon, Hugh Cleghorn, wrote in 1799 that "two different nations, from a very ancient period, have divided between them the possession of the island. First the Cingalese, inhabiting the country in its southern and western parts . . . and secondly the Malabars [Tamils] who possess the northern and eastern districts. These two nations differ entirely in their religion, language and manners."[9]

On their departure 149 years later, the British bequeathed a system of government modeled on their own to one of their least troublesome colonies, which in contrast to India had not produced any popular nationalist movement against colonial rule. The independent country's first constitution, which remained in effect until 1972—when it was replaced by an openly Sinhalese-supremacist constitution that renamed Ceylon as Sri Lanka and declared a republic—was handed down by a commission chaired by a British peer, Lord Soulbury (again in contrast to India, where Indian elites wrote their own constitution between 1947 and 1950). The "Soulbury Constitution" created a parliamentary democracy within a highly centralized state structure, in which statutory, legislative, and fiscal powers would be concentrated in the institutions of the central government. The key institution, consistent with the Westminster model, was the national parliament, to which the prime minister and his or her cabinet would be accountable. In the parliament elected in 1947, just prior to the British withdrawal, Sinhalese held 58 of the 95 seats, Sri Lankan Tamils 15, plantation Tamils 14, and Muslims (who speak Tamil or Sinhalese depending on their location in the country) 8. There were no checks on this parliament, whether in the form of "robust bicameralism" with an upper chamber in which the communities are more equitably represented, a classic feature of federal-type systems, or the devolution of some powers to lower tiers of government, as in India, which also bears the imprint of the "Westminster" legacy but is a decentralized state consisting of numerous autonomous units with their own legislative, executive, and judicial institutions.

Shortly after independence, in 1948–1949, this Sinhalese-dominated parliament passed legislation that took away rights of citizenship—and in the process franchise—from the Tamil population of the plantation sector, on the grounds that these people were descendants of guest workers who did not belong in Sri Lanka and should be repatriated to India. One result was that from 1952 onward, when the second parliament was elected, Sinhalese accounted for close to 80 percent of the lawmakers.

Buddhist revivalist groups had been active in Sinhalese society since the late nineteenth century. Monks are revered even today by most Sinhalese, who tend to be devout and regard their religion as the basis of their identity. But the ecclesiastical organizations lacked a coherent and cogent political expression. This was largely due to the restricted sphere of politics, dominated by a small Anglicized (and multiethnic) elite under the colonial regime.

The mass-based nationalism conspicuous by its absence in colonial Ceylon was ready to erupt, once the country became a sovereign state and a democracy, from its social base of revivalist Buddhism. It needed a prophet, however. That prophet turned out to be Solomon West Ridgeway Dias Bandaranaike, an Oxford-educated member of the Anglicized elite and a senior leader of the country's largest political party, the United National Party (UNP), Sinhalese-dominated but inclusive of some elite Tamils. Bandaranaike had high political ambitions, which led him to leave the UNP and float his own party, the Sri Lanka Freedom Party (SLFP) in 1951. He cannily spotted a reservoir of untapped political potential in the masses of small-town and rural Sinhalese, not educated in English, who had remained outside of the narrow ambit of politics sanctioned under colonialism. He also realized that the timing was propitious for a bold political move. The third general election was due in 1956, and that year was also the 2,500th anniversary of the establishment of Buddhism on the island. One influential treatise, published in Sinhalese and English in 1953 and "composed to commemorate 2,500 years of the Land, the Race and the Faith" advanced the thesis that "the history of Sri Lanka is the history of the Sinhalese race . . . [and] Buddhism is the golden thread running through the history of the Race and the Land."[10]

The prophet in turn needed a simple, seductive slogan to win over the masses. The slogan he devised was "Sinhalese Only!"—a commitment that an SLFP government would make Sinhalese the sole national and official language of the young state. Ironically Bandaranaike, scion of an Anglicized family, had himself mastered the Sinhalese language only as an adult. The slogan worked brilliantly, aided by enthusiastic endorsements from the high Buddhist clergy and the grassroots activism of hundreds of monks who spread the message to towns and villages across the two-thirds of Sri Lanka predominantly inhabited by Sinhalese-Buddhists. The SLFP won a landslide victory. The "Sinhalese Only" promise was superficially targeted against English-centric elitism, but there was an important and, for Tamils, ominous underlying message. In the early postcolonial period English-educated Tamils, mainly from the Jaffna Peninsula, were somewhat overrepresented in the very large state sector of employment—not just as clerks but also as accountants, doctors, lawyers, and teachers—relative to the Tamil proportion of the population. The "Sinhalese Only" policy signaled not just the symbolic hegemony of the majority's language but the prospect of a drastic shift in job opportunities in favor of Sinhalese speakers at the expense of Tamils. Tamils were now doubly beleaguered as a minority, as a community that had arrived in Sri Lanka only a millennium previously as a result of Tamil "invasions" from south India, and as a group that had allegedly been unduly privileged under the colonial dispensation. An oddly hyphenated nationalism—Sinhalese-Buddhist—was elevated in 1956 from a simmering social movement to the official ideology of the postcolonial Sri Lankan state. Fifty years later, the island is still struggling to emerge from the aftermath.

Tamil politics also changed irrevocably in 1956. In the years before independence the main Tamil party, the All-Ceylon Tamil Congress (ACTC), had demanded that Sinhalese and non-Sinhalese have equal representation ("fifty-fifty") in the legislature of the sovereign state, but it dropped that demand and instead advocated "responsive cooperation" with the Sinhalese-led UNP after independence in 1948. But angered and alarmed by the treatment meted out to the plantation Tamils, a senior ACTC figure quit the party and launched his own party in 1951, the same year that Bandaranaike left the UNP and founded the SLFP. This dissident, Samuel James Velupillai Chelvanayakam, liked to describe himself as a minority four times over: as a Tamil in Ceylon, as a Christian in the Hindu-majority Tamil community, as a Protestant among the predominantly Catholic Tamil Christians, and as an Anglican among the predominantly non-Anglican Tamil Protestants. Chelvanayakam's party was named the Lanka Tamil State Party— the Tamil acronym is ITAK—but it has always been better known as the "Federal Party" (FP) among Tamils and Sinhalese alike. In its founding session in the east-coast port city of Trincomalee, the

Tamil federalists declared "the Tamil people's unchallengeable title
to nationhood, their right to political autonomy and desire for federal union with the Sinhalese."[11] The FP's platform fared poorly in
the 1952 general election, though, when the ACTC retained the
vote of the bulk of the Tamil electorate. Chelvanayakam himself
failed to gain a seat in parliament; he was defeated in his electoral
district on the Jaffna Peninsula by a Tamil standing for the UNP.
But the FP won all but one of the Tamil-dominated constituencies
in the north and east in 1956. From then until his death in 1977,
Chelvanayakam was the undisputed leader of the Tamil community in Sri Lanka and the FP was its hegemonic political representative.

Having achieved his ambition, Bandaranaike decided to mend
fences with the alienated and fearful Tamils and negotiated a pact
with Chelvanayakam in July 1957. The agreement, known as the
"B-C Pact" after the initials of its signatories, proposed moderate
legislative and limited fiscal autonomy for a Tamil-led regional authority in the north and east, and stipulated that Tamil should be
the primary language of administration and courts in the north
and east (the substantial east-coast Muslim population is Tamil-
speaking, so Tamil is the language of the overwhelming majority of
inhabitants in the north and east). Had the agreement been implemented, Sri Lanka would have become a unitary but decentralized
state—with sovereignty vested in the national parliament but political authority devolved to one or more regional tiers of government—much like the United Kingdom's transformation from a
unitary and centralized state after 1997, when Scotland and, to a
lesser degree, Wales were endowed with institutions exercising autonomous powers. Chelvanayakam also extracted a promise from
Bandaranaike that the question of the plantation Tamil population,
whose citizenship and franchise had been revoked by a previous
Sinhalese-led government, would receive sympathetic reconsider-
ation.

The B-C Pact was unilaterally abrogated by Bandaranaike in

April 1958. It fell victim to one of the most enduring dynamics in Sri Lankan politics unleashed after 1956—the phenomenon of *competitive chauvinism* in intra-Sinhalese politics. The UNP, licking the wounds of its election debacle, seized the opportunity to pay Bandaranaike back in his own coin. A top UNP leader, Junius Richard Jayewardene—who was later to be Sri Lanka's premier between 1977 and 1988, during the disastrous slide into civil war—led a "long march" through the country's Sinhalese heartlands to mobilize public opinion against Bandaranaike's alleged capitulation to Tamil demands. The Buddhist ecclesiastical hierarchy was outraged by their protégé's *volte-face*. They sent hundreds of monks to besiege Bandaranaike's official residence in Colombo. The siege was lifted only after he reneged on the agreement. Even then, he was not forgiven by all. A fanatic Buddhist monk assassinated Bandaranaike in 1959 in retribution for the attempted treachery.

The FP's response to the pact's abrogation was a prolonged campaign of civil disobedience, launched throughout the north and east but centered on the Jaffna Peninsula. This was met with repressive police action, and in 1961 the military was dispatched to the peninsula to help the police put down the agitation. FP lawmakers protesting outside parliament in Colombo were attacked by gangs of thugs. The accumulating tensions exploded in May and June 1958 in pogrom-like riots against Tamils, especially those living as a vulnerable minority in predominantly Sinhalese areas of the island.[12] This was the first episode of the gruesome, orchestrated mob violence that would recur and intensify two decades later, in the late 1970s and early 1980s, and play a catalytic role in escalating the conflict to civil war. In 1963 the first book with a title far removed from the Serendip image was published—*Ceylon: A Divided Nation*.[13] There were to be many more such books in the 1980s and 1990s.

The Sinhalese-Buddhist nationalization of the state originated as a revivalist ideology preached to the faithful by itinerant Buddhist monks.[14] It was given political form and articulation by an ambitious politician seeking a fast route to power, and was then reinforced by intraparty competition among the Sinhalese. The majoritarian definition of the identity of the Sri Lankan state after 1956, enforced by the centralization of political power, made Tamils feel like second-class citizens at best and unwelcome intruders at worst. After 1956 Sri Lanka became an "ethnic democracy"—to deploy a term used by Israeli political scientists to describe the character of the State of Israel. This type of state combines democratic institutions and procedures with the systematic, encompassing dominance of one ethnonational community (in both cases the majority, since Jews are almost 80 percent of Israel's population).[15]

Beyond questions of citizenship and equal rights, the ethnicization of the state opened up a deep conflict over a land and the right to that land. Once Sri Lanka was defined as a sacred geographic space giving its Sinhalese-Buddhist citizens privileged status, Tamils responded from 1956 onward with a defensive political construct of their own, by claiming that the north and east of the island constitute a traditional Tamil "homeland" in which Tamils are entitled to regional autonomy, if not sovereignty. Finding themselves at the receiving end of an ethnic-linguistic-religious definition of the concept of democracy as majority rule, Tamils invented their own quasi-sacred geographic space where they happened to constitute a 70 percent majority. The idea that the north and east constitute the inalienable and indivisible Tamil homeland has been the central shibboleth of Tamil politics in Sri Lanka for the past fifty years. What has changed is that while the moderate nationalists of the FP fruitlessly agitated until the end of the 1970s for regional autonomy within a united but decentralized Sri Lanka, the Tamil Tigers upped the ante to sovereignty in the 1980s.

This bitter conflict over the land called Sri Lanka has found a focal point since the late 1950s in the issue of Sinhalese relocating from other parts of the island to live in the north or east. All varieties of Tamil opinion, moderate and radical, have consistently described this as "state-sponsored colonization" of the Tamil homeland with the purpose of altering its demography and undermining Tamil claims to territorial autonomy (or later, to sovereignty). Sinhalese-Buddhist governments have retorted that this is conspiracy theory and that the only purpose has been to give poor Sinhalese farmers and fisherfolk some land and a source of livelihood. While Tamils have typically overstated the extent of "colonization" and have shown a knee-jerk proclivity to describe any and all Sinhalese residing in the north or east as state-sponsored colonists, Tamil claims are not fantasy. There is a clear pattern over several decades of many new Sinhalese settlements being placed in areas of strategic importance in the conflict over the land—for example, in the multiethnic eastern district of Trincomalee, which is contiguous to the overwhelmingly Tamil northern province, and in parts of the north close to the junction with the east. Once the conflict escalated to civil war from 1984 onward, these contested seam zones became the sites of some of the worst violence. Tiger guerrillas began to attack the settlements and settlers at the same time as the fortress-like Sinhalese settlements guarded by military and police emerged as a major element of the government's war strategy.

A UNP prime minister attempted to negotiate a compromise with the Tamils in 1965. The result, another pact with the FP leader Chelvanayakam, amounted to a more limited version of the 1957 autonomy agreement. Additionally, the 1965 pact tried to directly address the growing struggle over land and natural resources in the north and east by stipulating that "land in the two provinces [was] to be granted in the first instance to landless persons [already resident] in the [local] district; secondly to Tamil-speaking persons resident in the northern and eastern provinces [a category that covers the overwhelming majority of the population, including the region's Muslims, who are Tamil-speaking, in addition to the Hindu and Christian Tamils], and thirdly to other citizens of Ceylon, preference given to Tamil residents in the rest of the island."[16]

This agreement, too, was never implemented. It was perma-

nently shelved by the government, which developed cold feet and
jitters in the face of a hostile campaign launched by the opposition SLFP, backed by yet another mobilization of Buddhist monks,
which stoked fears among many UNP members of parliament
about adverse implications for their prospects in the next general election. It was the second time in less than a decade that
Chelvanayakam had been badly let down. The episode fueled distrust and acrimony between the elites of the two communities, and
the first incipient signs of radicalization among younger Tamils
date to its aftermath in the late 1960s.

The sustained dynamic of *intra*ethnic competitive chauvinism
among the Sinhalese, which had the effect of growing *inter*-
ethnic polarization with the Tamils, was driven by the nature of Sri
Lanka's electoral system. Typical of Westminster-style democracies,
Sri Lanka had a "first-past-the-post" electoral system, with lawmakers elected on the basis of a plurality of votes cast in single-
member districts. This type of electoral system tends to magnify
relatively slender pluralities of the national vote into disproportionately large majorities of seats (as in the United Kingdom, for example). For instance, in the 1970 general election an SLFP-led coalition won 115 of 150 parliamentary seats (77 percent) with 49
percent of the popular vote, while the UNP got only 17 seats (12
percent) although it won 38 percent of the vote. In 1977, by contrast, the UNP won 139 of 168 seats (80 percent) on the basis of 51
percent of the vote while the SLFP was reduced to just 8 seats (5
percent) although it secured 30 percent of the vote. This built-in
tendency for the front-runner party to emerge with massive parliamentary majorities also provided an incentive to the two major
Sinhalese parties to try to outbid each other in adopting the most
populist and intransigent positions on Tamil issues. Because of the
territorial concentration of the Tamils in the north and to a lesser
extent in the east, the vast majority of electoral districts, over 80
percent, had a negligible proportion of Tamil voters. Tamils domi-

nated only 11 percent of electoral districts, all in the northern and eastern provinces. This meant that in the rest of Sri Lanka, which contained the vast majority of electoral districts and where national electoral battles were won or lost, Tamil voters were not a factor that needed to be taken into consideration by vote-seeking Sinhalese politicians. To the contrary there existed an incentive to appeal for votes by taking strongly anti-Tamil chauvinist positions.[17]

An unusual exception occurred in the 1965 election, when the UNP failed to gain an outright parliamentary majority and had to depend on outside support extended by fourteen Tamil federalist lawmakers, all elected from the north or east, to form a government; hence the negotiations on autonomy and "colonization" with Chelvanayakam. However, even that pact failed to withstand the pressures of intra-Sinhalese competitive chauvinism. In six parliamentary elections between 1956 and 1977, the year of the last pre-civil-war poll, a great divide was apparent between the north and east—where the Tamil autonomists usually won about three-fourths of the electoral districts, including all or almost all of the Tamil-dominant constituencies—and the "Sinhalese south."

In 1972, almost a quarter century after independence, the "Soulbury constitution" framed by the British was finally replaced by a constitution written by Sri Lankans. The Sri Lankans in question were an SLFP government returned to power in 1970—Sirimavo Bandaranaike, Solomon Bandaranaike's widow, was the prime minister—who along with a motley collection of Sinhalese socialist and communist allies held a commanding 77 percent majority in parliament. These socialists and communists initially had resisted the rise of intolerant majoritarian nationalism but joined the bandwagon during the 1960s. The SLFP-led coalition rammed through a constitution that not only declared Sri Lanka a democratic socialist republic and formally renamed the country (from "Ceylon") but powerfully affirmed the Sinhalese-Buddhist nature of the state that had come to pass since 1956. The "Sinhalese Only" policy was now enshrined in the constitution, and the primacy and central-ity of Buddhism to the country's personality was emphasized. On the floor of the house, the approximately 10 percent of parliamen-tarians who were Tamils elected from the north and east protested this charter of Sinhalese-Buddhist supremacy, which was drawn up and enacted without any consultation with them. Their objections were brushed aside.

Turmoil was not confined to the chamber and corridors of par-liament. During the first half of the 1970s the SLFP-led govern-ment enacted measures intended to drastically reduce the number of Tamil students gaining admission to coveted university programs in medicine and engineering. Since 1956 Tamil representation in most sectors of state employment had fallen substantially, except among doctors and engineers, since high-achieving Jaffna Tamils, in particular, excelled in university programs in these fields. New government policies introduced district-based admission quotas that drastically cut the numbers of Jaffna Tamil students admitted to such programs. The beneficiaries were less-qualified, less-competent Sinhalese students from rural and small-town backgrounds, the SLFP's traditional following. The new policy caused deep disquiet and anger among the substantial educated stratum of Jaffna Tam-ils—the Tamil federalists' core base—and inflamed their youth. In mid-1975 the mayor of the city of Jaffna, an ethnic Tamil SLFP loyalist, was shot dead by a twenty-year-old Tamil. A year later in May 1976 the young gunman, Velupillai Prabhakaran, co-founded the Tamil Tigers organization. In the thirty years since then, Prabhakaran has achieved recognition, even among his numerous enemies, as an exceptionally determined and resilient political and military leader.

By the time of the 1977 general election, the divide between Tamils and Sinhalese had become critical, and radical ideas of na-tional liberation through armed struggle were beginning to take root among Tamil youth. The climate was reflected in the rhetoric used in the manifesto of the Tamil United Liberation Front (TULF), an ominously named amalgam of the autonomist FP and the smaller ACTC party:

> The Tamil United Liberation Front seeks in the general election the mandate of the Tamil Nation to establish an independent, sovereign, secular, socialist state of Tamil Eelam that includes all geographically contiguous areas which have been the traditional homeland of the Tamil-speaking people of the country.[18]

Prior to this, Tamil autonomists had always insisted on their commitment to the unity of Sri Lanka. The belligerent posture was partly a bombastic venting of discontent and partly a ploy to strengthen the TULF's bargaining position with the incoming central government. It worked well with the Tamil electorate. The TULF won all fourteen seats from the northern province and four of the ten in the much more multiethnic eastern province, so that eighteen of the twenty-four electoral districts in the north and east returned TULF candidates. On the thickly populated Jaffna Peninsula, the cultural and political heartland of Sri Lankan Tamils, the TULF won a staggering 79 percent of the popular vote. Nationally, consistent with the healthy democratic pattern of alternation in power of the two main Sinhalese parties, the UNP won a landslide victory, securing 80 percent of parliamentary seats on the basis of 51 percent of the vote.

In 1978 the UNP government enacted three significant constitutional reforms. First, a diluted form of proportional representation was introduced in parliamentary elections to reduce the wide discrepancies between votes and seats produced by the "first-past-the-post" system. Second, a strong executive presidency, modeled on the Gaullist fifth republic in France, was introduced, turning the polity into a semipresidential system. The apparent assumption was that the president would be above the divisiveness and outbidding of legislative politics. Third, Sinhalese and Tamil were given the status of joint national languages and along with English made co-official languages of the state.

This slew of reforms failed to check a severe deterioration of the Sinhalese-Tamil conflict in the late 1970s and early 1980s. The introduction of an electoral system based on proportional representation, while a positive step, had no impact in this critical period because the country's next parliamentary election was not held until 1989, primarily because of the descent into civil war through the 1980s. By the end of the 1980s, Sri Lanka had become one of the bloodiest arenas of ethnic war in the world. In short, the conflict had moved beyond the orbit of normal democratic politics. The president from 1978 to 1988 was the UNP veteran Junius Jayewardene, the same man who had instigated a chauvinist agitation against the Bandaranaike-Chelvanayakam pact on Tamil regional autonomy and language rights in 1958. Jayewardene miserably failed to measure up to the role of evenhanded leader, and indeed during the 1980s became the personification to most Tamils of a state that seemed to extend the "Sinhalese Only" worldview from the sphere of language to all aspects of policy. Recognition of the Tamil language turned out to be a case of too little, too late. The conflict was swiftly moving into a phase where growing numbers of Tamils, especially of the younger generation, no longer saw their goal as constitutional equality of the majority and minority languages; instead they sought security and collective ethnonational rights—self-determination—in a separate state.

The escalation rather than mitigation of ethnic conflict was powered by two interlocking developments occurring outside the framework of institutional politics. First, intercommunity relations were tense and troubled in the wake of the 1977 election, especially given the "mandate" accorded by Tamil voters in the north and east to the TULF's sovereigntist—in Sinhalese eyes blatantly secessionist—platform. Shortly after the election a serious wave of anti-Tamil ethnic rioting swept the Sinhalese-majority areas of the country, the first such outbreak since 1958. This was followed by further outbreaks in 1979 and 1981. Second, by the late 1970s a very small Tamil guerrilla underground had emerged in the north and was carrying out sporadic hit-and-run attacks, mainly against police officers. The appearance of a "terrorist" problem, even if minor, fanned the flames of Sinhalese anger. In July 1979 the government enacted a Prevention of Terrorism Act and sent an army brigadier to Jaffna with a brief to eradicate the terrorists within six months. Not only were the terrorists not neutralized, but the high-handed and often brutal behavior of Sinhalese military personnel in Jaffna deeply offended a population already seething with discontent. As in most ethnonational hegemonic regimes, the Sri Lankan military was then, and remains, overwhelmingly composed of members of the dominant community. In this environment desultory negotiations in the early 1980s between the UNP government and TULF leaders on autonomy formulae went nowhere.

In 1991 I interviewed Kittu, a top LTTE figure who was the Tigers' commander in the Jaffna Peninsula from 1985 to 1987, a crucial period when the Tigers "liberated" most of the peninsula from the government's military and secured their own ascendancy as the leading Tamil insurgent group. Killed in 1993, Kittu is one of the most revered figures in the LTTE's pantheon of martyrs. The LTTE's artillery corps is named after him, and a public park dedicated to his memory sits in the center of Jaffna city. Kittu, a peninsula Tamil of Hindu background, joined the Tigers in 1978 at the age of eighteen. When I asked him why he had done so, he cited the anguish and anger he felt when he worked as a volunteer in refugee camps established in Jaffna for Tamils who fled the south after the 1977 riots. The trauma and destitution of these innocent victims of mob violence affected him deeply, he said. In 2004 I interviewed another member of the Tiger vanguard, Sornam, a top commander who joined the movement in 1982, in his base near the strategic and multiethnic town of Trincomalee on the east coast.[19] Sornam, an east-coast Tamil from a Roman Catholic family of fisherfolk, went, like Kittu, from high school to insurgency. When I posed the same question about the motivation driving his decision, he replied without a moment's hesitation: "Riots."

The radicalizing effect of ethnic pogroms is unmistakable, but until July 1983 the active insurgents numbered in the dozens. After July 1983 the pioneers were joined by quite literally thousands of others who took up arms against the Sinhalese-Buddhist state. The catalyst was a horrific massacre of Tamils in Colombo and else-where in the south after an LTTE ambush on the Jaffna Peninsula killed thirteen government soldiers, all Sinhalese. It has been esti-mated that between 2,000 and 3,000 Tamils were slaughtered in the "Black July" carnage—including 53 young Tamil political detain-ees lynched in the capital's main prison—and about 150,000 made homeless. Some of these refugees migrated to the north in search of relative safety while others fled across the sea to the Tamil province in south India. Numerous eyewitness accounts of the July 1983 atrocities suggest that UNP activists organized and led the killings and the arson of Tamil homes and businesses, and that in many places police and even military personnel joined the rioters. Presi-dent Jayewardene failed to condemn the violence or express sym-pathy to the survivors; instead he blamed Tamils for bringing it upon themselves. The government then proceeded to bar TULF parliamentarians elected in 1977 from participating in parliamen-tary proceedings. Kittu was one of the Tigers in the ambush team on that fateful night in July 1983. He laughed as he recalled how the entire LTTE combat strength at the time—a total of thirty guerrillas—was mobilized for the attack. By 1987 the LTTE's core combat strength had multiplied by a factor of at least a hundred. Tamil insurgency has been transformed from a small-scale hit-and-run affair to a popular insurrection.

If the events of 1956 gave rise to the Sinhalese-Tamil conflict in its contemporary form, 1983 was the second watershed that tipped the conflict into civil war. A British scholar wrote in 1984 that "it is possible to view Tamil political history as a doomed and unconscious acting out of the most paranoid fantasies of the majority community. In the 1950s any suggestion of minor devolution [of power] to the Tamil areas was greeted with the response from Sinhalese chauvinists that this was just the thin end of the separatist wedge. By the 1970s, when twenty years of political frustration had led to popular support for separatism, the same chauvinists were able to claim that they had been right all along."[20]

In a sense Sinhalese-Buddhist nationalism is a success story. The agenda of ethnonational hegemony captured and was realized in the postcolonial state. The ideology of "race and faith" asserted its domination of the land. The collateral casualty was democratic stability, and the cost was one of the most protracted and bloody civil wars of recent decades.

The Forging of Peace

The Tamil Tigers divide the history of their armed struggle for independence into three phases: Eelam War I (1983–1987), Eelam War II (1990–1994) and Eelam War III (1995–2002). In 1987 and 1994, there were abortive attempts to terminate the armed conflict and find a political settlement. Both attempts were fundamentally flawed, and after their failure violence escalated dramatically. The period since February 2002, when a cease-fire came into effect, has seen war-torn Sri Lanka's first serious and substantive peace process. Its ultimate fate remains undecided, however, and in mid-2006 its prospects look bleak. The stakes are high, because a collapsed peace process is more destabilizing than none at all.

The mushrooming of Tamil insurgency in Sri Lanka since 1984 was enabled by India's support to the rebels. India is the region's economic hub and military power, its population and resources dwarf Sri Lanka's, and the coastline of its deep south, an area inhabited by ethnic Tamils, is a couple of hours by a fast boat from Sri Lanka's northern province. From September 1983 India's federal government authorized a clandestine program of training and arming the thousands of angry young men who swelled the ranks of Tamil guerrilla groups. This decision was partly motivated by an aspiring regional hegemon's desire to flex its muscles in its neighborhood, and partly was a response to the outrage expressed by south India's own ethnic Tamil population, who numbered at least fifty million at the time, at the suffering of their cousins in Sri Lanka. The Colombo government in turn sought assistance for its war effort from China, Israel, and Pakistan, all of which were regarded with hostility or suspicion in New Delhi—Pakistan as the archenemy, China as an unfriendly behemoth to the north, and Israel, with whom India did not have diplomatic relations until 1992, as a proxy for United States influence. Indian foreign policy was at the time dominated by progressive Third Worldism with a strong pro-Soviet tilt. The Colombo government's decision to build up its military with the aid of such countries augmented New Delhi's resolve to support the Tamil insurgents. As Mossad advisers reached Colombo to advise on counterterrorism strategy—it was they who urged fortifying militarized Sinhalese settlements in strategic areas and seam zones between ethnic groups—dozens of training camps for Tamil guerrillas sprang up in south India. Tamil insurgent groups openly operated offices in Madras (now known as Chennai), the capital city of India's deep-south Tamil province. A close nexus developed rapidly between Sri Lankan Tamil militants and the Indian military and intelligence community assigned to mentor and equip them.

This Indian policy was the brainchild of then prime minister Indira Gandhi, leader of the ruling Congress Party and daughter of the country's first prime minister, Jawaharlal Nehru. Indira Gandhi had successfully backed a popular revolt and insurgency in east Pakistan in 1971, which led to Pakistan's dismemberment and the birth of Bangladesh. Intensely charismatic and equally autocratic, she held strong ideas of India's natural dominance of the South Asian region. After Indira Gandhi's assassination in late 1984, a sympathy wave swept her son, political novice Rajiv Gandhi, who was anointed as her heir, to power on an electoral landslide. From 1985 onward, Indian policy toward the Sri Lankan conflict, which was becoming more and more brutal, began to undergo a gradual shift. The Tamil insurgents were still afforded sanctuary, staging areas, and material support, but the Indian political leadership and foreign service started to increasingly emphasize the need to stop the spiral of violence and find a political solution. In the mid-1980s many Tamils in northern and eastern Sri Lanka hoped for an Indian military intervention, on the lines of Turkey's in Cyprus in 1974, to save them from the depredations of the Sinhalese armed forces and carve out a de facto Tamil Eelam, like the "Turkish Republic of Northern Cyprus" that resulted from Turkey's 1974 invasion of the eastern Mediterranean island.

But in fact India had no interest in the dismemberment of Sri Lanka and the creation of a separate Tamil state, whether de facto or de jure, on part of the island's territory. The Indian relationship with Tamil insurgents was fundamentally shallow, born of circumstances and strategic perceptions that were open to change. The strategic imperative to dismember the archenemy and regional rival, which had existed in the case of Pakistan in 1971, was absent in the case of a small neighbor like Sri Lanka. In the mid-1980s India was gripped by its own violent secessionist demands, particularly from Sikhs, an ethnoreligious community concentrated in the northern province of Punjab adjoining Pakistan. Indian officials were also disturbed by the penchant for ruthless violence that was increasingly discernible among their Tamil protégés, particularly the LTTE. In response to indiscriminate military violence against

Tamil civilians in the war zones—which led to an exodus of Tamil refugees, not just to India but throughout the world, from Canada to Australia—Tamil insurgents were committing numerous atrocities of their own. In May 1985, for instance, a group of fourteen LTTE commandos driving a hijacked bus stormed Anuradhapura, an ancient city and Buddhist pilgrimage center located a short distance south of the northern war zone. They shot 148 pilgrims and other civilians dead before escaping. When in June 1987 Prime Minister Rajiv Gandhi unequivocally stated that "India wants a settlement across the table that has to be within the constitutional framework of Sri Lanka . . . [and] we will not support the Eelam concept,"[21] the evolution of India's Sri Lanka policy was complete. The categorical statement also betrayed an accumulation of Indian irritation with the recalcitrance shown by Tamil insurgents, especially the LTTE and its leader Prabhakaran, toward a number of Indian-sponsored negotiations and autonomy schemes between 1985 and 1987.

In mid-1987 the Rajiv Gandhi government, buffeted by growing domestic political troubles, decided to engineer a foreign-policy triumph to boost its sagging popularity. Around the same time, President Jayewardene apparently realized that Tamil insurgency could not be defeated militarily, and that the policy of confrontation with India, the regional giant, could not continue indefinitely. The result was a compact called the "India–Sri Lanka Agreement to Establish Peace and Normalcy in Sri Lanka," signed by Gandhi and Jayewardene in Colombo on 29 July 1987. The agreement was drawn up in secret, apparently over just a few weeks, by a small group of Indian and Sri Lankan officials. All Sri Lankan Tamil political factions—ranging from the LTTE, which by 1986 had emerged as the dominant Tamil insurgent organization, to the TULF, the party of marginalized but extant Tamil moderates—were kept in the dark. In late July, Prabhakaran was flown to Delhi and merely informed about the impending signature of the intergovernmental agreement, which had already been finalized. As one critical Indian commentator acidly commented, the Indian prime minister had "presumed to append his signature on behalf of the island's Tamil population" after murky and hasty negotiations from which all Sri Lankan Tamils were completely excluded.[22]

This was indeed a strange peace agreement, concluded without any representation or participation of one of the two parties to the Sri Lankan conflict, the Tamils, and their principal belligerent movement, the LTTE. The problems with the agreement went beyond questions of the lack of process and inclusiveness to matters of substantive content, although undoubtedly the glaring substantive problems stemmed directly from the absence of process. While the agreement temporarily merged the northern and eastern provinces into a single unit of administration—a key Tamil demand—the merger was made subject to a referendum in the eastern province, which the Tamils were likely to lose given their lack of an absolute majority in the east. A North-East Provincial Council was to be set up with legislative autonomy in a few minor subjects and without any fiscal powers. Such crucial subjects as policing and land settlement were entirely excluded from its authority; they were to remain exclusive prerogatives of Colombo. A Colombo-appointed governor, with extensive powers of intervention and control, was to supervise this "glorified local government authority."[23]

The agreement's provisions on security issues—crucial in any civil war or similar violent conflict—were simply bizarre. All Tamil insurgents were required to surrender all of their weapons within 72 hours, while the government's forces were left intact, subject only to a temporary confinement to barracks in the north and east. This clause was flatly rejected by the LTTE leader Prabhakaran. An Indian peacekeeping force, made up of Indian military formations, was to deploy in the north and east to maintain order and ensure the implementation of the agreement. In return, the Jayewardene government agreed to not allow countries considered unfriendly by India to interfere in the Sri Lankan conflict and committed itself to developing the fine natural harbor of Trincomalee, on the island's east coast, in cooperation with India. The Sri Lankan president gloated that "Tamil terrorism is over . . . India is [now] willing to tackle this terrorist problem as an active partner with me . . . Earlier, they were training the terrorists."[24]

The agreement, structurally flawed in process *and* substance, unraveled rapidly. By October 1987 the Indian peacekeeping force was at war with the LTTE in northern and eastern Sri Lanka and within months the Indians came to be regarded as repressive occupiers by most ordinary Tamils. The India-LTTE conflict, which at its peak pitted 105,000 Indian soldiers against about 3,000 Tiger guerrillas, dragged on until the peacekeeping force was extricated from the quagmire in March 1990. In all, 1,155 Indian soldiers and 711 LTTE members died fighting each other, and after the Indian peacekeepers withdrew, the Tigers, strengthened and more popular among their people from their ordeal, quickly seized control of most of the north and east. The agreement also led to massive violence in the Sinhalese-dominated parts of the country. The Indian intervention was deeply unpopular with most Sinhalese, who viewed the presence of tens of thousands of foreign troops on the country's soil as an affront to Sri Lankan sovereignty. This encouraged a group of Sinhalese ultranationalist radicals, the Janatha Vimukthi Peramuna (JVP) or "People's Liberation Front," to launch an armed insurrection to overthrow the UNP government in the south. In 1988–1989 a vicious intra-Sinhalese civil war engulfed most of the country as the government's police and military forces and the JVP's cadres slaughtered each other, and innocents and bystanders, by the thousands. The carnage ended only in early 1990 with the liquidation of almost all of the JVP's leaders and most of its hard-core activists. In June 1990, with the JVP finished and the Indians out of the way, the core conflict flared again with a vengeance after a brief lull, as the Tigers and the government turned on each other. Eelam War II was under way.

Eelam War II ignited in the summer of 1990 with an LTTE massacre of three hundred captured police officers in the eastern province's heavily Tamil Batticaloa district, followed by brutal reprisals against Tamil civilians throughout the east by the army and other security forces. Combat casualties during Eelam War II represented an exponential increase on Eelam War I. This was largely because during this phase of the fighting the Tigers expanded in numerical strength and developed the ability to carry out operations of a semiconventional nature. In the summer of 1991, for example, a failed Tiger offensive against a key government military garrison at Elephant Pass, which connects the Jaffna Peninsula to the mainland across a saltwater lagoon, cost the lives of 564 LTTE fighters—including numerous young women and children—while in November 1993 the Tigers successfully knocked out a nearby garrison, killing over one thousand government soldiers. In the early 1990s the Tigers began to develop their naval wing, the Sea Tigers. The government navy, usually using Israeli-supplied Dvora gunboats, responded by shelling coastal areas held by the Tigers in the north. In the east there was a severe escalation of the tensions and sporadic violence that had been evident since the late 1980s between the Tamils and the large Muslim community—who are ethnolinguistically Tamil but assert a distinct identity and political agenda. During Eelam War II the Tigers perpetrated several mass murders of Muslims on the east coast. In one such incident gunmen entered a mosque in a large Muslim village near the Tamil-dominated town of Batticaloa and slaughtered 166 Muslims who were at Friday prayer.

Two government policies instituted during Eelam War II deepened Tamil hatred of the state. First, the government imposed an economic blockade on the Tiger-controlled Jaffna Peninsula, causing severe hardship to its population. Second, it authorized large-scale aerial bombing of rebel-held zones. Civilians were usually the victims of strafing by U.S.-supplied helicopter gunships and bombing by Israeli-supplied Kfir jets. The Tigers responded with a decapitation campaign against the Sinhalese military and political leadership. In 1991 the Sri Lankan defense minister, a man known for his hawkish views, died when his convoy was wrecked by a huge car bomb in Colombo. In 1992 the commander of the Sri Lankan army was blown up by a land mine while visiting a government-held islet off the Jaffna Peninsula. In 1993 Ranasinghe Premadasa, Jayewardene's successor as president, was assassinated in Colombo by an LTTE suicide bomber who had managed to infiltrate the presidential household as a sleeper agent.

By 1994 Sri Lanka seemed mired in the depths of polarization and despair. At this juncture a peace candidate appeared on the Sinhalese political firmament. She was Chandrika Bandaranaike Kumaratunga, born in 1945 to Solomon Bandaranaike, the prophet of Sinhalese-Buddhist nationalism and architect of the "Sinhalese Only!" campaign, and his wife Sirimavo, who succeeded him as SLFP leader and who as prime minister from 1970 to 1977 led the country to the brink of civil war. Chandrika, as she is known among Sri Lankans, lost both her father and her husband to Sinhalese nationalist assassins. Her father was murdered by a Buddhist monk in 1959 for trying to negotiate compromise with the Tamils; her husband, a popular movie actor of liberal political views who advocated conciliation with the Tamils, was killed by the ultranationalist JVP movement in 1988. A newcomer to politics, Chandrika took over the leadership of the SLFP, the party founded by her father, shortly before the parliamentary election of August 1994. She campaigned energetically in the Sinhalese-majority provinces against the ruling UNP regime's seventeen-year record, since 1977, of grisly and escalating bloodshed both between Sinhalese and Tamils and among the Sinhalese people. She promised to end the civil war and start direct peace talks with the LTTE.

After almost two decades in opposition, the SLFP won a thin parliamentary majority—a result of the proportional-representation electoral system introduced in the late 1970s—under her leadership. As the newly elected prime minister, Chandrika spoke eloquently of rebuilding Sri Lanka as "a country where people can live without fear, a vibrant living democracy of new systems and new institutions." She also spoke of being inspired by "what has been possible in South Africa and between the Israelis and Palestinians."[25] (In 1994 South Africa had just completed its transition from apartheid to multiracial democracy, while the Oslo process in the Middle East seemed to most to be a viable route to forging peace between Israel and the Palestinians.) The LTTE's international secretariat, then based in London, responded that the Tigers would be "very, very willing and pleased to talk to Chandrika and have a negotiated settlement." This position was reiterated by the movement's chief ideologue, Anton Balasingham, and subsequently in a rare public statement issued by its reclusive supreme leader, Velupillai Prabhakaran.

In late 1994 Chandrika Kumaratunga decided to consolidate her personal authority and peace agenda by running for president, the crucial post in the country since its conversion into a semi-presidential polity in the late 1970s. She won a landslide with 62 percent of the popular vote even after the Tigers staged a grave provocation by sending a suicide bomber who assassinated her main opponent, a senior UNP politician who had been deeply involved in organizing the July 1983 pogrom against the Tamils (the dead man was replaced with his widow by the UNP). The result was the first definite sign of deep war-weariness among the Sinhalese public, while the overwhelming majority of Tamils who voted cast their ballots for Chandrika Kumaratunga. In January 1995 the government and the LTTE reached a cease-fire agreement.

It proved to be an ephemeral opening to peace. The war resumed in April 1995 with a seaborne LTTE suicide attack on the government's major naval base on the east coast, near the port of Trincomalee. The government retaliated with land and air attacks on the Tiger-held Jaffna Peninsula. The main casualties were civilians—for example, 120 Tamil men, women, and children sheltering in a church on the Jaffna Peninsula died in a bombing raid by an air force jet. In November 1995, after several failed attempts the government finally succeeded in retaking the peninsula and driving the Tigers out to their strongholds on the northern mainland, parts of which are heavily forested. Several hundred thousand civilians joined the retreating Tigers in the exodus, leaving the peninsula's towns and villages eerily deserted, although at least four hundred thousand gradually returned in the years until 2002. In January 1996 the Tigers devastated Colombo's downtown financial district with a massive suicide truck-bomb attack. The building housing the country's central bank was destroyed in the explosion, which killed 91 people and injured 1,400 others. During 1995–1996, President Kumaratunga metamorphosed from dove to hawk, pledging to wage a "war for peace" to finish the LTTE. Tiger leader Prabhakaran in turn warned that as long as Jaffna continued to be occupied by the Sinhalese military the doors to peace would remain closed.

What went wrong? Unlike the foolish and unsustainable Indian-instigated attempt to terminate the armed conflict and impose a settlement in 1987, the belligerents were now addressing and tentatively interacting directly with one another. This undoubtedly represented progress. However, the disastrous and counterproductive nature of India's third-party intervention in the late 1980s does not detract from the reality that *constructive* third-party involvement is vitally important to prospects of ending civil wars and hammering out durable settlements. In 1994–1995 in Sri Lanka this was the crucial missing link: the absence of a neutral and credible third party, an international actor that could through its involvement help bridge the deep distrust and animosity between the belligerents. (India has desisted from active meddling in Sri Lanka since 1990, and in any case would not be able to play the role of a neutral third party, given its history of involvement in the conflict.)[26] For example, unlike the 2002 cease-fire agreement, which was made possible by Norwegian mediation and has been monitored by a small Scandinavian peacekeeping mission, the 1995 agreement did not have any third party underwriting its observance and implementation. To compound the problem of the vital missing link, neither of the belligerents had reached the point in the mid-1990s where they viewed the conflict as a long-term stalemate in military terms—although both sides probably welcomed and exploited a temporary respite from incessant warfare. The Sri Lankan military hierarchy was not reconciled to the Jaffna Peninsula being controlled and administered by the LTTE, while the LTTE had war aims it was tempted to pursue, especially in the hotly contested east but also on the mainland of the north (an ominous sign, in retrospect, was that the LTTE's supreme leader, Prabhakaran, did not personally sign the 1995 agreement, unlike in 2002). The result was the conflagration called Eelam War III.

In contrast to Eelam War I, Eelam War III ended in February 2002 with a cease-fire agreement negotiated and signed by the belligerents—the "Government of the Democratic Socialist Republic of Sri Lanka (GOSL) and the Liberation Tigers of Tamil Eelam (LTTE)"—on the implicit but clear basis of mutual recognition and equality between "the Parties." Unlike the suspension of hostilities in late July 1987, which coincided with the shotgun Indian attempt to impose a procedurally flawed and substantively unsatisfactory settlement, the February 2002 agreement recognized the cease-fire to be an essential first step in setting the stage for an incremental peace process. Its preamble states that "the overall objec-

tive . . . is to find a negotiated solution to the ongoing ethnic conflict in Sri Lanka . . . [and] bringing an end to hostilities is seen . . .
as a means of establishing a positive atmosphere in which further
steps towards negotiations on a lasting solution can be taken."[27] In
contrast to the abortive attempt to end Eelam War II, the 2002
cease-fire was negotiated with the "facilitation" of an international actor—the foreign ministry of the Royal Norwegian Government—which played a crucial role both behind the scenes and
in shuttle diplomacy between the two sides. Indeed, the cease-fire
agreement came into force once both sides initialed copies and
sent them with a covering letter to the foreign minister of Norway. Unlike the short-lived January 1995 cease-fire, this agreement was signed at the highest levels on both sides—by Ranil
Wickremasinghe, who was the newly elected UNP prime minister
of Sri Lanka, and Velupillai Prabhakaran, the venerated and feared
thalaivar (leader) of the Tamil Tigers.

The agreement is relatively short but clear and comprehensive.
The preamble is followed by four articles, each with a number of
clauses. Article 1 lays down the logistical modalities of the cease-
fire, Article 2 specifies a number of agreed-upon measures to re-
store normalcy in the war zones, and Article 4 sets out the terms of
entry into force, amendments, and termination. Article 3 established the Sri Lanka Monitoring Mission (SLMM), composed of
cease-fire monitors from five Nordic states: Norway, Sweden, Den-
mark, Iceland, and Finland. The SLMM is small—just three dozen
or so monitors plus additional support staff—but it has played an
important although increasingly beleaguered role in dealing with
numerous localized flashpoints and incidents. It has a head office in
Colombo and a liaison office in Kilinochchi, the northern town
that serves as the LTTE's administrative and political headquarters. In addition it has six field offices, three each in the north and
east, excluding only the two northern districts of Kilinochchi and
Mullaithivu, which are under total LTTE control. The SLMM has

worked with committees made up of prominent local citizens in each of the other six districts—Jaffna, Vavuniya, and Mannar in the north and Trincomalee, Batticaloa, and Amparai in the east—all of which are divided by cease-fire lines on the ground into zones of government and LTTE military control. Each district-level cease-fire monitoring committee has five members, two each appointed by the GOSL and the LTTE plus one SLMM representative. The cease-fire agreement concludes with two annexes—one guaranteeing the free movement of nonmilitary goods to and from the LTTE-controlled areas of the north and the east, and the other setting out agreed-upon locations of checkpoints in the seam zones between the respective forces.

The cease-fire has been frayed to the point of breakdown by a growing proliferation of localized and piecemeal violations by both sides, the result of the peace process having been stalled since 2003. That it was reached at all—and that a relapse into full-fledged war has not yet happened as of mid-2006—is due to compulsions and constraints on both sides.

The first factor is military. By 2001 both sides shared a strategic perception that the conflict had arrived at a military stalemate. The road to this common ground of sorts had been incredibly bloody. After the Tigers' ejection from the Jaffna Peninsula in late 1995, their main fighting forces withdrew southward to bases on the mainland of the northern province, an area known as the Vanni. The country's main south–north arterial road, the A-9 highway, cuts through the Vanni on its way to Jaffna. About fifty kilometers of the A-9, a stretch starting just north of Vavuniya, the last government-held town on the northern province's mainland, passed through Tiger territory and was therefore inaccessible, meaning that the forty-thousand-strong government forces on the Jaffna Peninsula could be supplied only by sea, a route vulnerable to Sea Tiger attacks, or by air, a limited and costly mode of transport. In the late 1990s the government launched a series of large-scale offensives to open the A-9 road. The offensives met with ferocious LTTE resistance and ultimately failed—the A-9 is known as the "highway of death" from those years of bitter fighting. During the first half of 2000 the Tigers went on the strategic offensive. Large LTTE formations broke out from the Vanni and overwhelmed a huge government military complex at Elephant Pass, perched on a saltwater lagoon that connects the Jaffna Peninsula with the mainland. They then moved rapidly into the Jaffna Peninsula. At one point in May 2000, advance LTTE units penetrated to within one kilometer of the center of Jaffna city. But thereafter the offensive stalled, as the government forces regained their composure and the Tigers were driven back to peripheral areas of the peninsula. The Tigers retained a military foothold on the peninsula, but their do-or-die initiative to recapture the whole of their heartland failed in 2000.

The second factor is economic. By 2000, after five years of Eelam War III, the Chandrika Kumaratunga government's slogan of "war for peace" had been revealed to be not just militarily but financially bankrupt. The stark reality was that the Tigers could not be defeated militarily and Sri Lanka was burdened year after year with unsustainably high military expenditures in pursuit of an unachievable aim. In July 2001 the message was driven home when a Tiger commando unit mounted a suicide attack in commemoration of the July 1983 massacres on Sri Lanka's only international airport north of Colombo and destroyed almost all of the country's civil air fleet on the ground. The country's image as a war zone had adverse effects on the south's economic potential and tourist revenues. The Tigers' zones of military control, in turn, consisted largely of rural hinterlands and jungle areas. The entire north and east had been decimated by two decades of armed conflict. Most of its infrastructure was destroyed, and most of its Tamil population had been reduced to a wretched subsistence existence. The humanitarian crisis there had become unbearable.

The third factor, which applies to the Tigers alone, was a quest for international respectability. The Tigers like to claim that they are a legitimate national liberation movement born of severe oppression who are fighting for justice and democratic rights for their people. But after two decades of armed struggle the LTTE's international image was that of a fearsome terrorist movement incapable of compromise and capable of atrocious violence. The LTTE was proscribed in the early 1990s in India and in the late 1990s in major Western democracies like the United States and Britain. Virtually its only overseas friends during Eelam War III were the very effective networks of the Sri Lankan Tamil diaspora, scattered throughout the world, which provided an essential lifeline through propaganda, fund-raising, and weapons-procurement activities. The Tiger leadership belatedly realized that international opinion matters and that their isolated and ostracized situation needed to be rectified.

Hence the receptivity of both parties to the efforts of the Norwegians, who became involved from about 1999 just as their shining glory, the Oslo peace process in Israel-Palestine, was falling apart. The breakthrough came in December 2001 when a resurgent UNP, campaigning on a pro-peace platform, narrowly won parliamentary elections. The party's leader, Ranil Wickremasinghe, a youngish politician relatively untainted by the savagery of the 1980s, assumed the office of prime minister at the head of a UNP-led cabinet of ministers. The hard-line Chandrika Kumaratunga, who was partially blinded in one eye during a failed assassination attempt by a woman LTTE suicide bomber during her presidential reelection campaign in December 1999, continued to be president in a very uneasy cohabitation arrangement.

The year following the 2002 cease-fire accord was a period of unprecedented optimism in Sri Lanka. The Tigers opened the A-9 under the terms of the agreement, and LTTE cadres, unarmed and out of combat fatigues, were allowed to enter government-controlled areas of the north and east and set up political offices in its urban centers like Jaffna, Trincomalee, and Batticaloa. In six face-to-face meetings, high-level government and LTTE delegations discussed the framework of a political settlement. In September 2002 the Tiger representatives spoke of a negotiated restructuring of the unitary and centralized state to enable "substantial autonomy" for "northeastern Sri Lanka, the homeland of the Tamils and Muslims," and added that sovereignty would be "the last resort under the principle of self-determination if our demand for regional autonomy and self-government is rejected." In December 2002 they announced that the movement had decided to pursue "internal self-determination" for the Tamil people based on "regional self-government" and "a system of self-rule" for the north and east "within a federal structure." Prabhakaran used his annual address on the LTTE's "Heroes' Day"—27 November, in 2002 the twentieth anniversary of the death of the first LTTE fighter—to publicly endorse this watered-down line. This appeared to seal the movement's strategic shift based on pragmatic calculations of compulsions and constraints—a strategic shift is less than an ideological transformation but more than an expedient tactical repositioning. The head of the government delegation reaffirmed the Tigers' legitimate and equal status in responding that his side viewed all aspects of the peace process as "a partnership between the Government and the LTTE."[28] In November 2002 a major donor conference was held in Oslo to gather aid pledges for postwar reconstruction needs. A donor consortium was established with the United States, the European Union, Japan, and Norway as co-chairs.

Belying these early signs of tangible progress, the peace process remains deadlocked and in suspended animation three years later. The historical patterns of intra-Sinhalese and Sinhalese-Tamil political differences over the past fifty years have proved tenacious and cast a deep shadow over the prospects of Sri Lanka's transition from war to peace.

In 2002 Ranil Wickremasinghe, the UNP prime minister, emerged as the harbinger of peace on the Sinhalese side of the ethnic divide. While he received accolades from the international community for his vision and efforts, the SLFP president Chandrika Kumaratunga was left to sulk on the sidelines, marginalized as a failed warmonger. Meanwhile, the bonhomie between the prime minister's men and the LTTE foundered in April 2003 when the Tigers unilaterally suspended the talks "for the time being" while reiterating their "commitment to seek a negotiated political solution" and lauding the "cordial relationship, frank and open discussions and the able and wise guidance of the facilitators" that had characterized the talks until then.[29] The Tigers cited two reasons for their decision—first, their exclusion from a donor conference in Washington, D.C., that month, and second, the refusal of the Sri Lankan military to vacate "high-security zones" on the Jaffna Peninsula that occupy Tamil residential areas and farmland. Both were dubious justifications. The Tigers could not attend the Washington meeting because they are designated as a "foreign terrorist organization" by the U.S. government, alongside al-Qaeda, Hamas, and the Lebanese Hezbollah. But there was no such problem in the Tigers' attending the third and much bigger aid conference scheduled in Tokyo in June 2003. And although under the terms of the ceasefire agreement the forces of both sides were supposed to vacate school buildings, places of worship, and other public premises, there was an escape clause, excepting those areas either party considered to be of strategic military importance. It was neither surprising nor unjustifiable that the military would refuse to vacate such strategic zones on the peninsula, at least until a substantive settlement was in sight.

In fact the breakdown of talks had deeper causes that are not publicly known. During the second half of 2002 the government and LTTE delegations discussed the establishment of a transitional administration to govern the north and east pending a final settlement. The topic was shelved because the government team wanted any such body to be set up within the framework of Sri Lanka's constitution whereas the Tigers wished it to be an extra-constitutional body, pointing out that the constitution enshrines and enables Sinhalese-Buddhist majoritarian supremacy, which is the source of the conflict. The Tigers did acknowledge, however, that there was a practical problem with an extra-constitutional arrangement—it was more than likely that Sinhalese nationalist groups would appeal to the country's supreme court on grounds of illegality and that the court would agree.[30] In December 2002 the issue was finessed with an announcement that the parties intended to proceed to negotiations on a permanent settlement as soon as possible, avoiding the need for a transitional arrangement.

The lack of agreement on the issue reflects deeper underlying differences in Sinhalese and Tamil views on the nature of a permanent solution to the conflict. To Sinhalese doves, such a solution entails a moderately decentralized state in which some powers are devolved from the center to a Tamil-dominated political authority in the north and east. This was the essence of a proposal for reform published in 1995 by the Chandrika Kumaratunga government, which suggested devolving limited powers to eight autonomous regions comprising a reconfigured state, of which the north and east would be one region.[31] This blueprint is similar to the model of devolution from the center to regions implemented in the United Kingdom in the late 1990s and in Spain in the early 1980s. The author of that proposal, Gamini Lakshman Peiris, a constitutional affairs expert, was then a close Kumaratunga associate who subsequently fell out with her and joined Wickremasinghe. Peiris then headed the government team in the post-2002 ceasefire discussions with the Tigers.

The Tigers have a substantively very different conception of the nature of an adequate and lasting solution. In October 2003, after withdrawing from the talks, they convened a gathering of trusted experts in Ireland that formulated a proposal for an Interim Self-Governing Authority (ISGA) for the north and east. The ISGA proposal, made public on 31 October 2003, suggested sweeping self-rule powers for a transitional government lasting four to five years in the north and east in which the Muslim and Sinhalese minorities living in that region would be represented but the government would be dominated by the LTTE's appointees. The Tigers' ISGA proposal, if implemented, would transform Sri Lanka into a multinational confederation, similar to the Bosnian state created by the 1995 Dayton agreement or the structure for Cyprus proposed by the UN's Annan plan in 2004.

Within days of the Tigers' ISGA proposal the simmering divisions in the Sinhalese polity came to a head as President Kumaratunga precipitated a showdown with Prime Minister Wickremasinghe's government—while he was on an official visit to Washington in early November 2003—by dismissing his defense, interior, and information ministers and temporarily suspending parliament. The ensuing crisis led to a fresh parliamentary election in April 2004. The main contestants in this election were an UNP-led front and a coalition of Kumaratunga's SLFP and the JVP, the ultranationalist and socially populist group with a history of two violent putsches, in 1971 and 1988–1989, against Sri Lanka's democratic system. The reborn JVP has a one-point agenda of undermining the peace process with the Tamils. Its core support base is limited to a single-digit proportion of the electorate, but it is a crucial "swing" factor in Sinhalese politics between the UNP and SLFP, who have roughly equal levels of support. The JVP's rhetoric touches a chord with a substantial cross section of the Sinhalese people, who have been deeply socialized in the majoritarian-supremacist worldview and who feel, at the very least, discomfited by a process that acknowledges the Tamil minority as equals and the Tigers as a legitimate political movement.

The SLFP-JVP alliance won a narrow victory against the UNP-led front. The difference in votes polled by the two coalitions, 4.2 million versus 3.5 million, was largely due to the committed JVP vote of several hundred thousand, the reason for Kumaratunga's tie-up with the chauvinist group. The big gainer was the JVP, which increased its number of parliamentarians to 39 (of a total of 225 seats in parliament) and obtained ministerial portfolios in the government. In the north and east an LTTE-sponsored political front, the Tamil National Alliance (TNA), won an overwhelming victory. The TNA won 22 of the 29 seats from the north and east, and all but 1 of the 23 seats from the region filled by Tamil lawmakers. In the Jaffna Peninsula the TNA polled over 90 percent of the popular vote, surpassing even the TULF's performance in 1977. The TNA's election manifesto spoke of "the Liberation Tigers as the sole and authentic representatives of the Tamil people" and urged that "the Sinhalese nation should accept . . . the ISGA document put forward by the LTTE."[32]

This is a familiar historical pattern on both sides of the ethnic divide. Prospects of Sinhalese-Tamil accommodation are impeded by intra-Sinhalese rivalries and the persistent appeal of majoritarian hegemonism among a substantial section of the Sinhalese people. The Tamils, on the other hand, vote en masse for a self-rule agenda—in 2004 the TNA deliberately adopted the image of a house, the Tamil Federal Party's election symbol in the 1950s and 1960s, as its symbol. The continuities are all the more striking after two decades of civil war.

The stagnation and subsequent crisis of the Sri Lankan peace process is an example of the perils of an incremental strategy of peacebuilding that fails to capitalize on initial momentum and does not move forward toward settlement of the substantive, central issues defining the conflict. An incremental approach is in principle sensible and to some extent inevitable in the aftermath of protracted armed conflict. But foot-dragging and delay can provide a golden opportunity to spoilers—in this case the JVP and like-minded Buddhist clergy—to mobilize and gain support. It cannot and should not be presumed that time is on the side of peace.

International engagement has been instrumental in the origins of Sri Lanka's peace process and is vital to its survival. At the minimum, the internationalization of the peace process—the central and direct role of Norway, and the less direct involvement of the United States, Japan, and the European Union—has made a total breakdown and resumption of full-scale war significantly less likely than it would otherwise be. The continuous Norwegian role, which in Sri Lanka is positively regarded by all except extreme Sinhalese nationalists grouped in the JVP and sections of the Buddhist clergy, has been made possible by the fact that Norway is viewed by the principal parties as more or less neutral and benign, a small "do-gooder" country (although Norwegian involvement is formally described as "facilitation," it goes far beyond the modest extent suggested by that term). Yet this advantage enjoyed by the third party is also its major weakness. When the peace process hits a roadblock or becomes stalled in a logjam, the Norwegians lack the clout to extricate the process and move on, since they are ultimately not taken very seriously by either side. In such a situation a more robust third-party intervention by a more powerful player is necessary and desirable.

After the 26 December 2004 tsunami ravaged almost two-thirds of Sri Lanka's coastline, the establishment of a joint government-LTTE mechanism for rehabilitation and reconstruction became an urgent need because significant stretches of the affected coastline are under LTTE control. Despite its obvious necessity and strong international support, including from the four co-chairs of the donor consortium and organizations such as the World Bank, the issue sparked a heated political debate in Sri Lanka. The JVP and its Buddhist clerical allies took to the streets, protesting that such a mechanism would accord undue legitimacy and recognition to the Tigers and demanding that all international aid be centrally controlled and disbursed by and from Colombo. It took the intervention of the United States to turn the tide against the inveterate enemies of peace. Speaking in Colombo in April 2005, Christina Rocca, assistant secretary of state for South Asia, said: "We hope the government and the LTTE will agree soon to a joint mechanism for tsunami relief, to assure that assistance finds its way to people who need it—wherever they are in Sri Lanka." She added, "Our position on the LTTE has not changed. The United States continues to regard the LTTE as a Foreign Terrorist Organization. [This] will remain in effect until the group renounces terrorism in word and deed. This includes ending the murder of political opponents and the recruitment of children. The LTTE should understand that we would be willing to consider engaging with them once they undertake such a renunciation."[33]

Two months later, in June 2005, an agreement on a "post-tsunami operational management structure" was initialed, separately in Colombo and Kilinochchi, by middle-ranking government and LTTE officials. The JVP complained to Sri Lanka's supreme court that the mechanism is unconstitutional, and in July the court stayed its implementation. Nonetheless, the episode was a lesson in the impact of an unequivocal intervention by a powerful international actor. The conflict in Sri Lanka is not of global importance like the conflict in Israel-Palestine, nor is it a major regional conflict such as that in Kashmir or in Bosnia in the 1990s. But even periodic interventions by a global superpower, especially at critical junctures, can be effective. The joint mechanism idea was rescued, even if temporarily, by the vigorous support from the United States as well as the assent of India, the regional power (the leaders of Sri Lankan governments pay regular visits to New Delhi to inform and consult with Indian leaders, and the Tigers are keen to mend fences with India as well). International influence can be decisive in overcoming domestic obstacles to peace processes, especially those erected by spoiler groups. The JVP quit the government in a huff in June 2005. Chandrika Kumaratunga seemed to regard this as a case of good riddance to bad rubbish. She denounced her erstwhile coalition partner as "extremist" and "racist."[34]

The support of the international community for a joint post-tsunami mechanism was motivated partly by the hope that it would help kick-start the stalled peace process and enable progress toward a substantive settlement. That hope was not realized, but the broad framework of such a settlement is clear. A serious, durable settlement will involve the reconstitution of the Sri Lankan state into a federation of the north and east, as one unit, with the rest of the country. The autonomous government of the north and east will enjoy extensive self-rule powers characteristic of robust federal systems, including jurisdiction over such matters as internal security (policing)—after all, the Tigers have their own army, naval force, and rudimentary air wing, which are not going to disappear—as well as the disposal and use of land.

Federalism, however, is defined as "self-rule *plus* shared rule."[35] To effectively institutionalize shared rule at the common-state level, the Sri Lankan legislature needs to be reconfigured as a strongly bicameral institution where the upper chamber is constituted as a "House of Peoples" (Sinhalese, Tamils, and Muslims). The representation of communities in this chamber need not be exactly equal, but cross-community majorities should be required to change the country's constitution or to enact measures that affect the vital interests of any community. Such a reconfiguration of parliament would help integrate Tamils into common-state institutions in a meaningful and participatory way, which has been denied to them since the 1950s, and also balance out the extensive self-rule enjoyed by the Tamil-majority region. Sri Lanka should probably revert to a parliamentary system, relegating the executive presidency to a largely titular role as part of the restructuring (the abolition of the executive presidency was a popular promise made by Chandrika Kumaratunga when she was first swept to office in 1994).

The main problem for the institutionalization of the self-rule principle in the north and east is the presence of a community of Muslims, who are one-fifth of the region's population (over one-third in the east) and largely reluctant to be subsumed under an LTTE-dominated Tamil autonomous authority. There is a solution: implementing the principle of shared rule at the regional level. This would mean guaranteed representation and an effective voice for Muslims—who already have nonterritorial autonomy in the form of their own schools and religious authorities—in the legislative, executive, and judicial institutions of the north and east. (It is not feasible to detach most Muslim-dominated areas from the self-rule region because the main Muslim concentration occupies a noncontiguous leopard-spot pattern down the east coast, although limited truncations of the east to reduce the number of Sinhalese and Muslims under self-rule authority are possible and could be negotiated.) As for Trincomalee harbor, the prize of the east coast, a formula of shared federal and regional authority is both necessary and negotiable. International support for such a settlement must of course be conditional on the Tamil Tigers continuing and completing their transition from a fearsome insurgent organization to a political party.

The comatose peace process was dealt a body blow in November 2005 when Mahinda Rajapakse, a senior SLFP leader, succeeded Chandrika Kumaratunga as Sri Lanka's president. Rajapakse owed his victory over his UNP rival, the former prime minister Ranil Wickremasinghe, to support from the JVP and a similarly hard-line party formed by some Buddhist monks. In exchange for their support Rajapakse signed a pre-poll agreement with these Sinhalese-

Buddhist extremists repudiating the federal model. Even then he prevailed by only a razor-thin margin in a closely fought election—he polled 4,887,152 votes against 4,706,366 for Wickremasinghe. The dovish Wickremasinghe would have won had the LTTE not called on Tamil voters to abstain. Most Tamil voters heeded the Tigers, and Tamil turnout was negligible in the north and low in the east as well as in Colombo. In the Jaffna district, for example, turnout was just 1 percent of 701,000 eligible voters. A Wickremasinghe win would have recharged the island's peace constituency and opened up another opportunity—after the joint post-tsunami mechanism was scuttled by Sinhalese-Buddhist extremists—to revive the peace process. The Tigers' decision to urge a Tamil boycott, on the shaky reasoning that all Sinhalese politicians and parties are uniformly hostile to Tamils, was their second strategic mistake in the period following the cease-fire, after their equally misjudged decision to suspend talks with Wickremasinghe's government on flimsy grounds in April 2003.

The cost of missing successive opportunities was a severe escalation of violence in the north and east in late 2005 and early 2006. Shadowy groups of gunmen—defectors from the LTTE and members of other small pro-government Tamil paramilitaries—went on a killing spree that targeted both prominent and ordinary civilian supporters of the LTTE. Such elements were supposed to have been removed from the north and east under the cease-fire agreement; instead, the Tigers plausibly argued, they were being given protection and support by parts of the Sri Lankan military apparatus to wage a proxy war on the LTTE. The Tigers stepped up their own campaign of vicious mine and sniper attacks on Sri Lankan army and navy personnel, apart from attacking the military-backed Tamil paramilitaries. Until late 2005 the tit-for-tat killings were concentrated in the east's Batticaloa district, where the LTTE had suffered the defection of its top commander and a group of his die-hard adherents in 2004. But subsequently the dirty war spread to other areas, including Jaffna and Trincomalee, where government soldiers executed Tamil civilians in cold blood. The indefatigable Norwegians organized a crisis meeting of government and LTTE teams in Geneva in February 2006 to salvage the tattered cease-fire. But after a lull of a few weeks the violence resumed in April, and a scheduled second session in Geneva fell through. Particularly ominous were the confrontations and exchanges of fire in the seas off the war zones between the government and LTTE navies. The cease-fire agreement demarcates the front lines between land forces throughout the north and east but is silent about the seas abutting the war zone. Amid spiraling violence, the island was poised on a knife edge in mid-2006.

The dividends of a permanent peace beckon. After the cease-fire agreement, Sri Lanka's growth rate increased fourfold, from 1.4 percent in 2002 to 5.6 percent in 2003. Foreign direct investment and tourist arrivals also rose sharply.[36] Tamils will naturally want to share in post-settlement prosperity, which depends on a common economic space—a compelling reason why a hermetic sealing-off of the Tamil self-rule region from the rest of the country will never be possible. Over the medium term the economic future of a restructured Sri Lankan state lies in its integration into emerging arrangements of cross-border regionalism in the South Asian subcontinent, particularly through cooperation with its giant neighbor, India. Sri Lanka has already benefited from a free-trade agreement with India, and the fruits of a comprehensive economic pact, which was on the horizon when the peace process stalled, would be even more substantial.[37]

But prior to such a redemption of Serendip, Sri Lanka must complete its transformation into a society and polity with which all Sri Lankans can feel a sense of identity and belonging.

· TWO ·

Cyprus

In April 2003 a "revolution" shook Cyprus. The "Green Line," a 220-kilometer de facto border that since 1974 has cut across the eastern Mediterranean island and until 2003 formed an almost impenetrable frontier between the Turkish Cypriot northern third of the country and the Greek Cypriot south, was thrown open by the Turkish Cypriot authorities. By the afternoon of 23 April, 1,000 Turkish Cypriots and 350 Greek Cypriots had crossed the line to the other side at the main crossing point in Nicosia, the Cypriot capital contested between the two communities since 1963 and divided between the two jurisdictions since 1974. By the end of the day, 3,000 Turkish Cypriots and 1,700 Greek Cypriots had made it across the four authorized crossing points strung across the Green Line, as United Nations peacekeeping troops looked on in amazement. This was only the beginning of a torrent of people. By 2 May, 170,000 Cypriots of both communities had made the journey, and a joint demonstration by Greek and Turkish Cypriots against the American invasion of Iraq had taken place in the derelict, overgrown no-man's-land straddling the two sectors of Nicosia known as the buffer zone in UN parlance and as the "dead zone" to locals. One year later UN secretary-general Kofi Annan reported to the

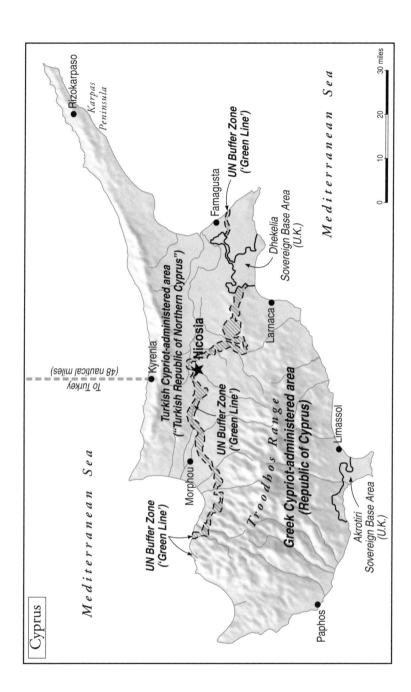

Cyprus

Mediterranean Sea

Rizokarpaso

Karpas Peninsula

To Turkey
(48 nautical miles)

UN Buffer Zone
('Green Line')

Kyrenia

Turkish Cypriot-administered area
("Turkish Republic of Northern Cyprus")

Nicosia

Famagusta

UN Buffer Zone
('Green Line')

Dhekelia
Sovereign Base Area
(U.K.)

Larnaca

Morphou

UN Buffer Zone
('Green Line')

Troodhos Range

Greek Cypriot-administered area
(Republic of Cyprus)

Limassol

Akrotiri
Sovereign Base Area
(U.K.)

Paphos

Mediterranean Sea

Mediterranean Sea

0   10   20   30 miles

Security Council that "as of 1 May 2004 3.7 million crossings by Greek Cypriots to the north and Turkish Cypriots to the south have taken place at the Ledra [Nicosia], Ayios Dometios/Metehan, Pergamos and Strovilia crossing points since 23 April 2003."[1] Cyprus's total population is about 900,000, of whom about three-fourths are Greek Cypriots and one-fifth Turkish Cypriots. The rest are Maronites, Armenians, and other minorities.

The Green Line revolution briefly catapulted Cyprus and its frozen conflict into the international headlines after many years. Exactly one year later, on 24 April 2004, a proposal developed by the UN for "the comprehensive settlement of the Cyprus problem"—popularly known as the Annan Plan after the secretary-general—was submitted to parallel, separate referenda in the Turkish Cypriot north and the Greek Cypriot south. It needed majorities in both jurisdictions to enter into force. This blueprint for a solution, easily the most ambitious and detailed attempt ever made to settle the Cyprus conflict, projected an umbrella "United Cyprus Republic" consisting of two largely self-governing Greek Cypriot and Turkish Cypriot "constituent states," supplemented by a limited central government constituted and operated on the basis of power sharing and equality between the two communities. The UN plan was supported by 65 percent of Turkish Cypriots but rejected by 76 percent of Greek Cypriots.

The outcome went against the grain of much established thinking about the Cyprus imbroglio, in which Turkish Cypriots have been viewed as the group bent on segregation and partition and Greek Cypriots as the group keen on reunification and a shared life. After the failure of the Annan Plan, Cyprus reverted to the *status quo ante* of de facto partition, except that the Green Line remains permeable, a soft border rather than a hard line of separation. Even so, any passage across the Line in Cyprus's divided capital city, Nicosia, conveys the unmistakable sense of an unresolved conflict suspended in limbo—the Greek and Turkish Cypriot police posts a few hundred meters apart, the visible presence of UN soldiers whose headquarters in the Ledra Palace Hotel straddle the Line, the propaganda posters and hoardings displayed by both sides near their respective checkpoints, and above all, the huge Greek national and Greek Cypriot flags and Turkish national and Turkish Cypriot flags that demarcate what Turkish Cypriots call "south Cyprus" from the entity Greek Cypriots refer to as the "pseudo-state" in the north.

The opening of the Green Line and the massive public response renewed hope in the international community and among Cypriot peace activists that a Cyprus settlement might still be feasible, just a month after UN-mediated negotiations between the Cypriot leaderships had ended in deadlock in March 2003. But the challenge of forging peace turned out to be more complex and daunting than anticipated, and a lesson in the limitations of international peacemaking intervention in a society deeply scarred and fissured by more than four decades of ethnonational conflict.

Amidst the gathering euphoria on 23 April 2003, as news spread like wildfire that the Green Line was open and more and more people made their way to the crossing points, a Greek Cypriot anthropologist noted a discordant scene:

> I also saw some Greek Cypriots standing [as if] paralyzed at the Ledra Palace checkpoint. They stood still watching others crossing, with tears flowing down their cheeks. Perhaps it was difficult for them to believe that this was happening. Perhaps they wanted to go too but felt it was not politically right. Perhaps they did not dare to visit their old home in case it was not there [any more]. Maybe they worried about their own reaction if someone else now lived there. Or perhaps they were not ready yet for the encounter between their memories and the current reality.[2]

The surge of people across the Green Line after three decades of rigid separation was partly the result of a very human curiosity among both Greek and Turkish Cypriots to simply see the forbidden space inhabited by the "Other." Forms of interaction mundane in "normal" contexts but novel in early twenty-first-century Cyprus flowered: "Prices were compared in detail, including those for Russian prostitutes [who have flocked to Cyprus since the mid-1990s]. Greek Cypriots marveled at the natural beauty of the [more unspoiled] north; Turkish Cypriots gaped at the flashy shopping malls of the [much wealthier] south. Greek Cypriots rushed to the casinos in the north, Turkish Cypriots to the horse races in the south."[3]

Yet there was a difference. Most Greek Cypriots who took the opportunity to go north went in search of a *past,* a life that had been brutally uprooted by the Turkish invasion of 1974. During the large-scale Turkish military invasion of Cyprus in the summer of 1974—the island is situated fewer than fifty nautical miles south of Turkey—165,000 Greek Cypriots fled and became refugees. In most cases the Greek Cypriots visiting villages and homes, abandoned in 1974, for the first time since the exodus were greeted politely by the Turkish Cypriots living in them, many themselves refugee families from the south (at least forty thousand Turkish Cypriots left their own homes to move north in 1974–1975). Food and drink were served and gifts given to the guests—there were instances of Turkish Cypriots turning over old albums of family photographs left behind by Greek Cypriot families in the haste of flight from advancing Turkish military formations. However, sizable numbers of Greek Cypriots also chose to spare themselves the emotional ordeal of such journeys to a lost past. The most common reason given was that it was an affront to their dignity, at the very least, to have to show passports to Turkish Cypriot police manning the Green Line in order to visit their former home in their own homeland.

The bulk of Turkish Cypriots, by contrast, crossed the Green Line in search of a better *future*. In the first few weeks after the opening, more than twenty-five thousand Turkish Cypriots took the opportunity to lodge applications for "Republic of Cyprus" passports with the Greek Cypriot authorities.[4] Just one week before the Line was opened, on 16 April 2003, the Greek Cypriot leadership signed the treaty of Cyprus's accession to the European Union (EU), culminating a process begun in 1990. This meant that anyone in possession of a passport issued by the Greek Cypriot authorities, who are the internationally recognized government of Cyprus, can live and work anywhere in the EU. In contrast, the Turkish Republic of Northern Cyprus (TRNC) is recognized only by the Republic of Turkey. On 1 May 2004, exactly a week after Greek Cypriots resoundingly rebuffed the Annan Plan, Cyprus was formally admitted as an EU member-state along with nine other countries, an enlargement that increased the number of EU states from fifteen to twenty-five. Because the island remained divided, the application of the *acquis communautaire,* the body of EU legislation and regulations, was suspended by the EU in the north pending a settlement of the ethnonational conflict. This meant that only the 63 percent of the island under Greek Cypriot authority was effectively admitted to the EU, while the Turkish Cypriot statelet covering the other 37 percent remained outside, diplomatically and economically isolated.

Cyprus experienced a political roller-coaster ride in 2003–2004. But the island is no stranger to turbulence. Virtually its entire history as a country since it gained independence from Britain in 1960 is a saga of turmoil and violence.

The Making of War

The opening of the Green Line would have enabled Greek and Turkish Cypriots to visit for the first time the national struggle museum of the other community, although it is unlikely many took the opportunity to do so. The two national struggle museums are located a short walk from each other in the divided city of Nicosia. The Greek Cypriot museum, created shortly after the independence of Cyprus in 1960, memorializes the struggle and sacrifices of the National Organization of Cypriot Fighters (EOKA in the Greek acronym), which fought an insurgency from 1955 to 1959 aimed at driving the British out of Cyprus and then uniting the island with Greece. The Turkish Cypriot museum, created in 1978, commemorates the heroes of the Turkish Resistance Organization (TMT), which was established as an armed "self-defense" organization in early 1958 in response to the EOKA campaign. In the Greek Cypriot museum the British colonizer is presented as the principal enemy, and the Turkish Cypriots are depicted as collaborators of British repression of Greek Cypriot aspirations during the EOKA struggle. In the Turkish Cypriot museum the Greek Cypriot community is foregrounded as the enemy and as a mortal threat to the very existence of Turkish Cypriots on the island after independence, and there are only marginal references to the period of British rule, which lasted from 1878 to 1960. The historical narratives accompanying the exhibits are not just antagonistic but mutually exclusive. In the Greek Cypriot version:

> The island became Greek during the 14th century BC when the Myceneans settled. Since then the monuments, language, customs and traditions of the Cypriot people have all been Greek. None of the foreign rulers could change the national character of the Cypriot people. The Turkish occupation was succeeded by the British one . . .

If the Greek Cypriot history of Cyprus begins in the fourteenth century BC and follows a linear, unbroken trajectory of unvanquished Greekness thereafter, the Turkish Cypriot version begins

almost three millennia later. The first exhibits are drawings depicting the conquest of Cyprus by the Ottoman Turks in 1571. A connection is drawn between the valor of the Ottoman warriors and
the resistance of the TMT to the attempted imposition of majoritarian tyranny on Cyprus four centuries later. The prominently
displayed anthem of the TMT's fighters reads:

> A spark is burning inside the fighter, the flame of Turkishness.
> There is nothing like it on the face of this earth. Cyprus can
> never be Greek. The Turkish fighters will not cease. Either
> Turkish Cyprus will exist or the fighter will not live.

As the Greek Cypriot scholar Yiannis Papadakis has observed,
"In contrast to its Greek Cypriot counterpart the historical narrative of the Turkish Cypriot museum clearly attains closure."[5] This is
the aftermath of the so-called Happy Peace Operation—the Turkish invasion in 1974—which according to the narrative has finally
liberated the Turkish Cypriots from all anxieties and miseries inflicted upon them by the majority community and ushered in an
era of security, dignity, and prosperity. In other words, the Turkish
Cypriot question has been conclusively and permanently solved by
the motherland's intervention, even if belatedly. The Greek Cypriot museum, to the contrary, presents a narrative of unfinished
struggle. According to this account, "After four years of unimaginable heroism and sacrifice [the EOKA revolt] the fight ended
with the unjust London-Zurich agreements," the pact that established the independent state of Cyprus and that not only prohibited *enosis* (union) with Greece—the clarion call of the EOKA rebellion and indeed of Greek Cypriot politics throughout the
twentieth century until 1974—but even denied the Hellenic character of the island, and the demographic fact of a 77 percent Greek
Cypriot majority in 1960, by institutionalizing complex power-
sharing arrangements designed to prevent majoritarian domination.

There are some uncanny similarities in the mutually incompatible nationalist histories and discourses presented by the two museums. The first is the use of photographs of fallen fighters in both museums to spell out the respective acronyms "EOKA" and "TMT." The second is "a complete dehumanization of the other group which is portrayed as . . . kind of monstrous . . . a crude caricature of a remorseless killer."[6]

The fate of Cyprus has been caught up for two centuries in the vortex of the broader Greek–Turkish conflict. In 1821 the Orthodox bishops of Cyprus were executed by the Ottoman regime for alleged complicity in Greece's war of independence from the Ottoman Turks. After 1878, the year the British gained control of Cyprus from the weakened and unraveling Ottoman empire, the problem on Cyprus resurfaced. In 1896 a revolt against Ottoman rule erupted on Crete, another Mediterranean island predominantly inhabited by Greeks, in the final and decisive episode of a series of Greek uprisings on Crete during the nineteenth century. This precipitated an outpouring of "nationalistic and anti-Turkish feeling" among the Greek population of Cyprus. As many as 682 volunteers set off from Cyprus to fight alongside the Cretan insurgents, and most fought in the Greek–Turkish war that broke out in 1897 catalyzed by the fighting on Crete. When the volunteers embarked from Cypriot coastal towns, "the population gathered on the wharves to wish them farewell and the boatmen transported them to the ships free of charge." When they returned, a newspaper published in Limassol, a large town on the southern coast that is Cyprus's second most populous city after Nicosia, reported that "the good lads have returned in high and lively spirits and are ready to have another go." A delegation of Turkish Cypriots met with the British authorities to complain "that the Christian . . . and the common class of the Greek community . . . had adopted a menacing attitude" toward them.[7]

By the end of the nineteenth century the *Megali* Idea (Great

Idea)—which "looks back on the power and glory of the Macedo-
nian and Byzantine empires and envisages the establishment of an
expanded Greek state to include all Greek communities in the eastern Mediterranean"[8]—was firmly implanted in Cyprus. Crete has
been an important reference point for both communities since that
time. In 1898 Crete became an autonomous entity under the protection of the major European powers, and enosis with the motherland, Greece, was achieved in 1913 after the Balkan Wars of
1912–1913. For Greek Cypriots this was the establishment of a
welcome precedent. The "Hellenic" character of the island and the
fact of a Greek majority had determined Crete's status, despite the
presence of a sizable Turkish minority. For Turkish Cypriots this
was a very ominous precedent. Should Cyprus go the way of Crete,
the very existence of Turkish Cypriots would be in peril. The
Turkish population of Crete was halved during the decade and half
of interim autonomy and in the 1920s declined to negligible levels
as Greeks were expelled from the new Turkish state created in
Anatolia and Turks were expelled from Greece on a massive scale.[9]
The nightmare scenario of Crete was used by Turkish Cypriot
leaders like Rauf Denktash, future president of the TRNC, to mobilize their community from the late 1950s onward.

Although the first Turkish Cypriot political party was formed
only in 1942 and the community's level of political organization remained rudimentary until the mid-1950s, there is evidence that
Turkish Cypriots much earlier saw the prospect of enosis as a threat
to their collective survival. In 1930, for example, a Turkish Cypriot
member of Cyprus's legislative council, a body sanctioned by the
British, spoke on the topic:

> We vehemently protest this representation [for enosis] as we
> have always done in the past. We believe that if Cyprus were
> annexed to Greece there would be no chance of life for the
> Moslems in Cyprus. We know that the Greeks are in the ma-

jority in Cyprus, but there are many other countries in the world being administered by foreigners in spite of the majority of the people belonging to another race. There is no principle in international law providing for the annexation of every country to the country which is homogenous to it. I am surprised my honorable Greek colleagues base this claim on international law. It would benefit the island if the question were set aside and all members of the Council united in taking measures to promote the development and progress of the country . . . [Otherwise] the divergent national feelings and sentiments prevailing on the island would make its administration impossible.[10]

In the following year, 1931, pro-enosis riots erupted in Cyprus, leading the British to suspend the limited "representative" institutions until elected municipal councils were cautiously restored during World War II.

The potential for a direct conflict between the British regime and Greek nationalism had been present in Cyprus from the beginning of British rule in 1878, even though Greek Cypriots initially welcomed their liberation from the Ottoman Turkish yoke. In 1881 the *Cyprus Herald,* the island's English-language newspaper, scornfully dismissed Greek Cypriot demands for an elected legislative council: "We do not think that the natives of Cyprus are ripe for an innovation of so extensive a nature." In response to Greek Cypriot demands for greater participation in the island's administration, the paper commented: "When they are educated and Europeanized they can expect posts in Government." According to a Greek Cypriot historian of the period, the British abandonment of "the Ottoman tradition of formal respect for Christian Orthodoxy made them at times outrightly detested. During Good Friday 1885 the epitaph procession through the streets of Limassol was grossly insulted from the balcony of the English club, causing a riot in the town and a wave of anti-British feeling across the island." A week after the fracas the *Cyprus Herald* stoked its embers by asking "the Greek community to remember that they form but a portion of the population, and [that] many of other religious denominations consider what they describe as Christ's funeral as downright buffoonery and rank idolatry."[11]

The tension between British colonial power and Greek nationalist ideas and the aspirations they engendered, latent since the late nineteenth century, simmered throughout the first half of the twentieth century before exploding in armed revolt. In 1954 the government of Greece raised the issue of "self-determination" for Cyprus at the United Nations, triggering much excitement both among Greek Cypriots and nationalists in Greece who considered Cyprus to be an integral part of the motherland. In April 1955 a series of bombings and hit-and-run attacks announced the beginning of EOKA insurgency on the island.

The EOKA oath of allegiance swore recruits to fight "for the liberation of Cyprus from the British yoke."[12] There was no explicit mention of enosis, but this was universally understood among Greek and Turkish Cypriots alike as the ultimate aim of the movement. The group's military leader was George Grivas, born in Cyprus in 1898, who had spent almost his entire adult life in Greece as a professional military officer. A colonel in the Greek army, Grivas was known to hold strongly nationalist convictions and had close links to right-wing political circles in Greece. Grivas assumed the nom de guerre "Dighenis" after a folkloric hero of Greek mythology. EOKA's political leader and spiritual mentor was Archbishop Makarios, the head of the autocephalous Greek Orthodox Church of Cyprus. He had risen to prominence after organizing a plebiscitary exercise in 1950 in which 96 percent of Greek Cypriots supported enosis with Greece. Makarios was to be the dominant figure of Greek Cypriot politics until his death in 1977.

The British response to the outbreak of insurgency was draconian. Nine captured EOKA men were executed by hanging in 1956. Makarios was exiled to the distant Seychelles islands, and numerous abortive attempts were made to capture or eliminate Grivas, who operated from hideouts in the Troodos mountain range that sprawls across south-central Cyprus, where he and his comrades were often sheltered and abetted by the inmates of Orthodox monasteries. In March 1957 an eighteen-year-old youth called Pallikarides was executed after being caught with a firearm—illegal possession of such weapons carried a mandatory death sentence under recently introduced emergency regulations. He was hanged despite pleas for clemency from forty parliamentarians of the Labor Party in Britain and a U.S. congressman.

The brutality of British counterinsurgency did not break the resolve of the EOKA hard core, and had the effect of recruiting more fighters and thousands of active supporters and sympathizers to its powerfully articulated cause. Although EOKA ruthlessly assassinated Greek Cypriots it deemed traitors—communists and collaborators with the British regime were the principal targets—its struggle acquired a halo of heroism among a very substantial section of the Greek Cypriot population, who considered its goal legitimate and the tactics unavoidable given the British reluctance to cede Cyprus. The martyred guerrillas of EOKA were its most potent recruiting and legitimating tool. The inspiring story of Gregoris Afxentiou, a top militant who refused to surrender after being cornered in his bunker near a remote monastery and fought a fierce battle for ten hours with British troops before his lair was blown up by the besiegers, was being told in Cyprus fifteen years after his death, a British writer discovered in 1972. According to local lore the soldiers "found beside his burnt body a copy of Kazantzakis' *Christ Recrucified,* lent to him by the abbot of Makheras [the nearby monastery]."[13] As in Northern Ireland in the 1970s, the British found themselves in a difficult situation in combating the

EOKA insurgency. The insurgent hard core always had fewer than a thousand members, as with the Irish Republican Army (IRA) in later decades. But like the IRA, EOKA's insurgents could count on a far larger popular base. Almost a half century later, all the major Greek Cypriot cities have one of their central avenues named after Grivas-Dighenis.

The British-EOKA war severely aggravated the ethnonational divide in Cyprus. Beleaguered by the EOKA campaign, the British authorities recruited significant numbers of Turkish Cypriots to serve as auxiliaries in the counterinsurgency effort. In July 1958 the regular police force consisted of 462 British personnel, 932 Greek Cypriots, and 891 Turkish Cypriots (a census in 1960 showed that Greek Cypriots comprised 77.1 percent of the island's population and Turkish Cypriots 18.2 percent). An auxiliary force of 1,770 special constables, formed to assist the military and police in counterinsurgency, was made up of 70 Greek Cypriots and 1,700 Turkish Cypriots, while a 542-strong mobile reserve unit was entirely Turkish Cypriot.[14] The Turkish Cypriot auxiliaries were frequently used to do the "dirty work" of torturing Greek Cypriot suspects to extract information, as is demonstrated in this account given in 1972 by a Greek Cypriot in Paphos, a town on the southwestern coast who joined EOKA as a high-school student:

> They brought me in . . . The English colonel was standing . . .
> As I was led past him a dead man was carried out . . . I saw his
> face . . . He was Giorgos Christoforou . . . The colonel said "If
> you don't speak you will be like that by the end of the day" . . .
> The colonel was short and rather fat. He had strange eyes. He
> spoke very good Greek . . . [Then] a Turkish sergeant with
> black gloves bawled at me to put my hands up then hit me
> with his fist. I have seen that man in Paphos since . . . I found
> many of my friends sitting on the concrete, including my
> school-teacher . . . [Next] the sergeant clubbed me on the

back of the head. I fell unconscious . . . The Turkish auxiliaries did the torturing, the British officers cross-examined. I was tied down to a table. They blocked my nostrils and dripped water on a scarf over my mouth . . . When my stomach was full they started to punch it. They did it again and again, day after day. The pain was like nothing I can explain. In the end I was glad when more of my friends were captured. When they were torturing them they had less time to torture me . . . In between a British captain questioned me. The first words he said to me were "Hello, Dracos"—my secret name, meaning Dragon. "Dragon," he said, "I'm going to turn you into a sheep."[15]

By the summer of 1958 the island was plastered with EOKA leaflets warning Greek Cypriots of an "Anglo-Turkish front."

During the first half of 1958 the clandestine Turkish Cypriot armed organization TMT emerged under the slogan "*taksim* [partition] or death." It used the emotionally charged rhetoric of holy war, even though the vast majority of Turkish Cypriots were secularized Muslims, and drew analogies with the 1919–1923 Greek-Turkish war in Anatolia. Apparently the TMT were "convinced that Turkey would send troops to their aid," and their "posters showed the island partitioned beneath the figure of a helmeted Turkish soldier."[16] That sort of partition would have to wait until 1974, but piecemeal partition began to emerge on the ground in the late 1950s. In June 2004, I asked Kutlay Erk, the mayor of Turkish Cypriot northern Nicosia, why the building housing his offices—labeled the "Turkish Municipality of Nicosia"—displayed the founding year 1958 on its façade. He replied that the British authorities facilitated the de facto formation of a separate municipality for two reasons—in response to Turkish Cypriot grievances that they were discriminated against by the Greek Cypriot mayor of the unified city administration, but also as a reward for cooperation against Greek Cypriot nationalists and as an incentive to further cooperation. Indeed, as the EOKA campaign continued, Turkish Cypriot leaders began to press insistently for local communal self-government through the creation of separate ethnic municipalities in the main towns—Nicosia, Famagusta, Limassol, Larnaca, Paphos, and Kyrenia—all of which except Nicosia are coastal towns. Cyprus's multiethnic towns, as well as most of the minority of its several hundred villages that were not entirely monoethnic, already had a pattern of residential segregation—separate districts, neighborhoods, or quarters for the two communities. The Turkish Cypriot demand for the establishment of separate municipal governments in the cities was their first demand for territorially based self-rule.

In the summer of 1958, tensions boiled over and Cyprus was convulsed in an orgy of violence between Greek and Turkish Cypriots. This was sparked by a bomb blast outside the Turkish Cypriot press office in Nicosia, which was later exposed as the work of TMT provocateurs, and rioting erupted as Turkish Cypriots attacked the Greek Cypriot quarter of Nicosia's Venetian old town. On 12 June eight Greek Cypriots were ambushed and killed by Turkish Cypriots in a rural area northwest of Nicosia, and a spiral of vicious tit-for-tat killing ensued. When the violence died down in September, 109 people had been killed—56 Greek Cypriots and 53 Turkish Cypriots—substantial casualties in a population that totaled 573,566 in 1960. The grave "burden of keeping the two communities apart fell to the British troops. Despite the presence of 30,000 troops incidents could not be avoided."[17] This crisis and predicament appeared to hasten and crystallize Britain's resolve to extricate itself from Cyprus. Just two years later in August 1960 Cyprus became an independent state, with the caveat that the British retained two military bases on the island, considered necessary given the geopolitical confrontation with the Soviet Union and its allies and the presence of a sizable communist element among

Greek Cypriots. Today those bases still occupy 99 square miles of the island's total area of 3,572 square miles.

In India in 1947 and Palestine in 1948 the British exit strategy was based on partition. In Sri Lanka in 1948 they bequeathed a Westminster-type model of majoritarian government in a centralized state on their departure, which was taken over by nationalists of the Sinhalese-Buddhist ethnic majority within a decade (see Chapter 1). The structure of government put in place in Cyprus in 1959–1960 was strikingly different, and indeed rather novel for its time.

This may have been because the British had little direct input into the process. In early 1959 the constitutional structure of independent Cyprus emerged from negotiations between the governments of Greece and Turkey held in Zurich in which Swiss experts had an advisory role. The tentative agreement was then sent to London. Once the agreement was approved by the British government, the leaders of the Greek and Turkish Cypriot communities were summoned to London and "presented with a *fait accompli*."[18]

The "London-Zurich agreements" codified in the 1960 Cyprus constitution expressly forbade both enosis and taksim. Instead a complex power-sharing formula was adopted with the following key features:

- A bicameral legislature. A 50-member house of representatives composed of 35 Greek and 15 Turkish Cypriots elected by their respective communities. The president (speaker) of this chamber would be a Greek Cypriot, the vice president a Turkish Cypriot. A simple majority would suffice for most legislation but on matters regarding taxation, municipal governance, and electoral laws separate majorities of both community blocs were required. In addition, a Greek Cypriot communal chamber of 24 members and a Turkish Cypriot communal chamber of 30 members would be elected by the respective communities. These chambers were empowered to legislate on religious, educational, and cultural matters pertaining to their own community.

- The executive arm would consist of a Greek Cypriot president and a Turkish Cypriot vice president, each elected by his or her own community. Either the president or the vice president could veto legislation passed by the house of representatives in the areas of foreign affairs, defense, and internal security, although no such veto right was given for legislation passed in the communal chambers. The cabinet consisted of a ten-member council of ministers, including seven Greek Cypriots and three Turkish Cypriots. A Turkish Cypriot had to hold one of the three major portfolios—defense, foreign affairs, or finance. Council decisions could be made by an overall majority vote but could be vetoed by either the president or the vice president.

- Constitutional issues and disputes were to be decided by a three-person supreme constitutional court. The court's president would be a neutral foreign judge and the two Cypriot communities would have one representative each. The high court of justice would similarly be presided over by a foreign national, who would have two votes, along with two Greek Cypriots and one Turkish Cypriot, who would have one vote each. Each community would also have communal courts, composed of civil and ecclesiastic branches, to deal with issues of personal status and religion.

- The Cyprus civil service would be apportioned among Greek Cypriots and Turkish Cypriots on a 70:30 basis. The police and gendarmerie, with a strength of two thousand, would also be 70 percent Greek Cypriot and 30 percent Turkish Cypriot.

- The army of the new state would have two thousand personnel, 60 percent Greek Cypriot and 40 percent Turkish Cypriot.

- Greek and Turkish would be the co-official languages of the Republic of Cyprus.

Alongside these detailed provisions on the internal governance of Cyprus the constitution incorporated two international treaties. The Treaty of Guarantee made Greece, Turkey, and Britain co-guarantors of the independence, territorial integrity, and security of Cyprus, and Greece and Turkey agreed not to sanction any activity by Cypriots aimed at enosis or taksim. The treaty allowed the guarantor states to act either in concert or unilaterally in Cyprus should this ban be violated. The Treaty of Alliance established a tripartite military command on the island, with command shared by Greece, Turkey, and the new Republic of Cyprus. This joint command would be led in annual rotation by an officer from each of the three states and would be chaired by a committee consisting of the foreign ministers of those states. Under this treaty, contingents of 950 Greek and 650 Turkish military personnel were to be stationed on the island, nominally subordinated to the tripartite command.

Of the 199 articles in the constitution, 48 were classified as "basic articles" that could not be discarded or amended. The rest could be amended subject to a two-thirds majority among both the Greek and the Turkish Cypriot caucuses in the parliament's house of representatives.

The 1960 constitution clearly recognized the binational reality of Cyprus and the need for institutionalized power-sharing and checks and balances between the two communities. The international treaties it incorporated recognized the international dimension of the Cyprus question and the risk of the troubled island becoming the flashpoint of a major regional conflict in the eastern Mediterranean. It therefore sought to build in security guarantees and safeguards against such a contingency. Overall, the Cyprus settlement of 1959–1960 was an attempt at a comprehensive, interlocking solution to the internal, regional, and international dimensions of the problem.

The settlement is remarkable for another reason. It was the first systematic application *in practice* of an approach to structuring government in "divided societies" that would be developed by academic political scientists in the 1970s and 1980s. This approach, most commonly known as "consociational," has four pillars:

1. Government by "grand coalition" between the groups, via their respective elites, at the political center
2. "Segmental autonomy," which can take a variety of forms, territorial or nonterritorial or both
3. "Proportionality" in the allocation of public employment and resources between the groups
4. "Veto" rights, either for the minority (or minorities) or for all groups on any constitutional changes or legislation considered detrimental by any community's representatives to its basic interests

Cyprus's experiment in consociational government far predates its academic elaboration.[19] The only comparable example is Lebanon's National Pact of 1943, which, however, was an unwritten "gentlemen's agreement" between the leaders of that country's Maronite Christian and Sunni Muslim communities. Moreover, since consociationalism emerged in comparative political science in the 1970s its proponents have usually limited themselves to the domestic domain of politics, disregarding the suprastate regional and international dimensions that characterize many of the most polarized and incendiary conflicts. The Cyprus settlement stands out in its attempt to devise a comprehensive, mutually reinforcing solution to *both* levels of conflict, the domestic and the international. In retrospect, it is the first example of accords of similar design concluded in recent years in Bosnia (November–December 1995) and Northern Ireland (April 1998).[20]

For Turkish Cypriots the 1960 constitution was a satisfactory outcome. It proscribed enosis and created a state on the basis of their constitutional equality with the ethnonational majority in which they enjoyed guaranteed rights, representation, and protections generous by any standards, given their 18 percent proportion of the population. Even territorially based self-governance had been conceded to their community in a piecemeal fashion, at the local level in the island's five largest urban centers. Article 173, one of the basic articles of the constitution, stipulated the establishment of separate Greek Cypriot and Turkish Cypriot municipalities in the cities of Nicosia, Famagusta, Limassol, Larnaca, and Paphos, as Turkish Cypriots had been demanding and attempting to create on the ground since 1958. A coordinating mechanism of the two sets of municipal councils, consisting of two members of each council and a "neutral" chair, was to be formed in these cities to enable essential cooperation.[21]

For Greek Cypriots the settlement was a bitter pill for precisely the same reasons. The nature and provisions of the constitution were in their view a denial of the Hellenic character of the island since antiquity *and* a violation of the modern democratic principle of majority rule. It conferred inordinate privileges on an 18 percent minority at the expense of the 77 percent majority. The pill was even harder to swallow in the immediate aftermath of the EOKA-led struggle, which had radicalized Greek Cypriot opinion. That the constitution proscribed taksim, the island's partition, was small consolation. As a prominent Greek Cypriot official put it in the late 1970s, Turkish Cypriots regarded the settlement "as a victory" while "for Greek Cypriots Zurich was a defeat."[22] On his return from London the Greek Cypriot leader Makarios apparently told his close associates that this was "an imposed solution which had to be temporarily accepted."[23]

The state of affairs established by the constitution lasted only three years. Chronic disagreement, growing deadlock, and mounting acrimony between the communities characterized those years. The multiethnic Cypriot army failed to materialize because of disagreement between the president and the vice president. While President Makarios wanted the force to be integrated at all levels, Vice President Fazil Kuchuk argued for separate monoethnic units. The 250 officer cadets—150 Greek and 100 Turkish Cypriots—were mostly EOKA and TMT members not disposed to cooperate with each other. Enough Turkish Cypriots could not be found to fill the community's 30 percent quota in the civil service, which had to be met in every department of the service. Civil service appointments became embroiled in legal wrangles, leading to near dysfunction of the island's administration. The issue of separate Turkish Cypriot municipalities in the five cities became a political football and a focal point for severe discord. Greek Cypriot leaders stonewalled their formation while Turkish Cypriot politicians demanded their speedy implementation so that Turkish Cypriot neighborhoods in these cities could achieve de jure autonomous status. This became "the problem . . . symbolizing the essence of the intercommunal conflict. The municipal crisis remained unresolved. Its progress through the council of ministers, the house of representatives and the constitutional court only served to polarize the Cypriot communities and harden their positions."[24] There were also debilitating disputes over how taxes should be shared between the communities. Greek Cypriots preferred to do this strictly on the basis of population ratios, while Turkish Cypriots protested that this was unfair and would perpetuate the relative poverty of their people.

As Cyprus sank into a political quagmire, both sides made preparations for armed confrontation. On the Greek Cypriot side the preparations were overseen by a trio of senior leaders including Tassos Papadopoulos, the labor minister, and Glafcos Clerides, president of the house of representatives. Clerides was much later elected president of the Republic of Cyprus—effectively the Greek Cypriot south—for two terms, lasting from 1993 to 2003, and Papadopoulos was elected president in 2003. These two men were to play important roles during the international community's renewed effort to craft a Cyprus settlement between 1999 and 2004. In the early 1960s the Greek Cypriots apparently developed a contingency plan for lightning military actions to overrun the Turkish Cypriot districts of the major towns and other "enemy" strongholds. EOKA veterans and arms caches formed the nucleus of an effort to train several thousand men constituting an officially sponsored paramilitary force. Although the government of Greece declined to support this venture, citing its international treaty obligations under the London-Zurich agreements, weapons were smuggled in from the motherland. The TMT organized paramilitary units to defend Turkish Cypriot urban neighborhoods and villages and conduct reprisals for abductions and murders. Direct assistance from the treaty-bound government of Turkey was not forthcoming but weapons shipments were nonetheless smuggled in from the motherland.

On 30 November 1963 President Makarios presented a list of thirteen proposed constitutional amendments to Vice President Kuchuk titled "Suggested Measures for the Smooth Functioning of the State and the Removal of Certain Causes of Inter-communal Friction." Its key elements were abolition of the presidential and vice presidential veto powers on parliamentary legislation and ministerial decisions, abolition of the requirement for cross-community concurrent majorities for legislation on specified subjects in the house of representatives, modification of the constitutionally prescribed composition of the civil service, police, and army to reflect the ethnonational ratios of the population, and the establishment of unified municipalities in the major urban centers. This was a proposal for a drastic overhauling of the state established in 1960 in a majoritarian direction. It was also a recipe for the outbreak of violent strife on an already tense island.

On 16 December 1963 the government of Turkey rejected Makarios's proposals. The archbishop retorted that the matter concerned only Cypriots. Kuchuk and his colleagues were finalizing a negative response when on 21 December 1963 a shooting incident in Nicosia in which two Turkish Cypriot civilians and a Greek Cypriot police officer were killed triggered a large-scale eruption of violence across the island. Until August 1964, after which the violence declined to more sporadic and localized eruptions, Cyprus was in the grip of civil war conditions despite efforts by British soldiers to contain violence in early 1964 and the induction of United Nations peacekeeping forces—the United Nations Forces in Cyprus (UNFICYP), present on the island to this day—in March 1964. Between December 1963 and August 1964, 191 Turkish Cypriots were killed and another 173 listed as missing, presumed dead. Of the Greek Cypriots, 133 were killed and 41 others were missing. Major towns, including Nicosia, Limassol, Larnaca, and Paphos, turned into war zones, with hostile neighborhoods separated by barricades and tense dividing lines patrolled by UN troops. Perhaps most important, about 90 percent of the Turkish Cypriot population retreated during these months into some thirty pockets or enclaves spread across the island, created around existing demographic and paramilitary strongholds. They abandoned scores of vulnerable Turkish Cypriot villages and largely or wholly evacuated dozens of mixed (if largely segregated) villages in the process.

Was the 1960 settlement fatally flawed? It is of course easy and tempting to answer in the affirmative. But it is far from clear what the alternative could have been—apart from a continuation of colonial rule. Territorially based formulas—partition, federation, or so-called "double-enosis," meaning the absorption of one part of the island into Greece and another into Turkey—all ran up against one social and demographic reality. When the state was founded in 1960, both Greek and Turkish Cypriots lived all over the island. Scores of exclusively or overwhelmingly Greek Cypriot villages were scattered across the northern parts of Cyprus. The island's northernmost settlement, the village of Rizokarpaso, located near the tip of the scenic Karpas Peninsula, had 3,151 Greek Cypriot residents and just two Turkish Cypriots. Karavas, a village near the port of Kyrenia—the staging ground for the 1974 Turkish invasion—had 2,416 Greek Cypriots and nine residents classified as "others" (neither Turkish nor Greek). Dozens of exclusively or overwhelmingly Turkish Cypriot villages dotted the southern parts of the country. The village of Mandria in the southwestern Paphos district was inhabited by 413 Turkish Cypriots and one Greek Cypriot. Klavdia in the southeastern Larnaca district had an exclusively Turkish Cypriot population of 524 people. All the towns—Kyrenia in the far north and Limassol in the deep south, the capital Nicosia located inland and the main port of Famagusta perched on the eastern coast—had mixed populations.

At the same time the social underpinnings of a state of individual citizens—rather than one constructed primarily on the basis of collective communitarian identities—did not exist (as in Bosnia in the 1990s and beyond; see Chapter 3). According to one estimate there were 114 "mixed" population centers on Cyprus in 1960 alongside 509 homogeneous settlements—392 Greek Cypriot, 117 Turkish Cypriot. This count used a very modest criterion for classifying a settlement as mixed, however—the presence of just ten people from the minority group—and even its author admits that "mixed centers were invariably divided into distinct ethnic quarters between which there was little social and economic contact."[25] Intercommunal marriage was nearly nonexistent. While 38 percent of Turkish Cypriots spoke some Greek at the advent of independence—the result of being a territorially dispersed minority—only 1 percent of Greek Cypriots knew any Turkish. The school system had fostered communitarian identities at the expense of a common Cypriot identity. This was partly the legacy of the Ottoman *millet* system—which provided for educational autonomy for different religious groups in the empire—and partly the result of later developments, such as the network of Greek Pan-Cyprian gymnasiums established in Cypriot towns since the late nineteenth century that turned out generations imbued with Greek nationalism.

In retrospect, the infant Cypriot state's experiment in conso-

ciational government was doomed to break down because it lacked
a support critical to the prospects of such complex solutions to the
problems of deeply fractured societies. That is, it lacked any provision for close, neutral, international supervision and mediation during its implementation. The turbulent history of Northern Ireland
since the Good Friday Agreement of 1998 has shown that robust
international support is vital if such agreements are to survive in
deeply torn societies.[26] The Dayton agreement that ended Bosnia's
1992–1995 war has been dependent on a protracted and multifaceted international supervisory regime for its implementation.[27]
Given the large-scale sectarian violence that wracked Cyprus in
the summer of 1958, there was a compelling case for an UN-led international military and police presence to ensure security on the
ground from 1960 onward. There was also a vital need for international supervision of the implementation of the London-Zurich
constitutional settlement and for mediation between the parties,
given the inevitability of disputes and deadlocks. The parties were
instead essentially left to swim or sink on their own, with tragic
consequences.

In 1966 Peter Loizos, a young British anthropologist of partial
Greek Cypriot descent, arrived in Cyprus to do fieldwork in his father's ancestral village, Argaki, situated about twenty miles to the
west of Nicosia. In 1960 Argaki had 1,219 Greek Cypriot and 72
Turkish Cypriot residents. By the late 1960s "the Argaki Turks
were about fifty in number, mostly elderly and rather poor . . . their
young people had gone off to the Turkish Cypriot enclaves and did
not visit them. They seemed quiet even subdued in the face of the
1,500 Greeks in the village."[28]

The enclave in question was centered on a village called
Ghaziveran, about twelve miles west of Argaki, which in 1960 was
an exclusively Turkish Cypriot village of 469 persons. The fate of
these two villages is a microcosm of the Cyprus conflict between
1963 and 1974.

In March 1964 "Greek Cypriot forces launched an attack on the Turkish Cypriot village of Ghaziveran. The village occupied a very strategic position on the shores of Morphou Bay, an obvious landing ground in the event of a Turkish invasion. Of even more significance, the only coastal highway passed through Ghaziveran . . . Seven Turkish Cypriots and one Greek Cypriot were shot dead before British troops were able to arrange a ceasefire agreement."[29] Eight years later, sitting inside the fortified enclave, the son of Ghaziveran's *mukhtar* (headman) recalled the battle:

> "The Greeks set up floodlights on us in the small hours," Hussein said. "They demanded we remove roadblocks and surrender our arms. My father went out to talk to the Greeks and the commanders showed [him] a list of the arms they wanted. It was ridiculous. The list read: so many sten-guns, so many grenades. We didn't have any of these things. We had twelve rifles and a few shotguns. At four in the morning they attacked. We had made bombs from lead piping and dynamite and laid them under the road. The Greeks had no tanks but they had armored a bulldozer and tried to force an entry that way. It blew up on the mine. Next they tried to encircle us with infantry. I think there were several hundred. We were far fewer, with only those twelve rifles to go round. So my father drew us into the village center and we fought from our houses until almost midday [when the attackers withdrew]. I was only thirteen but I was waiting to take the place of one of the men with a rifle if he got killed."[30]

Turkish Cypriot political identity was forged through such experiences in the enclaves—which were under the authority of an overarching Turkish Cypriot "provisional administration"—during the decade 1964–1974. Even a relatively young Turkish Cypriot aged forty is likely to have some memories of life in the enclaves—the claustrophobic atmosphere, the chronic insecurity about Greek

Cypriot intentions, the deep uncertainty about the future, and the hardships caused by a partial economic blockade imposed by the Greek Cypriot authorities on the enclaves. A visitor to the town of Paphos in 1972 "went into the Turkish quarter, which saw bloodshed in 1964 . . . Sentries sauntered in a no-man's land of abandoned houses, whose streets seemed old and haunted . . . The Turkish air of regulated, conservative living had been tainted by isolation and displacement. People had come in from outlying villages where they felt unsafe and there was nothing for them to do. The blue-painted shacks of the United Nations squatted on salient roof-tops, from which bored Scandinavian and Irish soldiers examined each other through binoculars."[31] Indeed in March 1964, after heavy fighting, "the size of the Turkish Cypriot-controlled sector of Paphos was reduced to an area of a few hundred square yards, where the majority of the town's Turkish Cypriots became refugees."[32]

For Greek Cypriots the watershed of a half century of conflict is July and August of 1974, when the Turkish military invaded and partitioned the island by force. For Turkish Cypriots the watershed was reached much earlier, in December 1963, when in their view Greek Cypriots effectively abrogated the London-Zurich constitutional settlement and declared war on them. Turkish Cypriots observe the period of 21–25 December annually as "national struggle and martyrs' week." Visitors to northern Nicosia are routinely taken to a house in the Kumsal neighborhood, on 2 Irfan Bey Street, which is preserved as a "museum of barbarism." The house, rented by a Turkish army officer posted with the Turkish military contingent in Cyprus, was raided by armed Greek Cypriots on the night of 24–25 December 1963. The officer's wife and three small children were shot dead in the bath, where they had hidden, and another woman was killed in the toilet. The bath and toilet are preserved in the pristine condition, complete with long-dried bloodstains and bullet holes. Until a few years ago this grisly museum was a mandatory excursion for Turkish Cypriot schoolchildren in the Nicosia area.

The fighting across Cyprus from December 1963 to August 1964 was a series of localized conflagrations that British and subsequently UN troops found almost impossible to control. In January 1964 a mass grave containing the bodies of twenty-one Turkish Cypriots—many bearing marks of torture or execution at point-blank range—was exhumed in the same area near Nicosia where eight Greek Cypriots had been killed by a Turkish Cypriot ambush in June 1958, the incident that sparked three months of intense violence that summer. The Turkish Cypriots had been murdered on 24 December. In June 1964, Grivas, the erstwhile EOKA chief of operations, returned to Cyprus from Greece; he was considered the only person capable of curbing the activities of armed Greek Cypriot bands. The same month the Greek Cypriot leadership authorized an increase in the strength of its National Guard, the now completely monoethnic army, to fifteen thousand men. Between June and August five thousand personnel of the Greek army arrived in Cyprus to serve under Grivas's command. In August, National Guard and Greek troops launched a major offensive against a Turkish Cypriot coastal enclave, Kokkina, in the west of the island. The offensive was called off only after Turkish air force jets bombed and strafed the attackers, causing heavy casualties, and Turkey threatened a full-scale land invasion. Turkey had already threatened to invade in March, but in August an invasion seemed imminent if hostilities continued.

Fighting tapered off after August 1964. There was another war scare in November 1967 when Turkey issued an ultimatum to Greece after an outbreak of fighting centered on an inland Turkish Cypriot enclave in the island's southeast, near the town of Larnaca. The crisis dissipated after Grivas was repatriated to Greece along with the unauthorized Greek military presence on Cyprus (excepting the 950 personnel permitted under the London-Zurich accords), which had swelled to twelve thousand men. This relative calm was what Peter Loizos experienced during his research in the late 1960s and early 1970s, in the course of which he studied social customs and political alignments in Argaki, focusing particularly on the left–right ideological cleavage in Greek Cypriot society. In reality these years were no more than a protracted lull. By the time Loizos published his findings in 1975 Argaki—and Cyprus—had been transformed.[33]

After the crisis of late 1967 blew over, the Greek Cypriot leadership under Archbishop Makarios resumed contacts with Turkish Cypriot leaders. This thaw was at least partly—and possibly largely—the fall-out of events in Greece, where in April 1967 a group of colonels seized power and formed a military junta. Makarios, for all his faults an elected leader with a large popular following in his community, had a relationship of mutual dislike and distrust with Greece's 1967–1974 military dictatorship. In 1970–1971, talks were held between the prominent Greek Cypriot leader Glafcos Clerides and Rauf Denktash, then on the brink of displacing the aging Fazil Kuchuk as the top Turkish Cypriot leader. The Turkish Cypriots wanted Greek Cypriot recognition of autonomy for their patchwork of enclave communities, in return for which they seemed ready to concede Greek Cypriot wishes on reforms to the structure mandated in 1959–1960 for the island's central government. The talks were inconclusive, consistent with a pattern that still persists today in which Greek and Turkish Cypriot elites have proven unable to make any progress on resolving their differences in the absence of third-party involvement. In March 1971 Makarios reiterated the core shibboleths of Greek Cypriot nationalism in a widely publicized speech:

> Cyprus is a Greek island. It was Greek from the dawn of history and it shall remain Greek forever. We have taken it over as

a wholly Greek island and we shall preserve it as an undivided Greek island until we hand it over to mother Greece.[34]

This definition of the island's identity and destiny is of course unacceptable to Turkish Cypriots. When in 2004 I interviewed Serdar Denktash, Rauf's son and the TRNC's deputy prime minister and foreign minister, he became visibly upset when I mentioned to him the abiding Greek Cypriot belief in the "Greek" character of the island.

Makarios's speech was very likely an expression of deeply held conviction, but it was *also* very likely an attempt to assuage and fend off a rapidly growing challenge to his authority from the far-right wing of the Greek Cypriot political spectrum. Encouraged by the 1967 military coup in the motherland, far-right Greek Cypriots led by a core of very hard-line EOKA veterans became more and more organized and confident through the late 1960s and early 1970s. They regarded the Makarios leadership as indecisive and overly moderate. In Argaki, Peter Loizos noticed the growing strength and assertiveness of these elements, who were constituted into a heavily armed island-wide paramilitary organization called EOKA-B in 1972 under the patronage of right-wing officers posted with the Greek military contingent on Cyprus.[35] In mid-July 1974, internecine Greek Cypriot divisions climaxed in a violent EOKA-B coup, with the active support of the Greek military regime and its representatives on Cyprus, against the Makarios government. Makarios barely fled with his life, and the putschists jailed, tortured, and killed large numbers of his grassroots loyalists across the island. A few days later, on 20 July, Turkey invaded Cyprus.

The EOKA-B seizure of power lasted barely a week. Two days after the Turkish invasion of Cyprus the military regime in Athens collapsed and civilian rule was restored. On Cyprus Makarios's lieutenant Glafcos Clerides took charge in Makarios's absence—

the archbishop had fled the island on a British helicopter—as the putschist forces led by Nikos Sampson, a guerrilla in the original EOKA who had been sentenced to death by the British in the late 1950s, rapidly disintegrated. Advance Turkish units who had landed on the island's northern coast meanwhile faced tough resistance from Greek Cypriot forces. When a cease-fire was reached on 30 July, they were still confined to a relatively small area around the invasion's bridgehead in Kyrenia.

During late July and the first half of August two rounds of crisis talks were held in Geneva. The bottom line of Turkish prime minister Bulent Ecevit, supported by his generals, was that the Greek Cypriots must agree forthwith to "a federal state based on geographical separation" of the Cypriot communities—in other words, territorially demarcated Turkish Cypriot and Greek Cypriot regions.[36] Such agreement was not forthcoming from the Greek Cypriots and the Greek government. The second round of the Geneva conference broke up on 14 August 1974 at 3 a.m., and at 4:30 a.m. substantially reinforced Turkish forces launched a massive military offensive. This decisive phase of the war was "a rout for the Greek Cypriots. They had no aircraft and no significant armor with which to repulse Turkish tank advances supported by bombing and strafing planes."[37] In three days the Turkish forces overran 37 percent of the island. When the fighting stopped, the cease-fire line ran just south of Argaki.

When news arrived of the first Turkish landings on 20 July, Argaki's EOKA-B militants decided to exact revenge on the Turkish Cypriots enclaved since 1964 in the neighboring village of Ghaziveran. An EOKA-B militant later recalled the attack:

> We took up defensive positions in the first houses . . . Ghaziveran was silent. The captain wanted us to set fire to some houses, so we chucked petrol on them . . . Their *mukhtar*

called out from inside: "All right, we surrender." The shooting
stopped . . . Our commander Photis, a friend of mine, went
into the phone-box to relay that Ghaziveran had given in.
When he came out someone in a house gave him a bullet in
the forehead. Then someone else was hit . . . I burst into a
house. There were six people inside and a child. I swung the
machine-gun and mowed them down, all seven.[38]

On 14 and 15 August the vast majority of Argaki's Greek Cypriots evacuated the village and fled south, as the village and its surrounding areas were heavily bombed by Turkish air force jets—
napalm was liberally used in these attacks—and Turkish land formations approached closer and closer. Only the fifty or so Turkish
Cypriot villagers and some thirty elderly and infirm Greek Cypriot
residents were left when the Turkish forces arrived. At least two
old Greek Cypriot men were subsequently subjected to sexual
degradation by Turkish soldiers. But "the person who was perhaps hit harder by the war than anyone else was the village priest,
Papa Loizos." He was from Kyra, an exclusively Greek Cypriot village just north of Argaki. When Turkish soldiers took Kyra they
shot his elderly mother dead. His father then set off on foot for
Argaki to inform the son of his mother's death. The old man "just
disappeared . . . I simply do not know what happened to my father . . . If he remained unburied or whether the Turks buried him
I do not know." The old couple had been sheltering in the captured
village, Kyra, with another very elderly woman aged ninety. Three
days after the village was taken, Turkish soldiers gang-raped this
ninety-year-old woman. "I am glad they shot my mother when
they did," the Argaki priest said, "so that such a thing did not happen to her." He added: "I see my parents as Christian martyrs.
They died the death of martyrs for their religion and their native
land."[39]

The Forging of Peace

For a quarter century after the cataclysmic events of 1974, Cyprus seemed frozen in a time warp. The Green Line, whose name originated in Nicosia during communal violence in 1958 when a British administrator drew a line on a map of the city with a green crayon to identify the "front line," became an iron curtain of 220 kilometers running horizontally across Cyprus. Efforts at intercommunity dialogue either did not get beyond preliminaries and generalities, or were too localized and limited to make a significant difference to the status quo.

In 1977 and 1979 two "high-level agreements" were signed, the first between Makarios and Rauf Denktash and the second between Makarios's successor Spyros Kyprianou and Denktash. In the 1977 agreement the Greek Cypriots for the first time acknowledged the principle of *bizonality*—in addition to bicommunality—as essential to peace and coexistence on Cyprus. In other words, any future common state would be composed of distinct, self-governing Turkish Cypriot and Greek Cypriot regions. As it was put by David Hannay, a top British diplomat who was the United Kingdom's special envoy for Cyprus from 1996 to 2003 and has written an insider account of the UN-sponsored peace process leading to the rise and fall of the Annan Plan.: "These agreements were only skeletons of a settlement . . . but they did establish a framework for a solution based on a bi-communal, bi-zonal federation."[40]

A major setback to diplomacy occurred in November 1983, however, when Denktash declared the independence of the north of the country as the Turkish Republic of Northern Cyprus (between 1975 and 1983 the area, which today still has a Turkish troop presence of at least thirty-five thousand, had a more nebulous title: "Turkish Federated State of Cyprus"). The TRNC remained an international nonentity as it was recognized only by Turkey.

Through the 1980s the UN persisted in low-key diplomatic efforts that proved fruitless, in parallel to its military peacekeeping mission, UNFICYP, tasked with patrolling the buffer zone along the Green Line (as of 2004 UNFICYP comprised 1,201 military and 46 police personnel). In 1992, UN secretary-general Boutros-Ghali published a "Set of Ideas" on a settlement after talks in New York between Greek Cypriot president George Vassiliou and Denktash. This did not generate a structured, substantive peace process, one reason being Vassiliou's replacement as president in 1993 by Glafcos Clerides, who adopted a hard-line stance against Boutros-Ghali's proposals in his victorious campaign.

More piecemeal and locally grounded attempts at rapprochement occurred fitfully. In the late 1970s the mayors of the two sides of Nicosia, both political moderates, decided to cooperate on an essential necessity—a joint sewerage system for the divided city, which became operational in May 1980. The success of the subterranean enterprise encouraged the duo to bring together a bicommunal team of scholars, architects, and urban planners who in the late 1980s formulated a "Nicosia Master Plan," a scheme for cooperative regeneration of the city. The plan has two scenarios—one with the Green Line, the other without. The two mayors traveled together to Venice to seek funding for the restoration of the Venetian old town's walls—this pre-Ottoman old town is bisected by the Green Line—and to divided Berlin. Some elements of the master plan have been implemented over the years, but the full realization of its vision awaits a Cyprus settlement.[41]

In the 1990s an energetic and youthful bicommunal movement for change emerged, seeking to address the past and look to a shared future through dialogue. The UN's base at the Ledra Palace Hotel on Nicosia's dividing line became a major center for bicommunal activities—much to the annoyance of hard-liners on both sides—which were generously funded by Western foundations eager to encourage the development of civil society. Nonetheless, the bicommunal movement remained restricted to a relatively small circle of people and had a limited impact on society at large. In the second half of the 1990s the movement suffered a setback when the Denktash regime in the north imposed a ban on Turkish Cypriot attendance. And in August 1996 tensions flared anew after ugly confrontations at Derineia, a point in the buffer zone south of the port of Famagusta, in which two Greek Cypriots demonstrating against the division of the island were killed in brutal circumstances.

When in late 1999 the UN stepped up its efforts to mediate a settlement, its principal interlocutors were the respective presidents, Glafcos Clerides and Rauf Denktash. Both were political dinosaurs and British-educated lawyers. Clerides defended EOKA suspects in the second half of the 1950s while Denktash prosecuted them on behalf of the colonial regime.

Forty years on they had evolved very differently. Clerides, in David Hannay's shrewd judgment, "understood very well that the Greek Cypriots had made major mistakes with disastrous consequences when they hijacked the Republic in 1963 and precipitated the hostilities in 1974. He was determined to learn and apply the lessons of those mistakes."[42] Indeed, in 2005 Clerides spoke candidly of a series of costly misjudgments made by Greek Cypriot leaders: "We wanted to violate agreements when there was no international support [for such a strategy, a reference to 1963] . . . we could not evaluate that Greece was not capable of a face-to-face conflict with Turkey [in the event of an escalation] . . . [and that] we did not have the capability to protect Cyprus if Turkey intervened." He also spoke of the Greek and Greek Cypriot nonacceptance of Turkey's 1974 ultimatum on reconstitution of Cyprus as a federation of two regions as an error, given that it had led to a catastrophe and that the territorial principle had to be conceded anyway in 1977 after it became a fact on the ground.[43] Denktash, on the contrary, was an unreconstructed hard-liner. Hannay writes that "Denktash's preferred solution was that north Cyprus should become part of Turkey" and that "it gradually dawned on me that the only people he ever negotiated with were the Turks."[44]

Since its inception the Cyprus problem has had two dimensions—the internal conflict and the international aspect of the Greece-Turkey relationship in the eastern Mediterranean. By the time the UN's "good offices mission" went into high gear in the last weeks of the twentieth century a third dimension had entered the equation. It was clear that Cyprus's bid for entry into the European Union—started in 1990 by the Greek Cypriot authorities as the internationally recognized government of Cyprus, accepted in principle by the EU in 1995, and elevated to the stage of substantive talks in 1997—was progressing rapidly and that Cyprus would definitely become a member in the Union's imminent enlargement. The UN-sponsored talks thus acquired the character of a race against time to achieve a settlement so that Cyprus could accede to the EU as a united island that had put its past behind it. Between 1999 and 2003 the EU repeatedly expressed a strong preference for Cyprus joining as a united country, its conflict settled, but it did not make a settlement a condition for completion of the accession process. The EU also repeatedly said that it would flexibly accommodate any unusual or complex legal and constitutional aspects of a UN-mediated settlement that were not in concord with its normal requirements of acceding states—in recognition of Cyprus's particular history and contemporary situation—through temporary or even longer-term bending of the Union's charter, the *acquis communautaire*. The EU further undertook to fine-tune its structural funds mechanism to take account of the gap in development and living standards between north and south should a settlement materialize—in 2002 the Turkish Cypriot per capita income of $4,000 was a quarter of the Greek Cypriot level, although the difference is mitigated by cheaper prices in the north and huge subsidies granted to the TRNC by the Turkish government.

In July 2000 Alvaro de Soto, the Peruvian official heading the UN team, put forward general principles that the UN felt should guide the talks. His paper stated that "the aim is a comprehensive settlement covering all issues . . . [which] should leave nothing to be negotiated subsequently . . . Nothing is agreed until everything is agreed." This approach contrasts with the incremental strategy adopted in the 1993–2000 Oslo peace process between Israel and the Palestinians. After several rounds of "proximity talks" between the parties organized by the UN and discreetly overseen by the U.K. and U.S. special envoys for Cyprus (Hannay and Thomas Weston, respectively) over three years in New York, Geneva, and Nicosia, no such settlement was on the horizon by late 2002. At that point "the option that had from the outset seemed the most likely—for the UN secretary-general himself to table a draft comprehensive settlement—became the only viable one."[45] In fact it was also urgent, as time was running out. The separate track of accession negotiations between the Greek Cypriots and the EU had reached a satisfactory conclusion and the European Council, the biennial meeting of EU foreign ministers, was about to announce this outcome in its December 2002 session in Copenhagen.

In November 2002 the first version of the Annan Plan was circulated. There were to be four subsequent versions of the plan over the next year and a half incorporating minor modifications on various issues, but the fundamentals would remain unchanged. In December 2002 the EU announced that "Cyprus will be admitted as a new Member State to the European Union." The statement welcomed the continuation of UN-led efforts to find a settlement, reiterated "its strong preference for accession to the European Union by a united Cyprus," and "recall[ed] its willingness to accommodate the terms of a settlement in the Treaty of Accession." It also said that "in the absence of a settlement the application of the *acquis* to the northern part of the island shall be suspended until the Council decides unanimously otherwise."[46] At the same time the EU put off setting a date for the start of Turkey's accession talks with the EU by two years, despite a strong Turkish campaign. It merely said that if Turkey met further requirements for reform by December 2004 a date would be set then.

The EU announcement on Cyprus meant that a settlement would need to be agreed upon by the leaders *and* passed by popular referenda on both sides of the Green Line—this idea of popular ratification had featured in all UN proposals since Boutros-Ghali's 1992 "Set of Ideas"—prior to the signing of the treaty of accession set for mid-April 2003 if a united island was to accede to the Union. The clock was ticking against the UN mediation effort. The UN mediators made a spirited last-ditch attempt but talks at The Hague in March 2003 ended in failure.

The six months leading up to the anticlimax of March 2003 were a turbulent period for Turkey and for the Turkish Cypriots. In November 2002 the Justice and Development Party (AKP), a moderate and modernist Islamist party, won parliamentary elections in Turkey and formed the government. The leaders of this government were much more positively disposed to the UN's efforts in Cyprus compared to the previous government headed by the geriatric Bulent Ecevit, who had also been prime minister in 1974 and apparently believed that the military intervention had permanently solved the Cyprus problem. Between December 2002 and February 2003, meanwhile, several very large demonstrations in favor of a negotiated settlement occurred in the TRNC involving at least seventy to eighty thousand people, a huge number since the TRNC's total population is about two hundred thousand. Discontent among Turkish Cypriots had come to a head, catalyzed by severe economic problems in the north resulting from Turkey's financial collapse in 2002 and widespread disgust at the hidebound nature and bunker mentality of the Denktash administration. Clearly the Turkish Cypriot community had not attained closure and eternal liberation in 1974. In fact, more and more Turkish Cypriots seemed to be convinced that because of the Denktash regime's intransigence they were "missing an extremely important bus" that would simultaneously deliver them to a permanent resolution *and* the benefits of the EU.[47]

Nonetheless Denktash was for the time being still the key Turkish Cypriot player, and he managed to secure vital Turkish backing for his rejectionist stance at The Hague. It could be that the Turks could not work up the resolve to confront or abandon their longstanding client, and Denktash could probably still count on powerful friends in Turkey's bureaucracy and military at a time when the Islamists, long derided in Turkey's "secular" republic, were just settling into office. Supporting Denktash may also have been a churlish—and stupidly self-defeating—expression of Turkish disaffection at their own accession aspirations having been postponed by the EU. On the Greek Cypriot side a change of guard had also taken place. In February 2003 Tassos Papadopoulos, a veteran of the EOKA struggle, was elected to the presidency and Clerides bowed out of the scene. Papadopoulos did not take an openly hostile stance to the UN's settlement plan at the Hague talks in March. Given his outright rejection of the plan a year later it is likely that this was a clever tactical decision—he did not need to do so as it was near certain that Denktash would reject the plan and be blamed by the international community as the spoiler. This was exactly what happened. In his report to the Security Council, Annan assigned Denktash "prime responsibility" for the failure, noting that since the end of 1999 "Mr Denktash by and large declined to engage in negotiations on the basis of give and take."[48]

After this failure in March 2003 the Annan Plan was resurrected in early 2004. The catalytic event was a parliamentary election in the TRNC in December 2003 that brought a long-standing

Denktash opponent and political moderate, Mehmet Ali Talat, to office as prime minister in an uneasy coalition with Denktash's son Serdar, who became deputy prime minister and foreign minister. Serdar had been instrumental in the opening of the Green Line on 23 April 2003, a month after the collapse of the Hague talks and a week after Papadopoulos signed the treaty of accession to the EU. The consent of Turkey—probably in belated recognition by its military and bureaucratic elite that they had damaged their own international image and prospects of EU accession by colluding with Denktash, a known Euro-skeptic, in scuttling the Annan Plan—was crucial to the opening of the Green Line. Denktash Sr. remained president, but his authority, already eroded by popular protests, was severely weakened.

The UN sensed a post-eleventh-hour opportunity. If a settlement could be swiftly agreed upon, Cyprus could still join the EU as a united country on 1 May 2004, the formal date of admission. It reconvened talks, in New York in February and in Burgenstock, Switzerland, in March. This time it was the Greek Cypriot delegation led by Papadopoulos that resorted to stonewalling and delaying tactics. Of the Turkish Cypriot trio—Talat and the two Denktashes—Talat unequivocally supported the Annan Plan, Rauf opposed it, and Serdar occupied an ambivalent middle ground. The Turks, in a *volte-face* from 2003, threw their weight behind Talat—both Prime Minister Erdogan and Foreign Minister Gul strongly endorsed the plan. At the end of March, with time once again running out—the plan had to be put before parallel referenda in April—Annan used his discretion to finalize Annan V, the fifth version of the plan. The referendum date was scheduled for 24 April. If the plan was approved by majorities in both jurisdictions, it was projected that in June 2004 there would be UN-supervised elections to the institutions of the United Cyprus Republic and its two constituent states, as well as to elect Cypriot members of the European Parliament. On returning to Cyprus Papadopoulos gave a

television address on 7 April in which he, as Annan cryptically put
it in his report of yet another failure to the Security Council,
"called upon the [Greek Cypriot] people to reject the plan with
a resounding No."[49] In Hannay's less diplomatic language,
"Papadopoulos . . . in a lengthy, rambling and emotional television
address . . . launched a root-and-branch onslaught on the fundamentals of the UN's approach."[50]

The Annan Plan proposed a confederation in Cyprus—meaning a
loosely federal union in which the constituent territorial units
would have maximal autonomy—and stipulated that the limited
joint institutions at the federal level would operate on the basis of
consociational norms. The United Cyprus Republic would consist
of a Greek Cypriot constituent state over 72 percent of the island's
territory and a Turkish Cypriot constituent state over the other 28
percent. The constituent states would have jurisdiction over all
matters except foreign policy, EU affairs, and central bank func-
tions, which would be the province of the federal government. The
72:28 formula meant the transfer of 9 percent of the island's territory, comprising a swath of areas lying just north of the Green Line,
to the envisioned Greek Cypriot constituent state. This was considered necessary and just, given that since 1974 Turkish Cypriots,
roughly 18 percent of the population, had been in possession of 37
percent of the island and 57 percent of its coastline.

There was an additional powerful rationale, however. The areas
earmarked for transfer covered the 1974 residences of 120,000 of
the 165,000 Greek Cypriots who became refugees in 1974. The areas restored to Greek Cypriot administration would include villages like Argaki in the island's west, abandoned by 1,500 Greek
Cypriots in 1974, and towns like Varosha on the eastern coast,
just south of the port of Famagusta, which had been abandoned
by 40,000 Greek Cypriots. About one-third of Turkish Cypriots
would have to relocate from their current residences as a result. The

transfer would proceed under UN supervision in six phases ranging from three and a half months to three and a half years. In other words, while comprehensive terms were to be agreed to on this and all other issues as part of a one-stop encompassing settlement, its *implementation* would be incremental.

The remainder of the Greek Cypriot refugee population and their descendants, as well as all Turkish Cypriots who migrated from areas south of the Green Line after 1974, were entitled to compensation for lost property. A property board consisting of an equal number of Greek and Turkish Cypriots, plus foreign nationals nominated by the UN, would administer this process. Special provisions applied to persons over 65, who were to be given an accelerated right of return on a priority basis, and to the protection and maintenance of religious sites of both communities. On the especially sensitive Greek Cypriot concern about people from Turkey settled since 1974 in northern Cyprus—claimed to number 119,000 in 2004 by the Papadopoulos government—the Annan Plan proposed a compromise.[51] A total of 45,000 such persons would receive Cypriot citizenship, as well as complementary citizenship of the Turkish Cypriot constituent state, on a onetime basis under the settlement. It was further provided that "to preserve its identity a constituent state may adopt specified nondiscriminatory safeguard measures in conformity with the *acquis communautaire* in respect of the establishment of residence by persons not holding its internal constituent-state citizenship status." The cap on such persons was projected at 18 percent of each constituent state's population until such time that Turkey joined the EU.

On security issues the plan stipulated that "Cyprus shall be demilitarized and all Greek Cypriot and Turkish Cypriot [military] forces, including reserve units, shall be dissolved." The Greek and Turkish military contingents stationed on the island would be limited to a maximum of six thousand personnel each immediately, with a further cut to three thousand in 2011. In effect this meant that the thirty-five-thousand-strong Turkish military forces in northern Cyprus would be drastically reduced immediately, and halved again in 2011. By 2018 or Turkey's accession to the EU, whichever was sooner, the Greek contingent was not to exceed 950 and the Turkish contingent 650 (the numbers permitted under the 1959 London-Zurich agreement). Subsequently there would be reviews every three years "with the objective of total withdrawal" of non-Cypriot forces from the island. A UN peacekeeping presence on the ground would continue until at least 2010 and be reviewed thereafter.

The Annan Plan's proposals on the structure of the federal government were clearly descended from the 1959–1960 settlement that established the binational consociational—but non territorialized—state. The parliament would be bicameral. The upper house, the senate, would have forty-eight members equally divided between Greek and Turkish Cypriots. The lower house, the chamber of deputies, also with forty-eight members, would be constituted on the basis of the populations of each constituent state, but each constituent state (effectively the Turkish Cypriot entity) would hold at least one-quarter of the seats. Parliamentary decisions would be made by simple majority in both chambers, but "specified matters" would require cross-community majorities in the senate. Such concurrent majorities would elect a federal copresidency, to consist of six members including at least one-third from each constituent state (in effect Turkish Cypriots), and its chair and deputy chair would rotate between the two groups. The co-presidency would endeavor to act by consensus; if consensus was not forthcoming, a simple majority would suffice so long as that majority included at least one representative from both constituent states. A six-member federal council of ministers would consist of three Greek and three Turkish Cypriots. Of the island's six representatives in the European Parliament, four would be Greek Cypriots and two Turkish Cypriots.

The supreme constitutional court—empowered to "resolve disputes between the constituent states and between one or both of them and the federal government, and resolve on an interim basis deadlocks within federal institutions"—would consist of "an equal number of judges from each constituent state, and three non-Cypriot judges until otherwise provided by law." In his postreferendum report to the Security Council, Annan noted that "highly qualified individuals with a combination of experience in European law and federal systems were selected in close consultation with the parties" to serve as the foreign judges on the constitutional court.[52] He also noted that seven technical committees of Greek and Turkish Cypriots, chaired by the UN, had formulated 131 pieces of federal legislation, including four constitutional laws, 124 federal laws, and three cooperation agreements between the constituent states, and had finalized the composition of the federal government, including 6,181 positions at different levels. The cooperation agreements, intended to facilitate the conduct of the United Cyprus Republic's relations with the EU, were explicitly modeled on the example of Belgium, a federal EU member-state that uses similar agreements between its Flemish and Francophone constituent regions.

The preamble to the proposed accord "affirm[ed] that Cyprus is our common home" and "acknowledg[ed] . . . that our relationship is not one of majority and minority but of political equality where neither side may claim authority or jurisdiction over the other." It spoke of a "new bi-zonal partnership . . . within a peaceful environment in the Eastern Mediterranean" and "look[ed] forward to joining the European Union, and to the day Turkey does likewise."[53]

The Annan Plan asserted that the constitutional structure it proposed for Cyprus "is modeled on Switzerland, the status and relationship of its federal government and its cantons" (Foundation Agreement, Article 2). In fact, the UN's blueprint has a familial resemblance to contentious peace settlements undergoing a tortuous implementation in two places infinitely more troubled than Switzerland—Bosnia and Northern Ireland. The Annan Plan is remarkably similar to the confederal and consociational Dayton agreement that ended the Bosnian war at the end of 1995 and to the consociational Northern Ireland agreement reached on Good Friday in April 1998. The resemblance is not just generic. Particular provisions of the Annan Plan will be uncannily familiar to anyone acquainted with the Bosnian settlement (complementary common-state and constituent-entity citizenships, the presence of a cohort of foreign judges on the country's constitutional court) or the Northern Ireland accord (cross-community majorities for legislation, popular ratification through parallel referenda conducted separately in Northern Ireland and the Republic of Ireland).

On 24 April 2004, 64.9 percent of Turkish Cypriots said *Evet* (Yes) to the Annan Plan, an easily explicable and expected verdict. In Turkish Cypriot northern Nicosia, 68 percent of voters were in favor. In the TRNC town of Morphou—whose hinterland includes both Argaki and Ghaziveran—which would be given to the Greek Cypriot constituent state as part of the territorial adjustment if the plan came into effect, a large majority of residents approved the plan. Across the Green Line, 75.83 percent of Greek Cypriots said *Oxi* (No). In his postmortem Annan somberly noted that "the sheer size of the No vote raises . . . fundamental questions."[54] That feeling was shared by others. Mehmet Ali Talat, the TRNC's prime minister, told me in June 2004 that while he was expecting a Greek Cypriot 'No' majority of up to 60 percent, he was shocked by the magnitude of the rejection.

There are several proximate causes of the outcome of the Greek Cypriot vote. The Greek Cypriot communist party AKEL (Progressive Party of the Working People) called for a 'No' vote after its last-minute demand for a postponement of the referendum pending further assurances on implementation and the security provisions was rejected. AKEL's stance was important because the party has a disciplined following comprising almost one-third of the Greek Cypriot electorate. But its unhelpful intervention was not entirely surprising as the party has a decades-long record of dithering and pusillanimity at critical junctures of the Cyprus conflict. Skeptics noted that the party was enjoying the spoils of office in a governing coalition with the party of Papadopoulos, the right-wing president, and had a strong vested interest in not upsetting the arrangement. A top AKEL ideologue praised the Annan Plan in a television appearance, but this was at variance with the official party line and in the end only 20 percent of AKEL supporters voted yes. However, even though the leadership of the other large Greek Cypriot party, the center-right DISY (Democratic Rally) whose members include ex-president Clerides, endorsed the plan, 62 percent of DISY supporters still voted no. The tide of negative opinion among Greek Cypriots was aggravated by some flaws in the international community's "selling" of the plan. Advertising the settlement as the "Annan Plan" fed into rejectionist propaganda that the plan was an imposition. Many Greek Cypriots were also annoyed by the international community's insistence that this was the "last chance" for a settlement. They felt railroaded, if not bullied.

The root causes of the overwhelming 'No' vote run much deeper. In January 2003, shortly after the first versions of the UN plan were publicized, a prominent Greek Cypriot academic published a scathing attack on the proposals. He argued that the plan would "establish a divisive and dysfunctional system of governance . . . [that] legitimizes and institutionalizes the division of the island," and that "its adoption is a worse option than partition." He asserted that "bi-communality should be an integral but not the exclusive characteristic of the framework for a solution [and] regarding bizonality, although initially there would be two states we should not exclude the possibility . . . of evolution into a system that would combine elements of federation and unitary state." An updated version of the critique published in May 2004 called for "the reintegration of the northern part of the island into the Republic of Cyprus" and an alternative model of settlement in which "the importance of both the individual citizen and the [ethnonational] community is recognized."[55]

This is precisely the kind of argument that appears to have struck a deep chord among the Greek Cypriot people. The idea of enosis (union of Cyprus with Greece) has almost disappeared from Greek Cypriot public discourse over the past three decades, and the Athens government's endorsement of the Annan Plan apparently made no difference to Greek Cypriot opinion. But the twin ideas that Cyprus is historically and culturally a Greek island, and that as the majority group Greek Cypriots have the right to have a *dominant* say, not just an *equal* say, in determining and running its polity have *not* disappeared. The principles and provisions of the Annan Plan go against the grain of these deeply held beliefs, even though most variants of Greek Cypriot discourse have undergone a shift since 1974 in which Turkey's interference, rather than the Turkish Cypriot community, is assigned prime blame for the Cyprus conflict.

If these deeply rooted and resilient beliefs provided the underlying basis for the huge 'No' vote, that vote was crystallized by two characteristics of contemporary Greek Cypriot society—a culture of grievance and what Peter Loizos, borrowing a term from John Kenneth Galbraith, calls a culture of contentment. Even those Greek Cypriots who acknowledge that "mistakes" were made and the Turkish Cypriot minority suffered serious mistreatment after Cyprus's independence tend to harbor passionate convictions that an intolerable injustice was inflicted on their community in August 1974. That injustice not only was not being rectified but in basic ways was being allowed to stand, in this view, by the complex compromise engineered by the UN and supported by the EU, the U.S., and the U.K. In the typical Greek Cypriot perception, they have never had their day in court. A powerful and widespread sense of grievance was vented on 24 April 2004.

The popular culture of grievance was reinforced by the "culture of contentment." The southern two-thirds of Cyprus is an affluent society. Greek Cypriot Nicosia looks like a wealthy town in Florida. The prosperity extends to the dispossessed of 1974. Many of Argaki's refugees have built successful careers and businesses in the south. Although the Annan Plan promised the return of their village, many of them "seem to feel that they would prefer to live in a smaller, richer, safer, nearly all-Greek state than shoot the rapids in untrustworthy company on a raft engineered by Annan's team."[56] The level of the 'No' vote was more or less uniform across Greek Cypriot society, between young and old, men and women, leftists and rightists, refugees and nonrefugees.

The integration of conflict-torn, fractured societies into wider networks of transnational and regional cooperation provides a way of locking in peace settlements and guaranteeing long-term stability. But it is the settlements that are stepping stones to the flowering of transnational cooperation and regional integration, not vice versa. In the anomalous case of Cyprus, because the Greek Cypriots knew that they would join the EU club regardless of a settlement, they had no countervailing incentive to support the Annan Plan that might just have outweighed their dominant underlying belief structure and their cultures of grievance and contentment. On the contrary, they had a perverse incentive to *not* approve a solution that would remove an obstacle in Turkey's long and bumpy journey to the EU. Of course, in playing the spoiler they may have "demonstrate[d] that they had not understood the first thing about the fundamental objectives of the [European] Union."[57] But there was a fatal gap between the two tracks of international engagement with Cyprus that enabled them to play the spoiler. The prospects of a Cyprus settlement fell into a large crack between the UN and EU stools.

In April 2005, two years after the opening of the Green Line and one year after the twin referenda, the Rauf Denktash era in Turkish Cypriot politics finally came to an end. The moderate Mehmet Ali Talat became the TRNC's president, the first person apart from Denktash to hold the post, after winning a solid majority of 56 percent of votes cast in the first round (his main opponent, a hard-liner, polled 23 percent). All the same, the Turkish Cypriots remain diplomatically and economically isolated. Yet even if their leadership and Turkey had not played the spoiler in 2003 it is likely, given the 2004 denouement, that the UN's ambitions would have foundered on Greek Cypriot opposition. In December 2004 the EU gave Turkey a date for starting accession talks—3 October 2005. To pave the way for these talks, Turkey signed a customs union agreement in August 2005 with all EU member-states, including Cyprus, even while insisting that this did not imply recognition of the Greek Cypriot authorities as the legitimate all-island government. In June 2005 Kieran Prendergast, the UN's undersecretary-general for political affairs, toured Cyprus and met with the principal protagonists but concluded that the time was not ripe for the UN to resume its third-party diplomacy.

The Cyprus endgame is yet to be played. As and when it unfolds, any settlement is likely to be within the parameters defined by the UN's ill-fated 2004 plan. Until then the island remains uneasily suspended between an elusive formula of unification and the sword of partition.

· THREE ·

Bosnia

Until 1991 the Bosnian city of Mostar was celebrated as a jewel of Yugoslavia, a country that exists today only in the history books. Although a small city of about a hundred thousand people, Mostar's celebrity status extended throughout Yugoslavia and beyond. There were several reasons for this. The first was the city's strikingly beautiful natural setting. Mostar spreads out on both banks of the Neretva River, whose emerald-green waters flow through the region of Herzegovina, the southern part of Bosnia—the official name of the country is "Bosnia and Herzegovina"—into the Adriatic Sea. The city is picturesquely framed by the rugged ranges of Herzegovina, a mountainous region. As the Neretva snakes through this starkly beautiful terrain, it narrows to treacherous rapids while negotiating gorges and widens into placid lakes while traversing valleys. The second half of the two-hour drive south from Sarajevo, the Bosnian capital, to Mostar is unusually scenic even by the standards of the now-extinct country called Yugoslavia, whose diverse topography included the black-granite peaks and ranges of the Dinaric Alps along with hundreds of miles of pristine Adriatic coastline.

The second reason is that Mostar represented in an urban microcosm the diverse cultural influences that over hundreds of years shaped the area of the Western Balkans that in the twentieth century became a country called Yugoslavia. This is most evident in the city's architecture. The city's famed architectural treasure was a bridge connecting the two banks of the Neretva, built in 1566 on the orders of the Ottoman emperor Suleiman, who is also known in history as the *kanuni* (lawgiver) sultan and the "magnificent" ruler. Bosnia was an Ottoman Turkish possession from roughly 1463 until 1878. Ever since 1566 Mostar has been identified with its *stari most,* or old bridge—indeed, the city's name is a derivative of the local word for "bridge." The site of the Ottoman bridge, a wonderfully delicate and graceful arched structure made of locally quarried limestone, is surrounded on both banks by the *stari grad,* or old town, a charming quarter of cobbled streets filled with Ottoman-era houses and mosques. Modern Mostar, however, was largely constructed during the late nineteenth and early twentieth centuries by Austro-Hungarian authorities who governed Bosnia from 1878 until 1918, when the first Yugoslav state was founded on the basis of the Wilsonian principle of national self-determination out of the ruins of the Ottoman and Habsburg empires. On the western bank the Austro-Hungarians built a variety of public buildings that bear the unmistakable imprint of late Habsburg architecture. An exemplar is the city's "gymnasium," or high school, built in the 1890s at a commanding point on the Boulevard, which runs parallel to the Neretva and abuts the elegant avenues and residential neighborhoods of the modern city. Beyond its richly eclectic architectural mix, Mostar has a curiously Mediterranean feel despite its inland location—the Adriatic coast, about an hour's drive south, has been important to the city's identity and prospects for centuries.

But Mostar was more than just blessed by nature or simply a fascinating confluence of bygone eras and traditions. Between 1945 and 1991 it was also renowned as a microcosm of the multinational country called Yugoslavia, resurrected at the end of World War II under communist leadership after the first Yugoslav state was invaded, occupied, and dismembered by Nazi Germany and its allies in 1941. The second Yugoslav state, like its predecessor, gathered multiple ethnonational groups (Serbs, Croats, Slovenes, the Slavic Muslims of Bosnia, Montenegrins, Macedonians, Albanians, and Hungarians) and religious communities—the Catholic and Orthodox branches of Christianity, and Islam—under one roof. Of the six republics that constituted the communist Yugoslav federation, Bosnia was by far the most multinational—about 45 percent Bosnian Muslim, 35 percent Bosnian Serb, and 18 percent Bosnian Croat in 1991. Of the 126,000 people who lived in the city of Mostar and its suburbs in 1991, 35 percent were Croat, 34 percent were Muslim, and 20 percent were Serb, while 11 percent chose, even in the last Yugoslav census, conducted that year in the twilight of the country's existence, to identify as "Yugoslav," a supranational category favored by urban, younger and highly educated citizens of the former Yugoslavia.[1]

Mostar was not simply one of the most multinational urban centers of Yugoslavia in the statistical sense. It had gained a reputation for cultural and political cosmopolitanism since the early twentieth century. The famous poet Aleksa Santic (1868–1924), a Serb, was a Mostarian. In the 1930s and during the years of World War II the city had a significant underground of communists, the only multiethnic political movement of the time. Herzegovina turned into a killing field between 1941 and 1945, as Nazi-sponsored Croat fascists murdered thousands of Serb civilians and a variety of sectarian political movements vied with each other and with the communists for supremacy. But "Mostar Croats saved Serbs, Serbs protected Muslims, and communal life revived faster in Mostar than anywhere else in Bosnia after the war."[2] For the next four and a half decades Mostar was a showpiece of the creed of *bratstvo i jedinstvo* (brotherhood and unity), the ideology of the resurrected Yugosla-

BOSNIA'S PREWAR DIVERSITY AND POSTWAR DIVISION

via formed under the leadership of Josip Broz Tito and presided
over by him until his death in 1980.

In 1992 this city was consumed by the flames engulfing Yugoslavia. The first round of warfare between April and June 1992, which
broke out as soon as Bosnia was recognized as an independent state,
pitted an alliance of Croat and Muslim militias against groups of local Serbs who were backed by units of the federal Yugoslav People's
Army (JNA). By June the Serbs lost the battle, the JNA's combat

units withdrew from the area, and Mostar and its suburbs were almost emptied of its substantial Serb population. During the fighting Mostar was heavily damaged by Serb forces shelling from the mountains overlooking the city. The Croat-Muslim alliance broke down in less than a year as radical Bosnian Croat nationalists patronized by the extreme nationalist regime in Croatia launched their own landgrab and expulsion campaign directed against Muslims in central Bosnia and in Herzegovina during the first half of 1993. A key strategic objective of this campaign was control of Mostar, which was to become the capital of a Bosnian Croat statelet appended to Croatia. In May 1993 Mostar exploded in heavy fighting between Croats and Muslims. The Boulevard in the city center became the front line, and its adjacent grid of neat, tree-lined streets turned into free-fire zones. The Croat-Muslim war stopped ten months later in March 1994 when the United States government mediated a truce during talks in Washington, D.C. The truce left Mostar divided along the front line between Croat-controlled west Mostar and a much smaller and less populous Muslim-held east Mostar, which included the old-town neighborhood. The division was similar to that of Jerusalem between 1948 and 1967 into a larger, more populous Israeli-controlled western part inhabited by Jews and a Jordanian-controlled eastern sector populated by Arabs.

By 1994 the city Mostar had been only three years earlier was unrecognizable. There were almost no Serbs left in the ruined, divided city. Forced population movements meant that there were almost no Croats left in the Muslim-held sector, while the vast majority of the Muslims who had lived in west Mostar had fled or been expelled. The bullet-scarred, shell-pocked ruins of the city center marked a no-man's-land and new border between mutually hostile and fearful zones. The bulk of the prewar city's highly educated, professional citizens had fled this necropolis. Something else was missing too. The spot where the sixteenth-century bridge spanned the Neretva was now a yawning chasm. On 9 November 1993, as Mostar reverberated to the sounds of intense combat, a Bosnian Croat tank positioned on Mount Hum, overlooking the city, fired a shell at the middle of the old bridge. It was a direct hit and the bridge imploded and collapsed in fragments into the Neretva. The wars that erupted in Bosnia and Croatia following Yugoslavia's disintegration were marked not just by systematic "ethnic cleansing" but by the deliberate destruction of hundreds of historic monuments and places of worship. The nineteenth-century Serb Orthodox church on Mostar's east bank, dynamited to rubble in 1992, was one such casualty. Yet the popular resonance of the Mostar bridge—both as a historical motif and as a symbol of solidarity and coexistence during the twentieth century—was so uniquely powerful that many across former Yugoslavia regard the moment of its destruction as marking the definitive death of Yugoslavism as an idea. In Mostar, many who suffered the personal loss of family and homes during the war cite the destruction of "the bridge" as a moment of exceptional, almost unbearable, pain and bereavement.

For a decade the stumplike remains of the old bridge's watchtowers on each bank were the only reminder of its 427-year existence until, on 23 July 2004, a replica of the structure was inaugurated in a grand ceremony attended by a galaxy of world leaders and international officials as well as heads of state and prominent politicians from across the former Yugoslavia. The event was covered live by major international broadcast media and featured on the front pages of many of the world's leading newspapers the next day. This was the culmination of a World Bank–UNESCO project that received additional financial support from the governments of Italy, the Netherlands, and Turkey. Its completion in 2004 coincided with a renewed effort by the international community—engaged since 1996 in a protracted state-building, democratization, and stabilization intervention in Bosnia—to set up a unified, multiethnic city government in Mostar, one of the most important and most difficult sites of that intervention. The international community's efforts in Mostar since 1994 had a record of only limited and piecemeal success in the face of tenacious local divisions and antagonisms.[3] Movement of pedestrians and vehicles across the city's dividing line picked up only from 1999, while reasonably significant returns of evicted and expelled people to their former homes materialized in Mostar only in 2001–2002.

Given the high profile of the frozen conflict in Mostar, it was little surprise that postwar Bosnia's international supervisors tried to derive as much mileage as possible from the inauguration. As a result the occasion became more an international jamboree than one with genuine significance for citizens. In predominantly Croat west Mostar the event evoked reactions ranging from studied indifference to surly hostility. But even in Mostar's predominantly Muslim eastern part, skepticism prevailed over enthusiasm:

> Local Bosniacs [Bosnian Muslims] poured scorn on the international obsession with the bridge's alleged wider meaning, such as that voiced by the international community's "high representative" [the top international official overseeing Bosnia's postwar transition] Paddy Ashdown, who said [in his speech] that the [new] bridge is a cornerstone of Bosnia's reconstruction as a multiethnic society. As if that were not enough Bosnia could according to Ashdown [a Briton from Northern Ireland] become a bridge between the Islamic world and the West, helping the two worlds overcome stereotyped and misguided views of one another. . . . "That may be too much reconciliation for one bridge," said a local Bosniac.[4]

When I lived in Mostar in 1998, the city was a tense and indeed frightening place, a graphic study in the meaning and consequences of ethnonational conflict and partition. Viewed from the perspective of that period, Mostar today seems almost "normal." Most of the war damage to infrastructure and buildings has gradually been repaired, the ruined city center has been rebuilt, people can cross the Boulevard and visit the "other" side without fear of abuse or attack, several thousand Muslims have reclaimed houses and apartments in west Mostar, and Western European and American tourists arrive by the busload from the Adriatic coast or the nearby Catholic pilgrimage site of Medjugorje (a remote Herzegovinian town where the Virgin Mary is said to have made an appearance in 1981) to gape at the new old bridge and photograph the few destroyed buildings that remain. Yet under the veneer of "normalcy" the city remains deeply fractured by political and psychological fault lines.

Mostar's quixotic situation is, yet again, a microcosm of Bosnia. The massive international effort to build a viable state and functioning polity in Bosnia since a peace agreement brokered by the United States on an air force base in Dayton, Ohio, in November 1995 ended the armed conflict that convulsed Bosnia for 43 months from April 1992 has been correctly characterized as "a highly visible testing ground for post–Cold War interventions in general, for the redirection of European and trans-Atlantic security organizations, and for the new agenda of development agencies in post-conflict reconstruction."[5] Since the end of 1995 Bosnia has been the site of one of the most challenging and high-profile peace processes of the contemporary era. How does the balance sheet look today? In particular, what does the Bosnian experience of peacebuilding illuminate about

- the prospects of federalism and power sharing—the pillars of the Dayton settlement—in deeply divided postwar societies?
- the efficacy of international intervention in such societies, given the large-scale and sustained international role in postwar Bosnia?

The Making of War

In early 1943 Fitzroy Maclean, a British intelligence officer, parachuted into Bosnia on an important and dangerous mission. His task was to ascertain the situation inside Axis-occupied Yugoslavia and take up the post of Allied liaison officer with the communist-led Partisan resistance movement, whose strongholds were at the time located in Bosnia. In his memoirs Maclean described his impressions of wartime Bosnia:

> Bosnia was in a sense a microcosm of the country [Yugoslavia] as a whole. It had been repeatedly fought over by Turks, Austrians and Serbs, and most of the national trends and tendencies were represented there, all at their most violent. The population was made up of violently Catholic Croats and no less violently Orthodox Serbs, with a strong admixture of equally fanatical local Moslems. It is hard to imagine the savage intensity of the passions that were aroused or the extremes of bitterness they engendered. Magnified and revitalized by the war the latent tradition of violence revived. The lesson we were having was an object lesson, of burned villages, desecrated churches, massacred hostages and mutilated corpses.[6]

This could equally have been a description of Bosnia at war fifty years later. Yet the view that regards Bosnia and its wider cultural and geopolitical region, the Balkans, as a part of the world populated by primitive people given to expressing atavistic hatred of one another through morbid spasms of violence—a view that reportedly influenced the thinking of then President Clinton about the Bosnian war—is far too simplistic.[7] The Bulgarian scholar Maria Todorova has argued that "as in the case of the Orient, the Balkans has served as a repository of negative characteristics against which a positive and self-congratulatory image of the 'European' and 'the West' has been constructed."[8] In fact the history and society of Bosnia are remarkably complex. American journalist Chuck Sudetic's luridly titled book *Blood and Vengeance,* a compelling account of the 1992–1995 Bosnian war, reconstructs the history of one mixed Serb-Muslim community in the Drina River valley in eastern Bosnia, adjoining Serbia, over a period of almost 150 years starting in the mid-nineteenth century. The focal point of the narrative is the July 1995 Srebrenica massacre of up to seven thousand Muslim men and boys by Serb forces, which occurred in this area. Sudetic's account reveals that relations between local Serbs and Muslims over the generations in and around the eastern Bosnian town of Visegrad were characterized by a peculiar cyclical pattern of extended periods of apparently friendly and peaceable neighborly coexistence punctuated by episodes of brutally violent conflict.[9] As British journalist Misha Glenny writes, modern Bosnia has been "both the paradigm of peaceful, communal life in the Balkans and its darkest antithesis."[10]

Bosnia was shaped on the cusp of the contending Habsburg and Ottoman empires for four centuries and then on the seam of two contending nationalisms—Serb and Croat—during the twentieth century. It is not surprising, then, that "Bosnia is a land where with extraordinary regularity other people's wars have nourished and been nourished by the internal conflicts of Bosnian society," in the phrase of the French scholar Xavier Bougarel.[11] The first major episode of intercommunal violence in Bosnia occurred as recently as 1875–1876 when Orthodox Serb peasants in eastern Herzegovina, an area located east of Mostar and adjacent to Montenegro, revolted against their Muslim landlords during the final years of the Ottoman regime. There is thus no evidence of "ancient hatreds." During the two decades of the first, interwar Yugoslavia and the four and a half decades of the second, communist Yugoslavia, Bosnia was generally stable and peaceful. But Bosnia erupted in intense violence during the troubled periods of World War I and World War II, when it turned into a killing field of different ethnonational and political factions, and finally in the wake of the unraveling of the communist federation in the early 1990s. Even though all these troubles were sparked by events and forces external to Bosnia, Bosnians were deeply complicit in the violence that ensued.

Because of Bosnia's history as a frontier society on the fault line first of contending empires and then of competing nationalisms, modern collective identities in Bosnia emerged and developed on the basis of ethnonational communities. During the first decade of the twentieth century the first political parties formed in Bosnia under the relatively permissive and modernizing Austro-Hungarian regime, which displaced the Ottomans in 1878. They were the Serb National Organization, Muslim National Organization, Croat National Union, and Croat Catholic Association (the last a smaller party). In Sarajevo and elsewhere in Bosnia, student groups opposed to Austro-Hungarian rule and committed to ideals of south Slavic solidarity against external domination—the word *Yugoslavia* means "land of the southern Slavs"—organized in the years leading up to the outbreak of World War I in 1914 as separate Serb and Croat societies (both societies had some Muslim members).[12] The Austro-Hungarian administration made failed attempts to promote an overarching Bosnian identity cutting across group boundaries. This strategy was motivated primarily by the need to counter irredentist claims to Bosnia emanating from the neighboring independent state of Serbia, which found powerful resonance among Bosnian Serbs, who were the single largest ethnonational community in Bosnia from the 1880s to the 1960s, when Muslims became the single largest group. During the communist period the vast majority of people in Bosnia and indeed across Yugoslavia continued to regard their ethnonational community as their primary identity. In the 1981 census only 8 percent of Bosnians declared their pri-

mary identity to be "Yugoslav"; the rest preferred the ethnonational categories of Serb, Croat, and Muslim. The proportion of
residents identifying themselves as Yugoslavs declined further to
5.5 percent in 1991, and these people were concentrated in urban
centers like Sarajevo, Mostar, Banja Luka, and Tuzla.[13] Only one-
quarter of Bosnia's 1991 population of 4.4 million people lived in
cities; most lived in small towns and rural areas.

This overwhelming preference for ethnonational categories of
identity was perfectly consistent, however, with the communist
conception of Yugoslavia as a supranational, federal union based
on equality between its constituent peoples. Those who professed
their primary identity to be Serb, Croat, or Muslim were *also* all
Yugoslavs. For most of the second Yugoslavia's existence complementary identities were no illusion. Canadian writer Michael
Ignatieff recalls traveling across Yugoslavia as a child in the late
1950s: "Everywhere I remember people telling me happily that
they were Yugoslavs . . . Everyone now says the descent into hell
was inevitable. Nothing seemed less likely at the time."[14]

Three interlocking legacies of the communist regime were responsible for the breakup of Yugoslavia and the subsequent tragedy in Bosnia. The first was the extreme decentralization of the
federal state in the last two decades of its existence, during the
1970s and 1980s, which made the federal units (the "republics"
of Slovenia, Croatia, Bosnia-Herzegovina, Serbia, Macedonia, and
Montenegro) radically autonomous, practically protostates. This
provided the communist elites in charge of these republics with a
ready-made institutional launchpad for sectarian and secessionist
agendas once the internal cohesion and popular legitimacy of the
communist regime eroded by the late 1980s. The problem was aggravated by a weak federal government constituted and operated
on the basis of consensus between representatives of the six republics (joined by representatives of the two "autonomous provinces"
of the Republic of Serbia, Vojvodina and Kosovo). By the end of

the 1980s, with the complicated system of governance and decision making in terminal decline, federal institutions were paralyzed by disagreement between representatives of the federating units.

The second divisive and destructive legacy stemmed from the communist regime's inordinate emphasis on recognition and institutionalization of different ethnonational identities, as a poor substitute for the pluralism of ideas and interests that the regime, wedded to one-party dictatorship, could never contemplate. This made ethnonationalism a tailor-made basis for political activity and mobilization in the immediate postcommunist period and a tempting strategy for political leaders looking to retain or win power. The third legacy was the entrenched ethos of authoritarian, manipulative politics practiced by unelected cabals, which could easily be exploited by the ascendant breed of nationalist politicians. Both Slobodan Milosevic, Serbia's leader from 1987 until 2000, and Franjo Tudjman, Croatia's leader from 1990 to 1999—the two individuals most culpable for the fate of Yugoslavia and its peoples during the 1990s—were products of the most perverse aspects of the communist system, except that Tudjman was a dissident under communism and a nationalist by conviction while Milosevic was a typical communist official who opportunistically reinvented himself with the changing times.

The dysfunction and crisis of the Yugoslav communist regime led to state failure.[15] It also impacted on certain features of Bosnian society in a way that ignited a catastrophe within Bosnia. During her research in a mixed Muslim-Croat village in central Bosnia in the late 1980s, the Norwegian anthropologist Tone Bringa found that while members of each community had a well-developed sense of sharing a locale and a history with the other group, they also had a strong sense of the boundaries of their own community and their differences of perception and interest, actual and potential, with the other group.[16] This sense of boundaries remained innocuous and the differences latent as long as the Yugoslav framework was stable. Once that framework crumbled, they provided the basis for competing ethnonational political mobilizations that rapidly escalated into violent conflict as Yugoslavia collapsed and imploded in the early 1990s.

In 1992 about three-fourths of Bosnia's 4.4 million people lived in the kind of rural areas and small towns studied by authors like Sudetic and Bringa. The ethos of intergroup relations in these places was very different from the secular cosmopolitanism that had taken hold to some extent during the communist decades in cities like Sarajevo, where there was significant intermixing including intermarriage. Yet even in Sarajevo, a city significantly expanded by urban-centric communist policies of developing higher education and industry, the ultimate effects on identity and intergroup relations are ambiguous. The wartime Bosnian Serb leader Radovan Karadzic, a migrant to the city from his native village in a remote part of Montenegro, was regarded as "a peace-loving and good-natured fellow" in his multiethnic Sarajevo milieu until his metamorphosis in 1991–1992.[17] In 1993 Bringa's village was destroyed by Croat-Muslim violence, and large-scale massacres, mostly of Muslims by Croat paramilitaries, occurred in the area. The area of Sudetic's expertise, the Drina valley of eastern Bosnia, was convulsed by Serb-Muslim violence from April 1992 onward and witnessed grisly atrocities including large-scale "ethnic cleansing" of the Muslim population by Serbs. In July 1995 the violence in the area climaxed in the Srebrenica massacre. Deeply held memories of past conflicts and wrongs, swept under the carpet for several decades by the glib slogan of "brotherhood and unity," reemerged in the context of breakdown and were stoked by demagogic propaganda. The mixed Serb-Muslim area in and around the town of Prijedor in northwest Bosnia, which witnessed massive Serb atrocities against Muslims in the summer of 1992, had seen genocidal violence against Serbs exactly fifty years earlier in 1942, perpetrated by German forces and Croat fascist militia abetted by some local Muslims.

The countdown to war in Bosnia began in November and December 1990, when multiparty elections were held in the republic. Three recently formed ethnonationalist parties—the (Muslim) Party of Democratic Action (SDA), the Serb Democratic Party (SDS), and the Croatian Democratic Union—Bosnia-Herzegovina (HDZ-BiH)—won a resounding victory in these elections by polling the bulk of votes in their respective communities. Indeed, "the election results read like a census of national identities in the socialist period," as large majorities of Muslim, Serb and Croat electors voted for the SDA, SDS, and HDZ respectively.[18] Overall, three-fourths of Bosnian voters cast their ballots for one or the other of these three parties. The two main nonethnic contenders—the Communist Party and a social-democratic party led by Ante Markovic, Yugoslavia's last federal prime minister and by origin a Bosnian Croat—fared poorly. The three victorious parties then formed a wobbly power-sharing coalition government, sharing out political offices amongst themselves.

The scale of the ethnonationalists' triumph in Bosnia's elections at the end of 1990 was unexpected. The outcome was partly a reflection of the unpopularity of the Communist Party in Bosnia, which benefited the ethnonationalist parties. Of all the republics composing Yugoslavia, the communists of Bosnia had the worst reputation for being dinosaurs, hidebound authoritarians out of touch with society. But there was an even stronger factor at work. Postcommunist democratization in Yugoslavia during 1990 followed a peculiar form and sequence. In January 1990 the League of Communists of Yugoslavia (LCY), the party that had run and monopolized power in the one-party state for four and a half decades, disintegrated into its republic-based components following

a confrontation at the party congress between the Serbian party
led by Milosevic and the Slovenian party, in which the Croatian
party eventually sided with the Slovenes. Following this rupture,
no country-wide political organization existed any longer in Yugoslavia that could steer the delicate process of dismantling the one-
party state and ushering in a new era of pluralism. No country-
wide democratic election was subsequently held in Yugoslavia;
consequently, an all-Yugoslav political space never developed. Instead, multiparty elections were conducted separately in the course
of 1990 in the different *republics* of the unraveling federation, starting with Slovenia and Croatia in April and May. In Slovenia the
winners were the communists, who campaigned on a platform of
"self-determination" and "sovereignty" for their republic. In Croatia
the elections brought to power an aggressively nationalist party, the
Croatian Democratic Union (HDZ; the Bosnian HDZ is its sister
party) led by the communist-era dissident Franjo Tudjman, who
made no secret of his ambition of making Croatia a sovereign state.

Unlike Slovenia, which has an overwhelmingly ethnic Slovene
population, Croatia at the time had a Serb minority of at least 12
percent. Many of these Serbs were survivors or descendants of victims and survivors of a genocidal campaign launched by Nazi-
sponsored Croat fascists against the Serb populations of Croatia and
Bosnia during World War II that claimed the lives of several hundred thousand Serbs. Over one-third of the six-hundred-thousand-
plus Serbs in Croatia in 1991 moreover lived in a swath of municipal districts with Serb majorities or pluralities, mostly adjoining
contiguous areas of Bosnia with large Serb populations. (This swath
of territory straddling the Croatia-Bosnia border was until 1881
the *Vojna Krajina,* or Military Frontier, established by the Habsburgs
in the late sixteenth century as a *cordon sanitaire* against the Ottomans and settled mainly by Orthodox Serbs from Ottoman-
conquered Bosnia and Serbia.) A militant Serb movement emerged
in the summer of 1990 in some of these districts in response to

the Tudjman government's assumption of power in Zagreb, and in August 1990 a major armed standoff between Serb irregulars and Croatian police commandos was defused only by JNA intervention. Confrontations between Serb militiamen and Croatian police continued through the subsequent months in flashpoint areas of Croatia. In Kosovo, Serbia's southern province, whose autonomy had been stripped away in 1989 by the Milosevic regime in Belgrade, representatives of the seething ethnic Albanian majority declared their own charter of self-determination in July 1990, encouraged by developments in Slovenia and Croatia. In October Milosevic's Socialist Party of Serbia decisively won elections in Serbia.

This was the context in which Bosnia had its tryst with democracy. Yugoslavia hurtled toward its demise during 1990 as one-party rule gave way to a pluralism dominated by competing ethnonationalist mobilizations that fed off each other. As fractures deepened across Yugoslavia, they were mirrored within Bosnia, the unit of the unraveling country that came closest, because of its multiethnic heterogeneity, to being a mini-Yugoslavia. This bore ominous portents. It is popularly said in the western Balkans that "without Bosnia there is no Yugoslavia, and without Yugoslavia there is no Bosnia." The wider, sheltering framework of a Yugoslav union was essential to Bosnia's internal stability. During the regime transition of 1990 no significant political force put forward an all-Yugoslav vision and agenda. The only attempt in this direction, Markovic's Alliance of Reform Forces of Yugoslavia, was formed belatedly and proved ineffectual. It was founded in late July 1990, after the elections in Slovenia and Croatia. The party subsequently won just 50 of the 735 seats in the parliaments of the other four republics.

In late June 1991 the governments of Slovenia and Croatia declared independence. In Slovenia the violent fallout was transient and limited. The JNA withdrew from Slovenia after a week of skirmishes with Slovenian armed formations organized from the republic's "territorial defense" structure (the second, auxiliary layer of military organization in communist Yugoslavia after the standing army, the JNA). But between July and December 1991 extensive areas of Croatia either dominated by ethnic Serbs or with mixed Serb-Croat populations were gripped by an intense civil war as Serbs in these areas rose in armed rebellion against Croatia's secession from Yugoslavia. The bitter fighting over the multiethnic Danubian town of Vukovar in eastern Croatia, near the border with Serbia, is the best known of many brutal battles waged in this war. The fighting in Croatia resulted in thousands of combatant and civilian deaths and produced several hundred thousand refugees. By the end of 1991, more than 27 percent of Croatia had been overrun by Croatian Serb insurgents supported by units of the JNA—formerly a multiethnic army in ethos and composition but by then dominated by ethnic Serb officers from Serbia, Bosnia, and Croatia following the departure of most officers of other nationalities, particularly Croats and Slovenes. On this territory, much of it reduced to rubble from the fighting, the insurgents declared a Republic of Serbian Krajina (RSK). In early 1992 the fighting in Croatia was frozen by the arrival in the war zones of a United Nations peacekeeping force, the United Nations Protection Force, or UNPROFOR. Their deployment was supported by Serbia's Milosevic government, reluctantly accepted by the beleaguered Tudjman government, and opposed—in rhetoric though not on the ground—by the most militant wing of the Krajina Serb leaders.

As Yugoslavia disintegrated and Croatia went up in flames, an eerie calm prevailed in Bosnia through 1991. In mid-October 1991 and again in late January 1992 the question of Bosnia's future was debated in the Bosnian parliament.[19] On both occasions the Muslim deputies belonging to the SDA party joined with the Croat deputies of the HDZ-BiH—the two parties together held a majority of parliamentary seats—against the outnumbered Serb parliamentarians of the SDS. The HDZ-BiH's hard-line stance against the continuation of a Yugoslav federation in any form, even as a truncated state minus Slovenia and possibly Croatia, was a product of the conflict in Croatia, the party's close nexus with the parent HDZ there, and the influence of Herzegovinian Croats, historically an extreme ethnonationalist element, within the Bosnian HDZ party. By autumn 1991 the leadership of the Muslim SDA party, whose stance was crucial because of its hegemony among Bosnia's single largest ethnonational community, decided to pursue Bosnian independence. They apparently preferred being big fish in a small pond, Bosnia, over being smaller fish in a bigger pond.

But the alliance of the SDA and the HDZ-BiH was built on quicksand, a fact that would be tragically exposed in Mostar and elsewhere in Bosnia in 1993. While the SDA calculated that it would secure a dominant position within an independent Bosnian state, substantial sections of the HDZ-BiH viewed Bosnian independence as simply a stepping stone to a "Greater Croatia" that would incorporate Croat-dominated areas of Bosnia like western Herzegovina. The SDS leaders protested bitterly against what they viewed as Bosnian Muslims and Bosnian Croats ganging up on the Bosnian Serbs, and objected to attempts by the SDA/HDZ-BiH duo to decide a question as incendiary as Bosnia's fate through a majority vote in parliament in violation of long-established socialist norms of equality and consensus between groups. From autumn 1991 the SDS withdrew its participation in the power-sharing Bosnian government established at the end of 1990 and embarked on a strategy of declaring "Serb autonomous regions," on the Krajina Serb model in Croatia, in areas of Bosnia with ethnic Serb majorities or pluralities. The party also began to build the logistical apparatus and operational structures for war and like the Krajina Serb insurgents developed a close relationship with the secret police of the government of Serbia. During the parliamentary

session of January 1992, SDS leader Radovan Karadzic issued a
chilling warning that the SDA and its leader Alija Izetbegovic were
leading the Bosnian Muslims to their doom.

The international response to the Yugoslav crisis would be critical to its evolution and outcome. In late 1991 the European
Union—then still known as the European Community—established a commission to recommend EU policy toward the crisis.
The commission's judgment that Yugoslavia was irretrievably in a
"process of dissolution" paved the way for international recognition of the emergence of the country's republics as sovereign states.
On the basis of the principle of international law known as *uti
possidetis juris* Yugoslavia's internal borders became international
frontiers. Germany took the lead in securing EU recognition of
Croatia's sovereignty and borders in January 1992. In Bosnia a referendum on sovereignty was organized by the government in
Sarajevo—which by early 1992 was bereft of almost any Bosnian
Serb participation—on 29 February and 1 March 1992, acting on a
suggestion contained in one of the EU commission's judgments. In
this plebiscite 63 percent of the eligible electorate voted, and 98
percent of the voters supported Bosnia's independence. The referendum was massively boycotted by Bosnia's Serb population. In
predominantly Serb areas, counterreferenda were organized that
produced overwhelming majorities against sovereign Bosnia and in
favor of a reduced Yugoslav federation in which Bosnia would be a
unit. After the official referendum the United States administration
took the lead in sponsoring international recognition for Bosnia
as a sovereign state, which was formalized on 6 April 1992. The
Bosnian war began the same day.

The international community's approach to the Yugoslav crisis
during those critical months has been controversial for two reasons. In the retrospective opinion of Lord David Owen of Britain,
who from 1992 to 1995 co-led the EU's mediation efforts in the
Croatian and Bosnian conflicts, "to have stuck unyieldingly to the

internal boundaries of the six republics as the boundaries of independent states was a greater folly than premature recognition [of Croatia in January and Bosnia in April 1992] . . . It is true there could not have been a total accommodation of Serb demands, but to rule out any discussion or opportunity for compromise was an extraordinary decision."[20] The application of the principle of *uti possidetis* to Yugoslavia, turning the internal borders of a federal country into international frontiers between sovereign states, has also been sharply criticized by some scholars.[21] These criticisms notwithstanding, demographic and other practical reasons would have made it extremely difficult, if not impossible, to redraw Yugoslavia's internal borders in a way more conducive to the maintenance of peace and regional stability.[22] In a fundamentally sounder approach, which was not attempted, the international community would have insisted on the continuation of a Yugoslav union, premised on nonrecognition of unilateral declarations of independence by component units and intensive international efforts to mediate accommodation between the chief protagonists.

The second source of controversy is the recognition of Bosnia as a sovereign state on the basis of a referendum decided by simple majority rule that was boycotted by a mobilized and agitated ethnonational group constituting at least one-third of the population. Such plebiscites inflame and polarize sensitive disputes over sovereignty because they "cannot measure intensities of belief" and they preclude "working things out through discussion."[23] Political theorist Frederick Whelan has observed that disputes over the legitimate boundaries of sovereignty and citizenship generate "the most intractable and bitter political conflicts," while political scientist Robert Dahl has pointed out that the conventional principle of democratic decision making, majority rule, is neither appropriate nor valid when "the rightfulness of the unit" of sovereignty and governance is itself contested.[24] By February 1992 Bosnia was poised on the brink of war. The referendum, and international rec-

ognition of Bosnia's statehood on its basis, precipitated the outbreak of war. The problem was not just that the overwhelming majority of Bosnian Serbs saw themselves as "orphans of secession" (to
use political scientist John McGarry's phrase), victims of a one-
sided international policy that validated Yugoslavia's breakup and
negated the rights and wishes of their community.[25] The majority
produced by the plebiscite was illusory because very substantial
numbers of Bosnia's Croats were motivated by an ulterior agenda,
approved by Tudjman's government in Zagreb and masterminded
within Bosnia by extreme ethnonationalists who took control of
the HDZ-BiH in February 1992. The stage was set for a triangular
war that would dominate the Western world's media for the next
four years.

The Forging of Peace

The 1992–1995 war catapulted Bosnia—until then a relatively ob-
scure unit of a middle-size communist country in southeastern
Europe—into the international headlines.[26] It also made Bosnia
a byword for the atrocious violence of ethnic war. The television
images were haunting—emaciated men behind barbed wire with
jutting ribcages and a chillingly glazed look in sunken eyes, relentless shelling of cities like Sarajevo and recurrent massacres of civilians queuing for bread, foraging for water, or burying family and
friends cut down by snipers, and above all the large-scale, merci-
less "cleansing" of entire populations who had become intolerable enemies to their neighbors virtually overnight. Public opinion in Western Europe and North America was horrified by such
carnage—not in some distant land perennially prone to war but in
a peripheral part of the Euro-Atlantic world on the eve of the
twenty-first century. The Bosnian war seemed like a bleak, disturb-
ing flashback to the Europe of 1939–1945.

The war spawned three armies in Bosnia—the Army of the Serb

Republic (VRS, the Bosnian Serb army), the Army of Bosnia-Herzegovina (Armija BiH, the Bosnian Muslim army), and the Croatian Defense Council (HVO, the Bosnian Croat army). The Bosnian Serb army was militarily the strongest of the three forces for almost the entire duration of the war. Large numbers of the JNA's ethnic Serb officer corps were Serbs from Bosnia, partly as a legacy of the leading role played by Bosnian (and Croatian) Serbs in the Partisan resistance during World War II. In April and May of 1992 this formidable cadre of professional military men turned into the core of the VRS. Ratko Mladic, a senior JNA officer born during World War II in eastern Bosnia who had already fought in the Croatian war in the second half of 1991, became the commander of the Bosnian Serb army. Both he and Karadzic were indicted in July 1995 for war crimes and crimes against humanity by the Hague-based International Criminal Tribunal for the Former Yugoslavia and have been fugitives since. The VRS inherited enormous quantities of lethal weaponry from the arsenals of the JNA. Consequently, during the war the Bosnian Serb military enjoyed a huge advantage in heavy weapons like artillery guns, tanks, and heavy mortars, particularly over their main adversary, the poorly equipped and comparatively ragtag Bosnian Muslim forces, which grew out of a nucleus of SDA-affiliated paramilitary groups and gangs of common criminals. The Bosnian Croat HVO, unlike the Muslims, enjoyed the support of the nationalist government of Croatia and rapidly became a strong force, although it suffered reverses at the hands of Muslim forces in 1993 in central Bosnia, an area relatively distant from Croatia where Muslims outnumber Croats.

By the end of 1992 Bosnian Serb forces seized two-thirds of Bosnia, expelling hundreds of thousands of non-Serbs, mainly Muslims but also Croats. The atrocities committed against non-Serbs by Bosnian Serbs—and by wild paramilitary groups from Serbia and Montenegro—were on a larger scale and more systematic in nature than those perpetrated by the Muslims, or even the Croats. But all three belligerents were guilty of brutal abuses from an early stage of the war. In the summer of 1992, for example, hundreds of Serb civilians were incarcerated, many tortured and some murdered, in Muslim-run detention camps in Tarcin and Celebici, villages located south of Sarajevo off the road leading to the Neretva valley and Mostar. Their fate was similar to that inflicted on Muslims rounded up in and around the northwestern Bosnian town of Prijedor around the same time, who were confined in camps located in the nearby villages of Omarska and Manjaca. In 1993 Muslim and Serb prisoners suffered hellish treatment at a Croat-run detention facility in Dretelj, a village south of Mostar. The Drina valley of eastern Bosnia was caught up in a spiral of ambushes and killings between Serbs and Muslims. The Serbs, though locally outnumbered, retained the upper hand in this conflict primarily because of the area's proximity to Serbia. The three prewar parties—the SDS, SDA, and HDZ-BiH—became the nucleus of militarized statelets and their leaders the political masters of the respective armies, although the relationships between military commanders and political leaders were intermittently, and sometimes severely, tense.

The Bosnian conflict frustrated and confounded international peacemaking efforts for more than three years. The UN's peace-keeping forces on the ground were reduced to the role of a beleaguered and usually ineffective fire brigade trying to contain eruptions of fighting in flashpoints around the country. The most significant attempt to end the conflict was the Vance-Owen peace plan, presented in the first half of 1993 and named after its formulators, former U.S. secretary of state Cyrus Vance and David Owen of Britain. The plan proposed a decentralized Bosnian state comprising nine cantons, three each with Serb, Muslim, and Croat majorities. In addition, Sarajevo and its environs would become a separate, neutral district under international administration (in April 1992, Greater Sarajevo's population was almost one-half Muslim, more than one-third Serb, and at least 10 percent Croat). The Bosnian Serb leadership rejected the proposal in May 1993 even after being urged to accept by Milosevic. Meanwhile the Bosnian Croat army, by early 1993 already embroiled in growing hostilities with Muslim forces in several areas, stepped up its campaign of violence and expulsion with the apparent objective of turning the Croat-*majority* cantons identified by Vance-Owen into Croat-*only* areas.

The Vance-Owen plan—which bore a strong imprint of the Swiss model of devolved canton-based government and in its proposal for Sarajevo carried echoes of the special internationally administered status proposed for Jerusalem in the UN's November 1947 partition plan for Palestine—was built on the premise that Bosnia's population being "inextricably intermingled, there appears to be no viable way to create three territorially distinct states based on ethnic or confessional principles."[27] This was true until March and April of 1992, when only about 20 percent of Bosnia's 110 municipal communities had an overwhelming majority of one ethnonational group. But in the intervening year Bosnia's ethnic map had undergone a brutal, tectonic shift driven by the basic logic of the Bosnian war—the creation of "facts on the ground," monoethnic territories carved out through "ethnic cleansing." A year after the war began it was already too late for the Vance-Owen formula. Any future settlement would have to accommodate the transformation of Bosnia's political geography and those cruel facts on the ground. At the same time, full-fledged de jure partition was precluded. The Bosnian state had been recognized in April 1992 and the international community clearly could not do a *volte-face* and sanction three statelets created by sordid means or the annexation of large parts of Bosnia to Serbia-Montenegro and Croatia.

It took resolute and coercive American diplomacy during the second half of 1995 to reach that complex compromise. The countdown to Dayton began in May 1995 when Bosnian Serbs took UN soldiers hostage and humiliated them by parading them in chains before the world media. In July Mladic's forces launched large-scale attacks on the remnant Muslim enclaves in eastern Bosnia, including Srebrenica, which had been designated as UN-protected "safe havens" two years earlier. Serb shelling and sniping continued to plague Sarajevo, where the Serbs held most of the mountain ranges overlooking the city as well as almost all of the suburbs. U.S. patience finally ran out. Starting in late August NATO warplanes, at American initiative, commenced a fortnight of aerial bombardment of Bosnian Serb military targets, including command-and-control facilities. The tide of war had already been dramatically reversed in Croatia earlier that summer when the Croatian army, massively built up since 1991, overran three of the four zones that made up the rebel Croatian Serb entity. Two hundred thousand Croatian Serbs fled these offensives, which had tacit American approval, into Serb-controlled Bosnia and farther afield to Serbia.

By mid-September 1995 the Bosnian Serbs were facing a military crisis. Croatian army units fresh from their triumph across the border swept into western Bosnia and parts of central Bosnia supported by the Bosnian Croat HVO and captured large swaths of Serb-held territory including several towns. Capitalizing on Bosnian Serb disarray, Muslim forces broke out of their enclave around the town of Bihac in Bosnia's northwestern corner and retook some territory from the Serbs, including the town of Sanski Most, which fell in late September. The Bosnian Serbs' largest town and political capital, Banja Luka in northwestern Bosnia, swollen with several hundred thousand Croatian Serb and Bosnian Serb refugees fleeing the enemy advances, was threatened with capture. The Croat and Muslim offensives stalled and the fighting tapered off by late September, leaving Banja Luka and nearby Prijedor in Serb hands. Yet as Richard Holbrooke, the U.S. assistant secretary of state tasked with the Bosnia brief, put it in a handwritten fax to Washington on 20 September:

The basic truth is perhaps not something we can say publicly right now. In fact the map negotiation, which always seemed to me our most daunting challenge, is taking place right now on the battlefield and so far in a manner beneficial . . . In a few weeks the famous 70–30 division of the country [favoring the Bosnian Serbs] has gone to around 50–50 [between Bosnian Serb control on the one hand and Bosnian Muslim and Bosnian Croat territories taken together on the other], obviously making our task easier.[28]

This leveling of the cleansing field enabled a determined and forceful American third-party (or more accurately fourth-party) effort to successfully mediate a settlement during two weeks of "proximity talks" on the Wright-Patterson Air Force Base in Dayton, Ohio, in November 1995.[29] The Bosnian Serbs, who had acquired a reputation for incorrigible intransigence and whose top figures, Karadzic and Mladic, were already indicted as war criminals, were effectively excluded from the negotiations. Instead Slobodan Milosevic negotiated on behalf of the Bosnian Serbs, and his cooperation was essential to the agreement. Milosevic was by now weary of his embarrassing Bosnian Serb ex-protégés and was motivated to rid Serbia of crippling economic sanctions and reinvent himself as a peacemaker on the international stage. Croatian president Franjo Tudjman, basking in his stunning military success in Croatia, attended the talks, and his assent was also vital (although he negotiated via his foreign minister and Bosnian Croat representatives were present). The Bosnian Muslim delegation presented a confused picture, its members at loggerheads with one another and its leader, Alija Izetbegovic, seemingly unwilling or unable to engage in the substantive details of negotiations. But in the end they too fell in line.

The talks were successfully wrapped up on 21 November, and

on 14 December 1995 the agreement ending the Bosnian war
was ceremonially signed in the Versailles palace near Paris. Under-
scoring the regional roots and dimensions of the conflict, the signatories were Milosevic and Tudjman, the two most powerful politicians in the region—rather than Bosnian Serb and Bosnian Croat
leaders—along with Izetbegovic. Although formally signed in
France, the agreement has gone down in history as the Dayton
peace agreement, one of the most famous and controversial settlements of recent decades.

The international community's first high representative in Bosnia
in 1996–1997, the former Swedish prime minister Carl Bildt, has
written:

> The peace agreement for Bosnia is the most ambitious docu-
> ment of its kind in modern history . . . A traditional peace
> treaty aims at [simply] ending a war . . . while here it is a ques-
> tion of setting up a state on the basis of little more than the ru-
> ins and rivalries of a bitter war . . . The peace agreement bal-
> ances the reality of division with structures of cooperation and
> integration and is based on the hope that over time the imper-
> ative of integration in the country and the region will be the
> dominant factor.[30]

To cope with this challenge the Dayton agreement devised a
complex, multitiered constitutional framework for the postwar
state.[31] Bosnia was structured as a confederation—a loosely organized variant of a federal state in which the powers of self-rule of
the territorially defined constituent units are dominant and the jurisdiction and competencies of the federal government are limited.
The state would consist of two "entities"—a radically autonomous
Serb Republic (Republika Srpska, RS) covering 49 percent of
Bosnia's territory, and a Federation of Bosnia and Herzegovina

(FBiH, often referred to as the Bosniac-Croat Federation) across the other 51 percent. The 51:49 division largely followed the front lines at the end of the war, but there were a few territorial adjustments—notably in the area of Sarajevo, where almost all the suburbs held by Serbs during the war were given over to Muslim control and authority, and in central Bosnia, where some of the land captured by Croats from Serbs in September 1995 was given to the RS. The two entities were demarcated by an Inter-Entity Boundary Line (IEBL) running across Bosnia in a meandering pattern for eleven hundred kilometers. The IEBL is the result of fighting on the ground and has no other logic or basis. It cuts through numerous prewar municipal districts and divides these between the entities.

While the establishment and recognition of the RS was the key concession to Bosnian Serb demands, the other entity, the FBiH, was a by-product of the Muslim-Croat war of 1993–1994. It was established in March 1994—when the U.S. government brokered a truce to that conflict during talks in Washington—to provide a political umbrella for the areas held by Muslim and Croat forces. The Americans viewed this as a way to stabilize the truce and to facilitate Muslim-Croat military cooperation against the Bosnian Serbs. This shotgun wedding between warring factions was confirmed at Dayton eighteen months later, but the Muslim-Croat entity was decentralized to alleviate Bosnian Croat concerns. The Bosniac-Croat Federation would be composed of ten cantons, and most powers were devolved to these cantons. This was a key concession to the Croats, outnumbered four to one by Muslims within the federation areas. Three cantons with large Croat majorities were thereby assured of self-government. Five other cantons have large Muslim majorities. The two cantons with substantial Croat *and* Muslim populations—central Bosnia and Herzegovina-Neretva, the canton centered on Mostar—were the focus of bitter Croat-Muslim hostilities during the war. These were endowed with special power-sharing regimes to ensure equitable status and treatment for the two communities. The institutions of the FBiH government, based in Sarajevo, were structured to ensure parity between Muslims and Croats. For example, if an FBiH ministry was headed by a Muslim, the deputy minister had to be a Croat, and vice versa.

The institutions of the common Bosnian state were similarly constituted. A three-member joint Bosnian presidency would consist of one Serb (elected from the RS) and one Muslim and one Croat (both elected from the FBiH). The chair would rotate between the three co-presidents, who would strive to operate through consensus (in practice, the joint presidency enjoys almost no substantive powers). The limited number of common-state ministries would have more or less equal representation of ministers from the three ethnonational groups, and the prime ministership would rotate between them. The upper chamber of the bicameral Bosnian parliament would consist of equal numbers of Muslim, Serb, and Croat lawmakers. Ethnonational caucuses in the common-state, FBiH, and cantonal parliaments were given the right invoke a "vital interest veto" on legislation they considered detrimental to the basic interests of their community. The Bosnian constitutional court, charged with adjudicating disputes between the common state and one or both entities, between the entities, or between institutions of the common state, would have nine members—two each from the three Bosnian communities plus three foreign judges who could not be from any of the other successor-states to Yugoslavia.

Two key principles underlie this complicated system of governance. The first is *ethnoterritorial autonomy*—for Serbs in the RS and for Croats as well as Muslims in the cantons composing the FBiH. The second principle is *institutionalized consociation*—see Chapter 2 for a discussion of the history and meaning of this concept—when the paths of the ethnonational groups do cross each other. Thus the consociational norms of grand coalition, allocation of public offices on the basis of ethnonational parity, and veto rights were all enshrined in the executive, legislative, and judicial institutions of the common state and the Bosniac-Croat Federation. The *degree* of ethnoterritorial autonomy—"segmental autonomy" is the other key feature of consociational government—was very great. Even in robust federal systems it is usual for foreign affairs, defense, and currency to be the purview of the central government and not the constituent ethnoterritorial units. The Dayton agreement gave the entities the right to maintain their own armed forces—in other words, a Bosnian Serb defense ministry and army would continue to exist alongside a FBiH army. (In practice, the FBiH army also consisted of separate ethnic Croat and Muslim formations, descended from the HVO and the Armija BiH, respectively.) Until 1998 three currencies were in circulation in Bosnia, including the old Yugoslav dinar in the RS and the kuna, the currency of Croatia, in the Croat areas of the Bosniac-Croat Federation. A common Bosnian currency—the convertible Bosnian mark, pegged initially to the German mark and later to the euro—was introduced in mid-1998 by the Central Bank of Bosnia and Herzegovina, an institution established and controlled by the international community.

The Dayton settlement was not just internally but *externally* confederal. The two entities were each given the right to establish and develop special ties of cooperation with neighboring states, meaning Serbia-Montenegro and Croatia. So Bosnia's internal *and* international frontiers would be "soft" borders. Just as the IEBL running across Bosnia would not be permitted to become a hard line of partition—a vital concern to Bosnian Muslims—Bosnia's borders with Serbia-Montenegro and Croatia too would be porous, in accommodation of the wishes of Bosnia's Serbs and Croats. In addition to their entity and common-state citizenships, Bosnians could hold parallel citizenship of these neighboring states.

This constitutional structure, which evidently accords primacy to ethnonational rights and demands, is outlined in Annex 4 of the Dayton agreement. At the same time the agreement incorporated ambitious commitments on safeguarding and upholding individual human rights. The most significant commitment was contained in Annex 7 of the agreement, which guaranteed an unconditional *right of return* to all who had been expelled from or otherwise compelled to abandon their homes in towns and villages across Bosnia during the war. The international community would do whatever it could to enable all those who wished to return to do so. Assuring freedom of movement across all former front lines and providing security to returnees would be a top priority of the military component of the postconflict international presence in Bosnia—sixty thousand NATO-led troops flooded into Bosnia in early 1996— who would be supported in this endeavor by their civilian counterparts in the UN, the Organization for Security and Cooperation in Europe (OSCE), the World Bank, and other agencies active in postwar Bosnia.

This represented a very ambitious commitment. About 2.3 million people—more than half of Bosnia's 1992 population of 4.4 million people—had been driven from their homes by the war. Around 1.2 million became refugees outside Bosnia—several hundred thousand in Serbia-Montenegro and Croatia, but countless others scattered throughout the world, mostly in the EU countries and in the United States and Canada—while another 1.1 million people were internally displaced within Bosnia.

The political structure of the Bosnian state established by the Dayton agreement is an attempt to reconcile deep polarizations within Bosnia. Opinion surveys in 1997 found that 91 percent of Bosnian Serbs and 84 percent of Bosnian Croats opposed the very idea of a united Bosnian state, whereas 98 percent of Bosnian Muslims supported it. Fundamental disagreement over the legitimacy of Bosnia's status as a sovereign state, which led to war in 1992, has persisted into the postwar phase. Students of politics from John Stuart Mill onward have argued that unless there is a consensus or near consensus among citizens of a polity about the legitimacy of the sovereignty and borders of the political unit to which they belong, sustainable democratic development is not feasible. Robert Dahl has written that democratic theory "cannot solve the question of the proper domain of sovereignty" where such disagreement exists over "the rightfulness of the unit" although "a crisp, unimpeachable solution would be a marvelous achievement."[32] He also says, however, that in such situations "we shall need to make complex and debatable empirical and utilitarian judgments" to "find reasonable answers" and "the result may well be a complex system with several layers of democratic government, each operating with a somewhat different agenda."[33]

This is precisely the nature of the Dayton settlement to Bosnia's theoretically and normatively insoluble problem—different ethnonational groups harboring incompatible notions of self-determination. Shortly after the formation of the first Yugoslavia at the end of World War I the Bosnia-born litterateur Ivo Andric, who would later win the Nobel Prize for Literature, wrote about the tragic essence of his homeland:

> Bosnia is a wonderful country, fascinating, with nothing ordinary in the habitat or people . . . But . . . Bosnia is a country of hatred and fear . . . You Bosnians have for the most part got used to keeping all the strength of your hatred for that which is closest to you. Your holy of holies is as a rule three hundred rivers and mountains away but the objects of your revulsion and hatred are right beside you—in the same town, often on the other side of your courtyard wall. And you love your homeland, you passionately love it, but in three different ways that are mutually exclusive, that often come to blows, and hate each other to death.[34]

The Dayton settlement and subsequent peace process attempts the Herculean task of devising and implementing a framework for the three different ways of being Bosnian to coexist, however uneasily.

That is a tall order. The Dayton formula for Bosnia—which can be plausibly regarded as contrived and convoluted, not just "complex"—risked dissatisfying all of the three Bosnian peoples, the Serbs and Croats by denying them the right to govern themselves in sovereign jurisdictions in Bosnia or to merge with their neighboring kin-states, and the Muslims by creating a highly decentralized, multilayered state of doubtful viability. There is little doubt that most Bosnian Serbs would have preferred their own fully sovereign statelet in Bosnia, probably in an associative relationship with the Serbia-Montenegro union, which dissolved in 2006. Most Bosnian Croats found their "federation" with the Muslims to be both contrived and unjust, and pointed to the asymmetry of Croats being denied their own ethnoterritorial "entity" in Bosnia in contrast to the Bosnian Serbs' RS. Most Bosnian Muslims regarded the recognition of the RS as an autonomous entity across almost half of Bosnia as a reward for Bosnian Serb genocide against Bosnian Muslims during the war, and the complicated political structure of the Bosnian state as a bad joke.

A decade later none of these underlying grievances have disappeared. But the Bosnian Serb stance has perceptibly shifted from angry recalcitrance to pragmatic acceptance of the state created by the Dayton agreement. As memories of the 1992–1995 war attenuated over time, most Bosnian Serbs realized that the Dayton agreement was not a bad compromise from their ethnonational perspective—above all because it gave the RS a constitutionally and internationally guaranteed autonomous status. Since the late 1990s almost all Bosnian Serb political elements, including the still-dominant SDS party, have foresworn the agenda of total separation in favor of the defense of the spirit and letter of the Dayton agreement, particularly against perceived encroachments on the RS's self-rule powers by the international community.

The HDZ-BiH, which continues to be the hegemonic party among Bosnian Croats, launched a protest movement against the international community in 2001, demanding full constitutional equality for Croats in Bosnia—code for a third entity. But this movement fizzled out. In reality most Bosnian Croat areas are self-governing in any case, especially the large swaths contiguous to Croatia that are virtually indistinguishable from Croatia and in all senses oriented toward it. The death of the Croatian nationalist strongman Tudjman in late 1999 deprived the most intransigent Bosnian Croat elements of patronage from Zagreb and sharply narrowed their room for maneuver.

Most Bosnian Muslims still think that the state is far too decentralized and that its structure of rights and representation panders excessively to the ethnonationalist claims of Bosnia's Serbs and Croats. Many Bosnian Muslims feel that this does not do justice to either their numerically superior status in Bosnia—no census has been conducted since 1991 but Bosnian Muslims likely constitute about half the population—or to their suffering as the greatest victims of the war. But despite their disaffection they too appear largely resigned today to the basic framework of the Dayton state. Most Bosnian Muslims know—even if they are reluctant to admit it—that a price had to be paid to Bosnia's Serbs and Croats to salvage any kind of united Bosnia from the ruins of 1995, and they are conscious of their own community's numerical and strategic weakness in the regional context of Bosnia, Serbia, and Croatia. They are also aware that the international community is both unable and unwilling to throw out or fundamentally alter the political structure put in place by Dayton, a binding international treaty. This is a bitter pill to swallow, but a decade after war's end a fragile equilibrium has emerged on the core question of Bosnian statehood and its institutional form.

The type of confederal, consociational settlement institutionalized by the Dayton agreement is susceptible to three potent criticisms:

- The settlement entrenches and perpetuates ethnonational boundaries and differences.
- The settlement relies on the empowerment of ethnonationalist
  segmental elites.
- Institutional frameworks built on territorially defined autonomy
  and shared decision-making at the political center provide the
  basis for democratic stability in moderately segmented societies
  like Switzerland and Belgium, but it is unlikely that they can do
  this in deeply divided postwar societies like Bosnia.

These are serious criticisms, but counterarguments exist. The
nature of such settlements is not a mindless indulgence of identity
fetishism but a practical response to intractable conflicts where
ethnonational fault lines *are* the dominant cleavage in society and
politics. While the formal, de jure partition of Bosnia has been
ruled out by the international community since the early 1990s, a
state based on a common, civic conception of national identity
is also infeasible in Bosnia. In 2003, opinion surveys run by the
United Nations Development Program found that "a state of citizens"—rather than a state based primarily on the autonomy and
rights of ethnonational communities—was favored by 52 percent
of Bosnian Muslims, 17 percent of Bosnian Croats, and 9 percent of
Bosnian Serbs.[35] This means that the civic model of government,
which gives primacy to individual citizens and priority to their
rights, would have to be imposed against the will of the vast majority of members of two of the three Bosnian groups, and would have
the support of just one-half of even the third group. Bosnians of *all*
three communities overwhelmingly vote in competitive elections
for parties and candidates who emphasize ethnonational identities

and interests—significant cross-ethnic parties are almost absent in Bosnia. In these circumstances, the framework of the Dayton state is not just the most feasible but the most democratic form of government for Bosnia.

The empowerment of ethnonational(ist) segmental elites is troubling but unavoidable. This is because supraethnic political alternatives are almost absent in Bosnia, as in other deeply divided societies like Northern Ireland or Cyprus. International supervision of these elites is, however, necessary and desirable for two reasons, as the experience of state building and stabilization in postwar Bosnia reveals. First, without external involvement the segmental elites typically lack the will and the capacity to interact and cooperate in the aftermath of a bitter, polarizing armed conflict. Second, a judicious mix of international sanctions and rewards—a "carrot and stick" approach—is essential to "civilize" and domesticate the most intransigent and extremist forces among those elites, who would otherwise play spoilers in the post-settlement peace process.

In Chapter 2 I noted that the UN's 2002–2004 peace proposals for Cyprus bore a remarkable although unacknowledged resemblance to the principles and structure of the Dayton settlement. That plan's failure to gain the acceptance of the eastern Mediterranean island's Greek Cypriot majority is indicative of the difficulties of making such settlements stick in societies with deep ethnonational divides. Lebanon's unwritten national pact of 1943, which was clearly consociational, broke down in the mid-1970s as civil war erupted, the cumulative effect of a slew of internal and external destabilizing factors. Northern Ireland's 1998 Good Friday agreement, an exemplar of the consociational model, has had a most tortuous career in the years since 1998 and its implementation remains suspended.

Clearly this type of settlement—whether confederal *and* consociational as in Bosnia and Cyprus, or simply consociational as in Northern Ireland or Lebanon, where ethnonational divides are not as territorialized as in Cyprus post-1974 or Bosnia post-1992—has difficult prospects in societies with a history of civil war.[36] Yet the paradox is that there seems to be no alternative path to peace-building in these societies. The Taif accord of 1989, which marked the end of the Lebanese civil war, is a renovated version of the national pact of 1943.[37] The crisis-prone career of the Good Friday settlement notwithstanding, there is near-universal agreement that its formula represents the only feasible framework for uneasy coexistence between opposed ethnonational identities and aspirations in Northern Ireland.[38] A future settlement in Cyprus is unlikely to deviate significantly from the ill-fated Annan Plan's blueprint. In deeply torn societies where integration around a common national identity is simply not possible, yet where partition and segregation are also infeasible and normatively undesirable, the type of settlement institutionalized in Bosnia by the Dayton agreement is, despite all its vices and flaws, the only option. In a crowning irony, the political structure of Dayton Bosnia replicates in a democratic and internationally supervised variant many key features of the confederal and consociational system of Yugoslavia that broke down in 1991–1992.

The Dayton settlement would not have materialized but for an American intervention during the second half of 1995 that combined energetic diplomacy with calibrated use of military power. Subsequently the Bosnian constitution, incorporated into the agreement as Annex 4, was largely written by lawyers from the U.S. Department of State. International engagement has been equally, if not more, vital to the post-Dayton peace process in Bosnia over the past decade. The scale of the international operation to stabilize and consolidate the Bosnian peace has been simply massive.

Since the winter of 1995–1996 hundreds of thousands of military and civilian personnel from scores of countries have served with international organizations in Bosnia. A variety of international organizations have worked on different aspects of the peace process. Until end-2004, when it was replaced by a lean seven-thousand-strong European Union Force (EUFOR) drawn from the militaries of EU countries, a NATO-led military peacekeeping force, known as the Implementation Force (IFOR) in 1996 and subsequently as the Stabilization Force (SFOR), provided the security guarantee. The OSCE was responsible for organizing and supervising elections to the municipal, cantonal, entity, and common-state levels of the political system—its powers included vetting parties and candidate lists—until 2002, when it relinquished its responsibilities to a Bosnian election commission composed of equal numbers of Muslim, Serb, and Croat members who were complemented by international members during a transition period lasting until 2006. Until the end of 2002 an International Police Task Force under the authority of the UN mission to Bosnia conducted a process of monitoring, reforming, and restructuring police forces across Bosnia—policing is devolved to the entity level in the RS and the cantonal level in the Bosniac-Croat Federation—to eliminate the worst forms of ethnonational prejudice and discrimination and ensure compliance with international standards. This UN-led operation was replaced by a smaller EU police mission in late 2002. The World Bank, International Monetary Fund, and United States Agency for International Development have been involved in the economic aspects of reconstruction.

The Office of the High Representative, staffed by several hundred Bosnian and international employees but led by internationals, has overseen all nonmilitary aspects of the effort and coordinated policy. At the end of 1997 the high representative was endowed with far-reaching powers of control and intervention vis-à-vis Bosnian politicians and institutions by the Peace Implementation Council, which gathers fifty-five governments and international agencies involved with the Bosnian peace process and meets twice a year. These sharply expanded powers included the right to formulate and impose legislation on deadlocked or incompetent institutions, dismiss elected officials deemed obstructive or corrupt and ban party leaders engaged in such behavior from public life, and close down media considered offensive to other ethnonational communities and/or the international community. The subsequent widespread use of these powers by high representatives has stirred a debate on whether the international peacebuilding operation in Bosnia has become a colonial-style civilizing mission that practices liberal imperialism in the guise of liberal internationalism.[39]

This criticism of the international role in postwar Bosnia has some merit. The international high representative and his minions do behave in a manner reminiscent of colonial viceroys and their lackeys, with more than a little arrogance and high-handedness, and Bosnia's international hierarchy is immune from accountability to Bosnians. But the critics have their own blind spots. They overlook the context of the international community's thankless task of stabilization, state building, and democratization in postwar Bosnia—an utterly broken society where local political elites are often descended from the criminalized party-statelets of the war years and the public are disoriented by the bloody implosion of the former political and social order and the plethora of postwar problems. The critics also focus their attack on the international high representative's decree powers, when in fact international engagement with postwar Bosnia has been multifaceted and mostly constructive. There is little doubt that Bosnia's international supervisors have postured as upholders of law, order, reason, and morality, and that an overly intrusive international role has the potential to damage the longer-term development of Bosnian capacities to run their country, where Bosnians emerge as active agents of their own future instead of remaining subjects in the shadow of an international guardianship. Yet overall the international presence in postwar Bosnia has done more good than harm and Bosnians would clearly be worse off without the international community in their midst.

The right of return promised by the Dayton agreement has not remained on paper because of the strong and activist international presence in postwar Bosnia. In the immediate aftermath of the war, few Bosnians would cross the Inter-Entity Boundary Line or de facto dividing lines, such as that represented by the ruins of the city center of Mostar, to "enemy" territory. By the late 1990s this situation changed, partly due to the passage of time but largely because of the improved security environment across most of Bosnia, which was enabled and sustained by the international civilian and military presence. By 2000 the border between Bosnia's two entities had become just a line on maps rather than what ethnonationalists would have liked it to be—a hard frontier of segregation between mono-ethnic zones. In most areas, less than five years after the war ended it was no longer possible to tell where the IEBL lay, and people traveled freely across the line in a manner unimaginable a few years earlier. In Mostar, too, the dividing line softened up considerably to movement of people and traffic.

Returns to their homes by refugees and internally displaced people remained sluggish until 1999. This was particularly true of the crucial category of *minority returns*—the return of the dispossessed to homes in areas dominated demographically and politically by another ethnonational community. If, for example, a Bosnian Muslim family expelled during the war from Banja Luka, Bosnia's largest Serb-dominated city, returned from their temporary refuge in Germany to Muslim-dominated Sarajevo, this would qualify as a return but *not* as a minority return. By returning to Sarajevo and possibly taking up residence in a house or apartment that formerly belonged to Serbs who left Sarajevo during the war, this family's return would actually contribute to the consolidation of forced population exchange and its effect, monoethnic territories. If instead the family returned to their original home in Banja Luka, the capital of the RS, this would be a minority return—the kind of return that runs directly against the aim of "ethnic cleansing."

Minority returns escalated sharply across Bosnia between 2000 and 2002. In these three years a total of 261,617 persons were recorded as minority returnees across Bosnia by the international authorities. They included Croats and Muslims reclaiming homes in areas dominated by the other group within the Bosniac-Croat Federation, Serbs returning to parts of Sarajevo and, most significant, Bosnian Muslims returning to the RS. The number of Bosnian Muslims living in areas that became the RS dropped from about five hundred thousand in April 1992 to fewer than thirty thousand by the end of the war, and returns were a feeble trickle until 1999. After 2002, minority returns tapered off as the pool of potential returnees approached saturation point. But by mid-2005 a total of 451,584 minority returns had taken place since the end of the war across Bosnia, including 159,601 (overwhelmingly Bosnian Muslims) to the RS.[40] These are not insubstantial figures, because Bosnia's total population is probably about 3.5 million today due to wartime fatalities and large-scale emigration during and after the war.

The prewar ethnic mosaic of Bosnia is no more, a collateral casualty of the extinction of Yugoslavia. But a decade after Dayton, enclaves populated by minority returnees have reappeared in a leopard-spot pattern across territories forcibly homogenized between 1992 and 1995, including in some of the most notorious locales of "ethnic cleansing." The minarets of mosques are once again visible in the landscape of Prijedor, close to Banja Luka in northwestern Bosnia, and parts of the Drina valley in eastern Bosnia, bordering Serbia, where attempts were made during the war to erase all traces, human and architectural, of Muslim presence and history. Several thousand of the Muslims evicted by terror from west Mostar have been able to reclaim their homes and a slice of their dignity.

So while "ethnic cleansing" has left a deep, permanent imprint on Bosnia—on the ground and in the memories of people—it has not had a total, untrammeled victory. This is due to the efforts of a raft of international community agencies that worked to translate Dayton's right-of-return provisions into a meaningful reality. A property law implementation plan sponsored by the international community assessed several hundred thousand claims submitted by the dispossessed. A dedicated task force on reconstruction and return, composed of staff of several international organizations, was created with a network of field offices. The reform of policing at the local level carried out by of the UN police task force, the security cover provided by SFOR soldiers, the efforts of the Bosnia mission of the United Nations High Commissioner for Refugees, and the aid supplied by donor agencies and governments for rebuilding houses and livelihoods all played a role in the complicated and difficult process of refugee return.

A peace process to settle an ethnonational conflict is missing a key element if it does not tackle the issue of the rights of expelled, dispossessed people. In November 2000 Kofi Annan spoke to this challenge in the context of Cyprus:

> Concerning property, we must recognize that there are considerations of international law to which we must give weight . . . The legal rights that people have to their property must be respected. At the same time, I believe that a solution should carefully regulate the exercise of those rights to safeguard the [ethnodemographic] character of the [Greek and Turkish Cypriot] "component states" [visualized by the UN's peace plan]. Meeting these principles will require an appropriate combination of reinstatement, exchange and compensation. For a period of time to be established by agreement there may be limits on the numbers of Greek Cypriots establishing residence in the north and Turkish Cypriots in the south.[41]

Such an acknowledgment in principle of the historic injustice suffered by Palestinian refugees in 1948 coupled with a mutually agreeable practical solution to the issue is essential to a settlement between Israelis and Palestinians.[42] In Bosnia, a rare positive example of recognizing and implementing the rights of refugees has been set at the beginning of the twenty-first century, after a grim twentieth century during which mass ethnonational expulsions—among them Palestinians in 1948 (and to a lesser extent also in 1967), east and central European Germans at the end of World War II, and Hindus, Muslims, and Sikhs in the Indian subcontinent in 1947—occurred with no hope of redress.

The Dayton agreement's constitutional structure resulted in two problems because of its emphases on decentralization of political authority and the rights of ethnonational peoples. First, in the initial postwar years, although Bosnia was nominally one state, there was a near absence of the common-state institutions needed for that state to be viable. Second, under the entity structure Serbs were not explicitly recognized as a "constituent people"—an important legal and constitutional concept carried over from the communist period—in the Bosniac-Croat Federation, while Muslims and Croats did not have the equivalent status, explicitly equal to Serbs, in the RS. In a political system where citizenship rights are mediated through membership in ethnonational groups, and the entities—and within the Bosniac-Croat entity the self-governing cantons—enjoy extensive autonomy, such nonrecognition implied inequality and exclusion. Both problems have been addressed through reforms of the Dayton structure initiated and supervised by the international community. In the process of reform the fundamentals of the Dayton settlement have remained intact but the agreement has been subject to modifications that make Bosnia a more functional and fairer polity.

Over the years international community action established the minimal institutional apparatus of a state, such as the Central Bank (which issued the common Bosnian currency in 1998) and a multiethnic State Border Service (in 2000) for air and land entry and exit points, and enacted essential legislation such as the statewide Election Law (2001) which facilitated Bosnia's admission to the Council of Europe. The jurisdiction and competencies of the common-state government, threadbare in the early postwar years, have been gradually strengthened and expanded under the supervision of the international community. Defense, for example, has been brought under the purview of the common state. This was a condition for consideration of Bosnia's membership in NATO's Partnership for Peace program, but it is also usual for defense to be under the central authority in federal systems. Separate Muslim, Serb, and Croat military units are still the norm, but they now coexist in a single Bosnian army of twelve thousand professional soldiers. In 2004–2005 Bosnia's first defense minister was Nikola Radovanovic, a Bosnian Serb who began his career in the JNA and fought in the Bosnian Serb army, in which he held the rank of colonel, during the 1992–1995 war. The number of common-state ministries has increased—possibly the most important in the longer term is the Ministry of European Affairs and Integration, which is responsible for negotiating Bosnia's ongoing process of entry into the EU. In the decade since Dayton, Bosnia has evolved from an unwieldy, implausible confederation toward a "normal" multinational federal state in which there is a rational balance of powers between the federal government and the constituent units.

The political institutions of the entities composing the state have also been reformed to facilitate equal treatment for members of all three ethnonational communities. In 2000 the Bosnian constitutional court called for such reform—by a split 5–4 vote in which the three international and two Muslim judges voted for reform and the two Serb and two Croat judges voted against it—in order to ensure statutory equality and equitable representation and participation for non-Serbs in the RS and Serbs in the Bosniac-Croat Federation. The reform process, completed in 2002 under the stew-

ardship of the international high representative, Wolfgang Petritsch
of Austria, coincided with the peak of minority returns across
Bosnia. As a result, fully one-half of the ministers in the Republika
Srpska government have to be non-Serbs (five Muslims and three
Croats), an upper chamber of the RS parliament has parity representation of the three ethnonational communities, and the RS
president, a Serb, has two vice presidents, one Muslim and one
Croat. Serbs are guaranteed reciprocal rights in the Bosniac-Croat
Federation's institutions, including parity representation with the
other two groups in the upper house of that entity's legislature and
a share of ministerial posts in the executive. These reforms have
further extended the paradigm of governance based on ethnonational group membership. But this paradigm is not unique to
Bosnia. It is an institutional necessity in deeply divided societies
with a history of civil war, such as Northern Ireland, Cyprus, and
Lebanon.

Bosnia still faces an arduous journey to the long-term stability
and relative prosperity promised by the EU. Following the incremental, rationalizing reforms to the Dayton structure under international supervision, the institutional framework of the state no
longer presents a structural obstacle to that journey. If a Cypriot
confederation of two ethnically defined "constituent states" with a
limited central government constituted on consociational principles could have been accommodated by the EU—which the EU
promised would happen if the Annan Plan came into force—so
can the Bosnian state, which has a similar configuration. Even a
long-standing EU member-state such as Belgium has since the
early 1990s had a structure of government—composed of two self-
governing ethnolinguistic regions, three recognized linguistic communities, and a bilingual if mainly French-speaking capital district,
Brussels, the seat of EU institutions—similar to Bosnia's. There is
scope for further reform of Bosnia's constitutional structure—one
proposal, advanced by a think tank in 2004, is to supersede the en-

tity framework with a more symmetric cantonized state in which the RS becomes the single largest and most populous canton of the country and the largely redundant Bosniac-Croat Federation tier of government is abolished, leaving its constituent cantons intact. "The result," the proponents argue, "would be a simplified, three-layered federal state . . . a normal European federal system with central, regional [cantonal] and municipal governments."[43] Such a reconfiguration would turn Bosnia's structure of government into a Balkan sibling of Switzerland.

But as a transitional postwar society Bosnia has other serious problems. The international community has not succeeded in building a viable Bosnian economy, and unemployment is rife. Until the meltdown of 1992 the mainstay of Bosnia's economy was a network of large industrial plants in towns across the republic. The large majority of these factories are defunct while the rest survive as pale shadows of their former selves. Nothing has taken the place of the "kaput" (finished)—as Bosnians describe it—socialist-era economy. In 1992 large-scale emigration began from Bosnia as hundreds of thousands fled the war. The wartime exodus totaled 1.2 million refugees, including the bulk of Bosnia's intelligentsia and highly trained professionals. By 1998 at least five hundred thousand of these refugees had become permanent emigrants resettled in dozens of host countries. Since the war Bosnia has lost many more citizens to emigration—at least one hundred thousand between 1996 and 2000—as more people, especially the educated and qualified, have taken the exit route from an impoverished, divided society only tentatively emerging from an inferno of violence.[44] Surveys have consistently shown that the majority of Bosnia's young people would leave the country if they could. These two phenomena—economic moribundity and human flight—make Bosnia's present gloomy and its future uncertain.

There are no near-term solutions to this predicament. The longer-term solution lies in incorporation into the EU as the

Union progressively enlarges into the western Balkans. That is going to involve a lengthy process, but it is likely to be completed before the twentieth anniversary of the Dayton agreement. In the meantime the aspiration to join the EU has the salutary effect of providing a shared focal point for Bosnians, overriding their ethnonational divisions. The development of a second, spatially more limited regionalism—renewed cross-border ties of cooperation across the former Yugoslav space—would be equally, if not more, necessary as a guarantee of shared stability and relative prosperity. If Yugoslavia had not violently dissolved into fragments, it would have had one of the easiest journeys among former communist states into the EU. The revival of ruptured relations among former Yugoslavs has become feasible only in the last few years, after the demise of the Milosevic and Tudjman regimes in Serbia and Croatia and the relative stabilization of Bosnia through the entrenchment of the (reformed) Dayton settlement. It is instructive that much of the meager foreign direct investment in postwar Bosnia has come from Slovenia, another republic of the former Yugoslavia and the only successor-state as yet admitted (in 2004) by the EU. The era of fraternal socialist solidarity is a receding memory but the construction of a regional bloc across former Yugoslavia is an imperative that beckons. In the pursuit of that imperative Bosnia—still a microcosm of much of the wider region after all its upheavals, and a country with soft internal *and* international borders—could play an important role.

The most important lesson of the forging of peace in Bosnia since 1996 for international state-building interventions in postwar societies is that such interventions entail a *protracted commitment.* There are no quick fixes or quick exits. Despite the gradual rollback of personnel and resources, the international community is still deeply involved in tending to and shoring up Bosnia's fragile postwar equilibrium and is likely to remain so during the Dayton state's second decade. It is unrealistic for such societies to be "expected to become democracies and market economies in the space of a few years . . . in the fragile circumstances . . . of emerging from war."[45] Despite an exceptionally high level of international attention and significant progress, the Bosnian peace process remains just that—an advanced but incomplete process—much like a semi-finished building adorned with scaffolding.

When the internationally sponsored construction of the replica of Mostar's old bridge began in 2001, it stirred hope in Emir Balic, a local resident in his late sixties. Mr. Balic is well known locally as the holder of the record for the highest number of dives, over a thousand, from the old bridge into the swirling green waters of the Neretva River. Diving from the old bridge into the Neretva had been a Mostar tradition for centuries, and an annual diving competition held every summer was a highlight of the town's calendar for decades until 1991. The traveler Evlija Celebija observed in 1664:

> Some dive head-first into the water, others dive sitting cross-legged like a Turk, and yet others dive together in pairs and threes. They then swim back to the bank, climb the rocks and come to the end of the bridge to receive gifts from the viziers and noblemen.[46]

"My biggest wish is to jump from the new old bridge, health permitting," Mr. Balic said in 2001.[47]

His wish has been fulfilled since. Yet many locals feel that the replica lacks the wondrous grace of the original, just as Mostar today is a pale shadow of the glittering melting pot of histories, cultures, and nationalities it was. But Mr. Balic can dive again, and the spot where the old bridge stood for four centuries is no longer eerily empty. That sums up the saga of catastrophic war and internationally engineered peace in Bosnia.

· FOUR ·

Kashmir

Kashmir is a Himalayan territory at the crossroads of India, Pakistan, China, and Afghanistan. India's Mughal rulers, who conquered much of the territory in 1586, were so taken by the beauty of its landscape that they called it *jannat*—paradise. For the last six decades Kashmir has been a paradise lost, its people trapped in the vortex of a bitter sovereignty dispute between India and Pakistan over their lives and land. It has repeatedly been a focal point of inter-state war—the first and second India-Pakistan wars, in 1947–1948 and 1965, were triggered by the dispute over Kashmir, and the territory also saw heavy fighting in the third war in 1971.

Since 1990 Kashmir has been in the grip of protracted guerrilla war with groups of Muslim insurgents pitted against Indian forces. The tourist brochure image of a vacation paradise—the Mughal monarchs used Kashmir as a summer resort from the sweltering heat of the Indian plains—has been replaced in the subcontinent and across the world for the past seventeen years by daily accounts of gun battles, bombings, body counts, and a traumatized population held ransom by a conflict in which they are subjects and participants but that is also beyond their control. Official Indian estimates cite a toll of at least fifty thousand killed—guerrillas, soldiers, police, and civilians—while parties in Kashmir opposed to Indian rule claim the real toll could be almost double that figure. Kashmir's best-known contemporary poet, Agha Shahid Ali, who died as an exile in the United States in 2001, wrote about the lost paradise in his poem "Farewell":

> At a certain point I lost track of you.
> They make a desolation and call it peace . . .
> Army convoys all night like desert caravans,
> In the smoking light of dimmed headlights, time dissolved . . .
> I am being rowed through Paradise on a river of Hell . . .
> If only somehow you could have been mine,
> What would not have been possible in the world?[1]

The most dramatic manifestation of the conflict is the Line of Control (LOC), a 742-kilometer de facto border that separates the Indian-controlled and Pakistani-controlled parts of disputed Kashmir.[2] Like similar de jure or de facto borders forged by ethnonational conflict in Israel-Palestine, Bosnia, Cyprus, and Sri Lanka, the LOC was carved out through war. It originated in early 1949 as a cease-fire line (CFL) at the end of the first India-Pakistan military conflict over Kashmir. The line was slightly modified during fighting in the subsequent wars of 1965 and 1971 and renamed the LOC—implying a status more stable than a cease-fire boundary but short of a recognized international frontier—by an agreement between the governments of India and Pakistan in 1972. It meanders through mostly mountainous terrain before terminating short of the Siachen glacier, situated in the inaccessible and uninhabited northern reaches of the disputed territory, where Indian and Pakistani soldiers have been locked in a standoff since the mid-1980s in what has come to be known as the world's highest-altitude battlefield, located at frozen heights of eighteen to twenty-one thousand feet above sea level.

Over the decades the LOC has been one of the most contested and most resilient features of the Kashmir conflict. Pakistanis typically think that the trajectory of the line is unjust because it leaves the greater part of the territory and the bulk of the population of Kashmir—eleven of fifteen million people—under Indian jurisdiction. Large numbers of citizens on both sides of the line who would ideally prefer Kashmir to be an independent state regard the LOC as a scar of India-Pakistan conflict that defaces their homeland. Indians on the contrary tend to be status quo-ist in their attitude to the LOC, and India's armed forces have successfully repelled large-scale incursions across the line attempted by the Pakistani military in 1965 and 1999. Until the mid-1950s the LOC (then known as the CFL) was a relatively porous border, and residents of areas near the line could often move across and back to visit relatives or conduct business with a permit granted by local administrative authorities. But for a half century since then the LOC has been a hard, forbidding dividing line of barbed wire, bunkers, and trenches guarded by several hundred thousand troops. This has been especially true since 1990, when insurgency erupted in Indian-controlled Kashmir. Since that time insurgents—from Indian-controlled Kashmir, Pakistani-controlled Kashmir, and Pakistan itself—who have been trained in bases on the Pakistani side of the LOC have been infiltrating the line to fight Indian forces, and the LOC has been the focus of a deadly game between the rebels and the Indian military units tasked to interdict and eliminate them.

So when in April 2005 a fortnightly cross-LOC bus service connecting Srinagar—the capital of the Kashmir Valley and the largest city in Indian-controlled Kashmir—with Muzaffarabad, a town that serves as the political center of Pakistani-controlled Kashmir, was inaugurated by agreement between the governments of India and Pakistan, the event sparked global attention. The trans-LOC bus was viewed as the consolidation of a thaw in Indian-Pakistani relations under way since early 2004, as a step signaling the beginnings of normalization in war-torn, insurgency-wracked Kashmir, and potentially as the first move toward transforming the LOC into a soft border. This was a major change for the better from the summer of 1999 when India's armed forces fought a sharp two-month battle with infiltrated Pakistani regular units on a very mountainous stretch of the LOC, or indeed the summer of 2002 when tensions escalated following a terrorist attack on India's parliament in New Delhi and India mobilized a huge fighting force on the LOC, sparking a Pakistani countermobilization and raising fears of war between the two nuclear-armed countries. At the LOC crossing point for the bus near the town of Uri, which falls on the Indian side of the line, Indian military personnel worked round the clock for weeks before the service commenced to repair a derelict wooden bridge across the Jhelum River straddling the line and the road leading to it:

> Not long ago this area was a minefield . . . soldiers in bunkers on either side, exchanging bullets and shells. Today they exchange pleasantries as bulldozers roll and the men work. Hundreds of men . . . are working on a war footing to rebuild the final 400-meter stretch of road [to the bridge], defusing mines, clearing undergrowth, and even building a complex for immigration, customs, a bank and other travel facilities.[3]

The bonhomie between the two sides soured somewhat when the Indians painted the restored bridge in the tricolor of the Indian national flag—saffron, white, and green—repainting in a neutral shade only after Pakistani protests. Nonetheless the bus service was launched on schedule and amid fanfare. Passengers from Srinagar disembark just before the bridge across the Jhelum and walk over to board another bus waiting on the Pakistani side, while those from Muzaffarabad follow the same procedure from the other di-

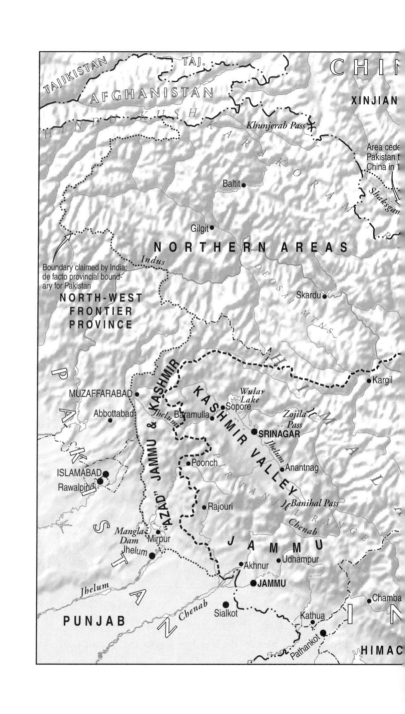

CHIN[A]

XINJIAN[G]

Khunjerab Pass

Area cede[d]
Pakistan t[o]
China in 1[

Shaksgan[

Baltit

Gilgit

NORTHERN AREAS

Indus

Boundary claimed by India;
de facto provincial boundary for Pakistan

NORTH-WEST
FRONTIER
PROVINCE

Skardu

Kargil

*Wular
Lake*

Sopore

MUZAFFARABAD

Abbottabad

Baramulla

Jhelum

Zojila
Pass

SRINAGAR

ISLAMABAD

Rawalpindi

Poonch

Jhelum

Anantnag

Banihal Pass

Rajouri

Chenab

*Mangla
Dam*

Mirpur

Jhelum

JAMMU

Akhnur

Udhampur

Jhelum

JAMMU

Chamba

PUNJAB

Chenab

Sialkot

Kathua

Pathankot

HIMAC[

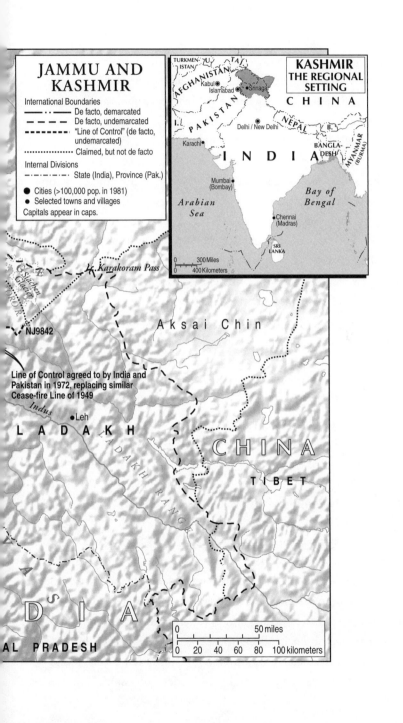

JAMMU AND KASHMIR

International Boundaries
— ··· — De facto, demarcated
— — — De facto, undemarcated
------- "Line of Control" (de facto, undemarcated)
············ Claimed, but not de facto
Internal Divisions
—··—··— State (India), Province (Pak.)
● Cities (>100,000 pop. in 1981)
• Selected towns and villages
Capitals appear in caps.

KASHMIR
THE REGIONAL SETTING

TURKMEN-ISTAN
U.
TAJ.
AFGHANISTAN
Kabul
Islamabad
Srinagar
CHINA
PAKISTAN
I.I.
Delhi / New Delhi
NEPAL
B.
Karachi
INDIA
BANGLA-DESH
MYANMAR (BURMA)
Mumbai (Bombay)
Arabian Sea
Bay of Bengal
Chennai (Madras)
SRI LANKA

0   300 Miles
0   400 Kilometers

Karakoram Pass

Siachen Glacier

NJ9842

A k s a i   C h i n

Line of Control agreed to by India and Pakistan in 1972, replacing similar Cease-fire Line of 1949

Indus

Leh

L A D A K H

LADAKH RANGE

C H I N A

T I B E T

D   I   A

AL PRADESH

0   50 miles
0   20   40   60   80   100 kilometers

rection. Two octogenarian men in Srinagar who had been bus drivers on the route until 1947—the scenic 170-kilometer road along
the Jhelum from Srinagar to Muzaffarabad, continuing onward to
the city of Rawalpindi adjacent to Pakistan's capital Islamabad, was
the region's principal artery of travel and trade until 1947—nostal-
gically recalled their memories of eighteen-seater Ford and Chev-
rolet buses plying the route with passengers, cargo, and mail on a
daily basis.[4] As some of the passengers traveling across the LOC on
the first runs of the bus service visited ancestral properties abandoned by their families in the late 1940s, when large numbers of
Muslims left Indian-controlled zones of Kashmir for Pakistani-
controlled areas while large numbers of Hindus and Sikhs fled in
the reverse direction, alarmist media reports appeared of the possibility of a rash of claims to refugee property.[5]

Meeting in Delhi in April 2005, Pakistani president Pervez
Musharraf and Indian prime minister Manmohan Singh "decided
to increase the frequency of the bus service and also decided that
trucks would be allowed to use this route to promote trade."[6] In
Washington, U.S. secretary of state Condoleezza Rice said that the
administration was "very impressed with what India and Pakistan
have achieved . . . It is quite remarkable when you see where they
have reached. They have opened the bus service in Kashmir, which
would have been unthinkable just a few years ago. They are looking at broader economic ties."[7]

Yet just as the opening of the Green Line in Cyprus in 2003 or
of the A-9 "highway of death" in northern Sri Lanka in 2002 did
not mean that a peace settlement was imminent in those disputes,
Kashmir remains far from a paradise regained. During the period
when the commencement of the Srinagar–Muzaffarabad bus service attracted world headlines, a very different drama was unfolding
in comparative obscurity along the LOC. Between 2002 and 2004
the Indian army erected a multitiered fencing system along 734 kilometers of the 742-kilometer LOC to deter cross-LOC move-

ment by insurgents. This fencing system comprises "two or three rows of concertina wire, about three meters or ten feet high, electrified and connected to a network of motion sensors, thermal imaging devices and alarms acquired from the United States and Israel,"[8] and was built without a fraction of the publicity attending Israel's construction of its controversial "security barrier" with the West Bank, labeled the "Great Wall of Palestine" by skeptics.[9] In the spring of 2005 the LOC fencing was obliterated along many stretches and badly damaged in others by exceptionally heavy snowfall across Kashmir. In April 2005, while attention was riveted on the beginning of the bus service, the Indian military was engaged in a race against time to reconstruct or repair the fencing prior to the beginning of summer, the season favored by insurgents for infiltration. During the summer months—despite a marked downturn in infiltration relative to previous years resulting from the India-Pakistan thaw and the Pakistani military's consequent lack of support and encouragement to infiltrating insurgents— groups of guerrillas did try to exploit gaps from collapsed fencing at several points along the LOC, sparking firefights with Indian troops.[10]

The bridge and fence imagery is illuminating of reality. The Line of Control in Kashmir remains a heavily militarized barrier—despite a cease-fire between Indian and Pakistani forces along the line that has been holding since November 2003—and is as yet far from being transformed into the bridge of peace that it must become as part of a settlement to the conflict. The aperture created by the bus service is symbolic of the incipient nature of the Kashmir peace process. The historical record is daunting. The Kashmir conflict has never seen a concerted peace process similar to that in Israel-Palestine in the 1990s or Sri Lanka in 2002–2003, let alone a final settlement as proposed in Cyprus in 2004 or concluded in Bosnia in late 1995. Efforts by the governments of India and Pakistan over the decades have remained limited to joint declarations of good intent—the most notable examples of these occurred in 1972 and early 1999—or to fitful episodes of dialogue and piecemeal confidence-building measures that have not added up to a coherent and purposeful peace process. International involvement in the conflict has similarly been limited to exhortations and appeals to India and Pakistan by world powers including the United States to tackle the dispute peaceably, and to temporary crisis diplomacy by the United States when the conflict has threatened to escalate dangerously (as in 1999 and 2002). A notable lack of clarity exists about the nature of a compromise settlement that can accommodate the antagonistic positions of India and Pakistan and assuage the aspiration to self-rule that appeals to a large proportion of the population of the disputed territory. Yet in the early twenty-first century Kashmir and the India-Pakistan conflict that revolves around it is, along with the Israeli-Palestinian conflict and the wider ramifications of that conflict in the Middle East, one of the two major regional flashpoints that must be addressed decisively to preserve international peace and advance global security.

In October 2005 an earthquake with its epicenter close to Muzaffarabad utterly devastated substantial zones of Pakistani-controlled Kashmir. The town of Muzaffarabad was practically razed along with other towns and scores of villages in adjacent districts. At least fifty thousand people were killed in Pakistani-controlled Kashmir. The calamity also hit parts of Indian-controlled Kashmir on the LOC in the northwestern Kashmir Valley, where almost fifteen hundred died. The town of Uri was heavily damaged, as was the bridge across the Jhelum into Pakistani-controlled Kashmir. The Srinagar–Muzaffarabad bus link was halted for a number of weeks after the catastrophe, perhaps a symbolic reflection of the halting nature of the India-Pakistan peace process over Kashmir (in April 2006 the first anniversary of the fortnightly service passed almost unnoticed locally and internationally as passengers dwindled to a trickle due to the disruption caused by the earthquake and frustrating bureaucratic and security procedures on both sides). The suffering of the hundreds of thousands of children, women, and men in Pakistani-controlled Kashmir who survived the earthquake, but received injuries and lost all their material possessions as their society and its infrastructure disintegrated around them on that Saturday morning, 8 October 2005, could have been efficiently alleviated had the governments of Pakistan and India collaborated extensively in rescue, relief, rehabilitation, and reconstruction operations, particularly because the official Pakistani effort proved inadequate and incompetent. But that road was not taken and the tragedy of the earthquake highlighted once again the plight of the people of Kashmir, caught as always in the crosshairs of the India-Pakistan conflict.

The Making of War

The Kashmir conflict is a by-product of the partition of the subcontinent into Hindu-majority India and the Muslim state of Pakistan in 1947.[11] The Israeli-Palestinian conflict developed in the period between the world wars as a struggle between two peoples, Arab residents and Jewish settlers, over possession of the land of Palestine and gradually acquired the character of a broader regional issue, especially after the exodus of about seven hundred thousand Palestinians from the newly formed State of Israel in 1948. The Kashmir conflict, on the other hand, began as a regional dispute between two newly sovereign states over rightful ownership of a land. Competing Indian and Pakistani claims to Kashmir, rather than an explosive internal conflict, turned Kashmir into a cauldron of armed hostilities.

When the sun set on Britain's Indian empire in 1947, as much as 45 percent of the subcontinent's land area was not directly administered by the British. Almost half of the subcontinent's territory was instead covered by a patchwork of 562 kingdoms and principalities

of varying sizes and populations that were ruled by Indian poten-
tates and enjoyed self-administration subject to their rulers' acceptance of the ultimate authority—known as "paramountcy"—of
British power. This vast network of "princely states," as they were
known, emerged gradually across the map of the subcontinent during the nineteenth century and constituted the pillar of the British
practice of "indirect rule."

Kashmir was one of the largest of the princely states of British
India. It was created in 1846 by a Hindu chieftain called Gulab
Singh, scion of a warrior clan from a region called Jammu, just
south of the Kashmir Valley, who cobbled together a sprawling,
polyglot princely state by partly conquering and partly purchasing
a number of adjacent areas. He was recognized as its *maharaja* (great
ruler) by the British in 1846, and his male heirs succeeded him over
the next century to the hereditary kingship of Jammu and Kashmir,
as the princely state was officially known. The princely state included the Kashmir Valley and the Jammu region as well as the remote and thinly populated high Himalayan areas of Ladakh, Gilgit,
and Baltistan, and was populated by diverse religious, ethnic, linguistic, and caste communities. The heterogeneity of the princely
state was noted in the early 1920s by Tyndale Biscoe, a British mis-
sionary and educator who worked there:

> To write about the . . . Kashmiris is not easy as the country of
> Kashmir, including the province of Jammu, is large and con-
> tains many races of people. Then again, these various coun-
> tries included under the name of Kashmir are separated . . . by
> high mountain passes, so that the people . . . differ considerably
> . . . in features, manners, customs, language, character and reli-
> gion.[12]

As decolonization approached in 1947, the princely states had
three options—to join one of the two new "dominions," India and

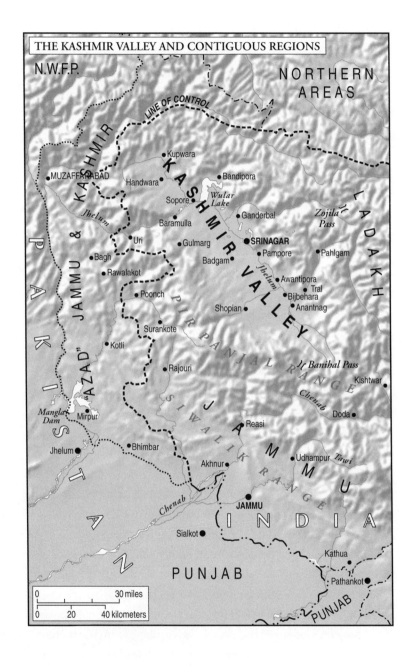

THE KASHMIR VALLEY AND CONTIGUOUS REGIONS

Pakistan, or to declare independence. However, Lord Mountbatten, the last British administrator of India, insisted categorically that the third option was merely nominal. He urged the princely rulers to make a decision to accede to either India or Pakistan on the basis of two considerations: the location of their fief in relation to the territories of the two emergent sovereign polities, and the preferences of their population of subjects. The large majority of princely states were enveloped by India's territory, and geography decided their fate regardless of whether they had Hindu, Muslim, or Sikh rulers. Problems arose in only two cases, where Muslim rulers favored Pakistan although the bulk of their subjects were Hindus and their kingdoms' location made incorporation into India a virtual fait accompli. Both of these princely states were integrated into India by 1948.

Kashmir proved to be the thorny exception to the generally smooth disposal of the princely states' status. It was geographically contiguous to *both* India and Pakistan, although its trade, transport, and commercial links were predominantly with areas that became part of Pakistan and a sizable population of Muslims who had migrated from the princely state in the late nineteenth and early twentieth centuries lived in Pakistan's Punjab province. Kashmir also had a solid Muslim majority of 77 percent (20 percent were Hindus and 3 percent others, mainly Sikhs), so the case for accession to Pakistan rather than India appeared stronger. However, the preferences of Kashmir's population were not as clear-cut as the demographic fact of a large Muslim majority. Kashmir's largest and best-organized political group in 1947 was a party called the Jammu and Kashmir National Conference (NC), led by a charismatic ex-schoolteacher, Sheikh Mohammad Abdullah. The NC was an offshoot of popular protest since the early 1930s against Kashmir's autocratic Hindu regime, whose incompetent and prejudiced policies were held responsible by a small but increasingly vocal nucleus of the princely state's educated younger generation of

Muslims for the mass poverty and illiteracy prevalent among the Muslim population. The NC's leadership and cadre were overwhelmingly Muslim, but the party sought to be inclusive, reaching out to Hindus and Sikhs who shared its agenda of reform and accountable government, and Sheikh Abdullah and his colleagues developed close ties during the 1940s with the leadership of the Indian National Congress, the party spearheading India's independence movement against British rule, particularly with Jawaharlal Nehru, who would become independent India's first prime minister. Nehru's family were Hindus from the Kashmir Valley—Hindus comprise a small minority in the overwhelmingly Muslim Kashmir Valley—who had migrated to the plains of northern India, and he took a special interest in Kashmir.

Kashmir's last maharaja, Hari Singh, vacillated on the issue. In August 1947, as India and Pakistan became independent states (Pakistan on 14 August and India on 15 August) he seemed to be inclined toward negotiating with the Pakistani leadership to preserve his throne and privileges, rather than with India's Congress leaders, whose disdain for the princely rulers was widely known. The Pakistani leadership, headed by Mohammed Ali Jinnah, appeared to regard Kashmir's incorporation into Pakistan as all but inevitable on the basis of territorial contiguity and religious demography. Indeed, Kashmir has been integral to the *idea* of Pakistan ever since its inception in the early 1930s, to the extent that the letter "k" in the term *Pakistan* denotes Kashmir. Jinnah and his colleagues were eager to court the maharaja since he was legally the authority entitled to decide Kashmir's future.

But a modus vivendi between the subcontinent's Muslim state and Kashmir's Hindu autocrat failed to materialize. By early October the maharaja's administration was accusing Pakistan's government of conniving in raids by armed groups from Pakistan into Kashmir's territory, of attempting to strangulate Kashmir by imposing a de facto economic blockade, and of supporting an armed re-

volt by Muslim subjects in an area of the princely state adjacent to
Pakistan. In the fourth week of October several thousand armed
men drawn from tribes in Pakistan's North-West Frontier Province
(NWFP) invaded Kashmir. The maharaja's forces proved no match
for them and within a few days the invading force was within striking distance of Srinagar. The maharaja then urgently requested India's military intervention to repel the invasion. The Indian government agreed, but asked that the maharaja first accede to India, so
that the Indian role would be in defense of Indian territory rather
than a military intervention in a territory whose status was yet undecided. The maharaja complied on 26 October, and the following
day airborne Indian units landed at Srinagar's airport.

The Indian soldiers rapidly rolled back the tribal invasion force
to the periphery of the Kashmir Valley in November 1947. Fighting resumed in the spring of 1948, in this phase between the Indians and the regular Pakistani army. When a cease-fire ended the
first India-Pakistan war in January 1949 the Indians were in control
of almost the entire Kashmir Valley, most of the Jammu region, and
the high-altitude region of Ladakh. The Pakistanis were left with a
considerably smaller territory and population, consisting of parts
of the Jammu region, a slice of the Kashmir Valley, and the high-
altitude regions of Gilgit and Baltistan.

The Indian successes in the 1947–1948 war were enabled by the
support Indian troops received from the NC's members and mass
base, particularly in the party's stronghold, the Kashmir Valley. In
the critical situation of late 1947 Sheikh Abdullah and his colleagues decided to throw in their lot with India. Constitutionally,
although Kashmir became a part of India with the maharaja's accession, under the terms of the accession the government of Kashmir
retained jurisdiction on all matters except foreign affairs, defense,
and currency and communications, which were ceded to the government of the Indian Union. Kashmir's statutory autonomy was
subsequently codified in Article 370 of India's constitution. For

Sheikh Abdullah and his followers, this recognition and institution-alization of Kashmir's right to self-governance represented the essential guarantee of the stability of Kashmir's relationship with the Indian Union.

The Kashmir dispute was also internationalized. While accepting Kashmir's accession to India, Mountbatten, the governor-general of the Indian dominion, wrote to the maharaja on 27 October 1947 that once the invading forces had been expelled and law and order restored, the accession should be ratified by "a reference to the people." On 2 November 1947 Nehru declared the Indian government's "pledge . . . not only to the people of Kashmir but to the world . . . [to] hold a referendum under international auspices such as the United Nations" to determine whether the people of Kashmir ultimately preferred India or Pakistan. In January 1948, in response to a complaint to the UN by the government of India against Pakistan-sponsored aggression in Kashmir, the UN Security Council established the United Nations Commission for India and Pakistan (UNCIP). UNCIP's mandate was to organize a plebiscite that would determine Kashmir's final status. Between 1948 and 1957 the Security Council repeatedly passed resolutions calling for the sovereignty dispute to be settled "in accordance with the will of the people, expressed through the democratic method of a free and impartial plebiscite conducted under the auspices of the United Nations." It was taken for granted that the internationally administered referendum would offer the people of Kashmir two choices: India or Pakistan.[13]

The plebiscite was never held. Instead, from 1953 onward Indian governments embarked on a strategy of incrementally revoking Indian-controlled Kashmir's self-rule powers and of governing the territory through client politicians in Srinagar who were subservient to New Delhi. The most significant casualty of this approach was Sheikh Abdullah, who had a large popular base in Kashmir—

particularly in his home region, the Kashmir Valley—and so could not be relied upon to be a client who would do New Delhi's bidding. Abdullah was deposed as head of Indian-controlled Kashmir's government in August 1953 by a Machiavellian political intrigue orchestrated by Nehru's government in collusion with disgruntled members of the NC leadership. Abdullah, popularly known as the "Lion of Kashmir," would spend most of the next twenty-two years, until 1975, in Indian prisons on suspicion of harboring subversive intentions. India's political establishment, led by the Congress Party, suspected him of aspiring to be the founder and leader of a sovereign state of Kashmir that would be neutral in the India-Pakistan conflict.

With Abdullah removed from the political scene, Indian governments set about the task of integrating Indian-controlled Kashmir securely into the Indian Union. Between 1954 and 1965, Indian-controlled Kashmir's political autonomy in the legislative, judicial, and fiscal spheres was effectively destroyed by a series of integrative and centralizing measures enacted from New Delhi. India's governments received active collaboration in implementing this strategy from compliant politicians who held office in Indian-controlled Kashmir at the mercy of their patrons in New Delhi. The presence of such compliant cliques was essential to New Delhi's strategy of coercive integration, since Article 370 of the Indian constitution stipulates that India's central government can take decisions even on matters related to defense, foreign affairs, and currency and communications "in consultation with the Government of Jammu & Kashmir," and on other subjects under the Indian Union's jurisdiction only with "the . . . concurrence of the Jammu & Kashmir Assembly [parliament]."[14]

Sheikh Abdullah's political career was merely the most immediate and obvious casualty of the Indian decision to impose hegemonic control. Indian-controlled Kashmir's democratic institutions and processes were subverted and permanently retarded by this policy. Elections were held to constitute Indian-controlled Kashmir's legislature at regular five-year intervals—in 1957, 1962, 1967, and 1972. All of these exercises made a cruel mockery of the principles and procedures of competitive democracy. They were fixed through a crude combination of fraud and intimidation to ensure the overwhelming victory of politicians favored by New Delhi. Sheikh Abdullah was himself no paragon of democracy. Indeed, in 1951 the NC under his leadership managed to "win" all seventy-five seats in Indian-controlled Kashmir's constituent assembly. But he also had the political strength and clout to negotiate a 1952 pact with Nehru's government that confirmed "maximum autonomy for the local organs of state power, while discharging obligations as a unit of the [Indian] Union."[15] His successors were stooges. Abdullah's former deputy, Bakshi Ghulam Mohammed, who took over with New Delhi's blessing in August 1953, informed Abdullah's handpicked constituent assembly in February 1954 that Kashmir "irrevocably acceded to India more than six years ago and today we are fulfilling the formalities of our unbreakable bonds with India."[16] In India's parliament Prime Minister Nehru praised the new leadership for "representing the wishes of the people of Kashmir."[17] The constitution framed for Indian-controlled Kashmir came into effect on 26 January 1957, the anniversary of India's proclamation as a republic in 1950, in a symbolic gesture of allegiance.

The strategy of hegemonic control could be sustained only by turning Indian-controlled Kashmir into a draconian police state in which civil rights and political liberties were virtually nonexistent. Mass arrests, arbitrary detentions, and violence by hired thugs against political dissidents became the norm. In 1953 large-scale protests against Abdullah's ouster were suppressed by police action, and thirty-three prominent NC leaders who sided with Abdullah against the New Delhi-instigated putsch were arrested under Indian-controlled Kashmir's Public Security Act (which had been used until then to harass Abdullah's opponents). When in 1955 Abdullah's followers formed an organization called the Plebiscite Front—which stood for "self-determination through a plebiscite under UN auspices, withdrawal of the armed forces of both nations from Kashmir, and restoration of civil liberties and free elections"—the government of Indian-controlled Kashmir prohibited the organization's public meetings and arrested its leaders.[18] After farcical "elections" in Indian-controlled Kashmir in 1962 produced a legislature in which the ruling clique held sixty-eight of the seventy-four seats, Nehru wrote to Bakshi Ghulam Mohammed, "It would strengthen your position much more if you lost a few [more] seats."[19] When in 1964 Bakshi fell out with his mentors in New Delhi, he was arrested with six of his leading supporters under a colonial-era law called the Defense of India Rules and incarcerated in the same jail in the Jammu region to which Abdullah had been consigned eleven years earlier.

When the Plebiscite Front, in a change of strategy in late 1970, announced its intention to contest elections to Indian-controlled Kashmir's legislature, due in 1972, "at least 350 officials and members of the Front were arrested under the Preventive Detention Act [of Indian-controlled Kashmir] in a series of police raids" and the organization was declared illegal under India's Unlawful Activities Prevention Act on the grounds that the Front had "on diverse occasions by words, either spoken or written, and signs and visual representations . . . asserted a claim to determine whether or not Jammu & Kashmir shall remain a part of India."[20] The areas of Pakistani-controlled Kashmir were also subject to draconian control throughout the first quarter century of the Kashmir conflict by the Pakistani government, acting through its Ministry of Kashmir Affairs (MKA).[21] But such policies were far less anomalous in Pakistan's military-bureaucratic authoritarian regime than in India's democratic and federal system of government.

In August 1952 Nehru told independent India's first parliament that he desired "no forced unions" and that if in a plebiscite the people of Kashmir decided "to part company with us they can go their way and we shall go our way."[22] But in March 1956 he told parliament that the plebiscite was "beside the point" and emphasized "Pakistani aggression in Kashmir and the legality of Kashmir's accession to India [in October 1947]," which he claimed had been ratified by Indian-controlled Kashmir's constituent assembly in 1954.[23] In April 1956 Nehru revealed that a year earlier, in May 1955, he had offered the Pakistani government a settlement based on the permanent, de jure division of Kashmir along the cease-fire line (this overture was naturally rejected by the Pakistanis since it meant ceding the bulk of Kashmir's territory and population to India on a platter).

The pronounced hardening of the Indian stance on Kashmir in the mid-1950s received support from a superpower, the Soviet Union. Eager to fortify itself economically and militarily against India, Pakistan joined United States–sponsored regional security alliances—the Southeast Asia Treaty Organization (the Manila Pact) and the Central Treaty Organization (the Baghdad Pact)—in 1954–1955. The Soviet Union responded by shifting its foreign policy in favor of India. In late 1955, Soviet leaders Khrushchev and Bulganin traveled to India and visited Indian-controlled Kashmir. Khrushchev announced in Srinagar, "That Kashmir is one of the States of the Republic of India has already been decided by the people of Kashmir," while Bulganin referred to "this northern part of India" and described its population as "part of the Indian people."[24] The constitution of Indian-controlled Kashmir promulgated by its constituent assembly in January 1957 declared that "the State of Jammu & Kashmir is and shall be an integral part of the Union of India," over objections from a small group of members who continued to be loyal to Abdullah.[25] The notion that Kashmir—including "Pakistani-occupied" Kashmir across the CFL/LOC—was an "integral part" of India was rapidly elevated to the core maxim of the official Indian position on Kashmir and came to be uncritically accepted across almost the entire range of India's political spectrum. The implications were that no quarter would be given to Pakistani claims and that dissent in Indian-controlled Kashmir would be criminalized and muzzled, even when that dissent was not of a pro-Pakistan nature. At the UN, the Soviet Union for the first time used its veto in India's favor in February 1957 to block the passage of a Security Council resolution that sought to reaffirm the necessity of an internationally supervised referendum to settle the sovereignty question.

According to Indian officialdom there was no longer a Kashmir question a decade after the genesis of the conflict. A corollary to the "Kashmir is an integral part of India" argument also became a dogma in India—that Indian-controlled Kashmir, as the Indian Union's only Muslim-majority unit, is essential and central to India's identity as a secular, civic state.[26] Stalled at the United Nations and rebuffed by the Indian leadership, the Pakistanis resorted to force to challenge the status quo in Kashmir. Encouraged by a flare-up of unrest with strong anti-Indian overtones in Indian-controlled Kashmir in 1963–1964, the Pakistani military regime, headed by the dictator Ayub Khan, formulated an ambitious plan, codenamed Operation Gibraltar, to seize Indian-controlled Kashmir. In August 1965 this plan was put into operation when several thousand Pakistani soldiers and armed volunteers from Pakistani-controlled Kashmir infiltrated the CFL into Indian-controlled Kashmir with the intention of fomenting a mass uprising. That intention was foiled when the population proved largely indifferent and in some instances hostile to the infiltrators. Memories of the late 1947 tribal invasion from Pakistan still rankled in the Kashmir Valley, when the undisciplined raiders committed numerous atrocities against the fellow Muslims they had ostensibly come to liberate, and Sheikh Abdullah's pro-independence followers were not willing to collude with Pakistani designs. The crisis in Kashmir triggered a twenty-two-day inconclusive war between India and Pakistan in September 1965, not just along the CFL in Kashmir but along the entire international frontier between Pakistan's western wing and India (Bengali-speaking east Pakistan, which emerged as sovereign Bangladesh with Indian support in December 1971, was largely spared the hostilities). Operation Gibraltar was a strategic failure, and the territorial status quo continued.

But the Kashmir question continued to simmer. In 1966 Jayaprakash Narayan, an Indian opposition leader, voiced a rare note of dissent in a letter to Indira Gandhi, India's prime minister and Nehru's daughter:

> We profess democracy, but rule by force in Kashmir. We profess secularism, but let Hindu nationalism stampede us into establishing it by repression. Kashmir has distorted India's image in the world as nothing else has done. The problem exists not because Pakistan wants to grab Kashmir but because there is deep and widespread discontent among the people [of Indian-controlled Kashmir].[27]

Prem Nath Bazaz, a veteran Kashmiri political activist and a member of the Kashmir Valley's small but high-profile Hindu minority, the Kashmiri Pandits, wrote in 1967:

> For a clear and realistic appraisal of the Kashmir situation it is necessary to recognize the fact that by and large the State's [Indian-controlled Kashmir's] Muslims are not very friendly toward India. An overwhelming majority among them are not happy under the present political set-up and desire to be done with it. But they are reluctant to bring about change through warfare and bloodshed.[28]

During a brief respite from jail in 1968 Sheikh Abdullah eloquently expressed Kashmir's predicament: "The fact is that Indian democracy stops short at Pathankot [the last town in India's Punjab province before entry into the Jammu region of Indian-controlled Kashmir]. Between Pathankot and the Banihal [a mountain pass that connects the Jammu region with the Kashmir Valley] you may have some measure of democracy, but beyond Banihal there is none. What we have in Kashmir bears some of the worst characteristics of colonial rule." In a message to the people of India on the occasion of their Republic Day on 26 January 1968 he added that

> Respect for the rule of law, the independence of the judiciary and the integrity of the electoral process are all sought to be guaranteed by the Indian constitution [enacted on 26 January 1950] . . . Many other countries have drawn on this constitution, particularly its chapter on fundamental rights. Yet . . . the constitution provides the framework, and it is for the men who work it to give it life and meaning. In many ways the provisions of the constitution have been flagrantly violated in recent years [in Indian-controlled Kashmir] and the ideals it enshrines completely forgotten.[29]

For all his rhetoric, Abdullah eventually concluded a rapprochement with the Indian government of Indira Gandhi in 1975. Its terms verged on abject capitulation to Indian power by the Lion of Kashmir. He was reinstated as the head of Indian-controlled Kashmir's government in exchange for abandoning the self-determination platform. Abdullah never spoke again about Kashmir's right to decide its own fate, a demand that he had tenaciously advocated for two decades since being cast out of office in 1953, about the promised but never realized UN-administered plebiscite, or about a role for Pakistan in settling the dispute. There was no reinstatement of any of the self-rule powers revoked by New Delhi since 1954. Abdullah was possibly worn down by age—he turned seventy in 1975—and by two decades of almost continuous incarceration. He also probably calculated that after Pakistan's dismemberment and the birth of Bangladesh in the December 1971 India-

Pakistan war the regional balance of power had shifted decisively in India's favor and he had no option but to seek accommodation with New Delhi.

The return of Abdullah did have a temporarily stabilizing effect on Indian-controlled Kashmir. After a hiatus of over two decades he and his party, extremely popular in the Kashmir Valley and the single largest party in Indian-controlled Kashmir as a whole, were participating in the political process. The National Conference Party led by Abdullah won a majority of seats in elections to Indian-controlled Kashmir's legislature in 1977 and formed the government, and after Abdullah's death in 1982 his son and political heir Farooq Abdullah led the NC to another resounding victory in elections in 1983. But Indian-controlled Kashmir's political climate started deteriorating again from 1984, when Farooq Abdullah's popularly elected government was dismissed at the behest of Prime Minister Indira Gandhi in a sordid abuse of New Delhi's emergency powers of intervention against governments of the States of the Indian Union. Indira Gandhi was apparently enraged because Farooq Abdullah had chosen to build links with Indian opposition parties as part of an effort to create an India-wide alliance against her ruling Congress Party. Indian-controlled Kashmir was governed directly from New Delhi until late 1986 as much of the population, especially the younger generation in the Kashmir Valley, seethed with discontent.

In late 1986 Farooq Abdullah, in a strategically disastrous political somersault, concluded a pact with the Congress Party in power in New Delhi, led by Indira's son Rajiv Gandhi since his mother's assassination in late 1984. He was reinstated as interim head of Indian-controlled Kashmir's government as part of the deal, pending fresh elections in March 1987. Farooq's *volte-face* was regarded as shameful opportunism by most of the NC's mass base, centered on the Kashmir Valley. An improvised coalition called the Muslim United Front (MUF), which brought together disparate factions with no coherent agenda beyond opposition to New Delhi's egre-

gious treatment of Indian-controlled Kashmir for decades, emerged
to contest the March 1987 election against the NC-Congress alliance. The MUF, while a ragtag alliance, evoked a significant popular response, particularly in the Valley, and acquired an army of
young volunteers who worked tirelessly in its campaign. Their efforts and hopes came to nothing when the election was blatantly
rigged by the bureaucracy and police at the behest of the NC-
Congress alliance, which won sixty-two of the seventy-six seats at
stake, while the MUF got just four. A vindictive crackdown on the
young men who had worked for the MUF followed—many were
incarcerated for months without charge or trial, and some were
tortured.

In 1988, as a dysfunctional government headed by the discred-
ited Farooq Abdullah stumbled on in Srinagar, some of these young
men, inflamed and radicalized by their experiences, crossed the
LOC in search of weapons and training. In 1989 the first groups of
trained insurgents returned from across the LOC. Through that
year the Kashmir Valley teetered on the brink of uprising as guerrillas carried out bombings and selective assassinations, and a mood
of fury against the government and its patron, "India," gripped the
Valley's population. The explosion came in January 1990, when
massive demonstrations for *azaadi* (freedom) broke out in the city
of Srinagar and other Valley towns, and panicked federal paramilitary police sent by New Delhi to contain the unrest opened fire,
killing hundreds of protesters. Four decades of authoritarianism—
the blatant disregard for civil rights and fundamental liberties,
the imposition of puppet governments through bogus or doctored
elections, and the effective revocation of Indian-controlled Kashmir's autonomy despite that autonomy being guaranteed by the Indian constitution—ultimately produced its nemesis in the form of
the AK-47-wielding insurgent.

Prior to 1990, Kashmir was primarily an arena of inter-state conflict, while the people of Kashmir remained on the margins. In

1947–1948, 1965, and 1971 the Indian and Pakistani states and their militaries fought over Kashmir. But in 1990 the conflict came home to roost with a vengeance as thousands of Kashmiri Muslim young men picked up the gun to fight Indian rule. In the seventeen years that have passed since then the insurgency has been through many twists and turns, flows and ebbs.[30] But the protracted war of attrition inside Indian-controlled Kashmir between thousands of guerrilla fighters and hundreds of thousands of Indian military, semimilitary, and police forces not only has had a massive impact on Kashmir's society but has transported the conflict to a plane very distant from the debating halls of the UN.

By late 2002, 15,937 insurgents had been killed, according to the Indian counterinsurgency command.[31] By 2006 this figure exceeded 20,000. Most towns and many villages in Indian-controlled Kashmir have "martyrs' graveyards" where the fallen *mujahideen* (holy warriors) are buried. The central martyrs' cemetery located in Srinagar's Eidgah neighborhood has more than a thousand *shaheed* (martyr) graves, including most of the pioneers and top commanders of the armed struggle. It is laden with a sense of desolation and pathos. The number of civilians killed over the years by the security forces, their auxiliaries, and the guerrillas is not accurately known, but is certainly in the low tens of thousands. At least six thousand Indian security personnel have also died.

The armed struggle was launched by an organization called the Jammu and Kashmir Liberation Front (JKLF). The JKLF was formed in 1964 in Pakistani-controlled Kashmir and until the late 1980s had negligible presence and support on the Indian side of the LOC. The JKLF believes in the reunification of the Indian-controlled and Pakistani-controlled parts of Kashmir in a fully sovereign state. One of the movement's founders, Amanullah Khan, elaborated this idea of "a united, neutral, secular and federal republic" of Kashmir as early as 1970.[32] The JKLF is a Muslim but not an Islamist movement—its flag is patterned on that of the Palestine Liberation Organization and like the PLO, which was founded around the same time as the JKLF was born, it sees itself as an anti-colonial national liberation movement. In 1990 this group emerged as the vanguard and spearhead of an uprising centered on the Kashmir Valley. The JKLF attracted a new generation of radicalized young men and drew inspiration from the Valley's traditions of mystical Sufi Islam.[33] The armed struggle spread like wildfire in the early 1990s in response to punitive Indian counterinsurgency policies that relied on "crackdowns" (intrusive and often brutal cordon-and-search operations targeted against entire villages and urban neighborhoods), shooting of unarmed pro-azaadi demonstrators, curfews, and widespread torture of detainees.

By 1993, however, the JKLF lost its leading role in the insurgency to the Jammu and Kashmir Hizb-ul Mujahideen (JKHM, "Warriors of the Faith"), a rival group. The JKLF did not have the organizational caliber and resources to withstand either the ruthless Indian counterinsurgency campaign or the growing hostility of its initial patron, the Pakistani military's notorious Inter-Services Intelligence (ISI), which supervised the U.S.-backed mujahideen war against the Soviet occupation of Afghanistan in the 1980s, on the other. The ISI never trusted the JKLF's independentists and from 1991 began to build up the JKHM even while engineering splits and defections in the JKLF. In contrast to the JKLF's rallying cry, *Kashmir banega khudmukhtar* (Kashmir will be sovereign), the Hizb-ul Mujahideen's slogan is *Kashmir banega Pakistan* (Kashmir will be one with Pakistan), and unlike the JKLF the JKHM is an Islamist group with close ties to a conservative Sunni Muslim political organization called the Jama'at-i-Islami (JI), which has separate but fraternal wings in Kashmir, Pakistan, and Bangladesh (Kashmir's Muslims are predominantly Sunni, although there is a Shia minority of about 15 percent). In mid-1994 the weakened JKLF ceased armed operations altogether, leaving the insurgency dominated by the JKHM. Despite their different conceptions of azaadi, both militant groups were born of a shared disillusionment with Indian policy toward Kashmir. Yusuf Shah, who has led the JKHM from 1991 under the nom de guerre Salahuddin, is a JI activist who stood in the rigged March 1987 election as an opposition MUF candidate, and Yasin Malik, who emerged in 1989–1990 as a top JKLF insurgent, had been his campaign manager in that election. Malik, only twenty-one years old in 1987, personifies the azaadi generation of Kashmiri youth.

The peak of insurgency lasted from 1990 to 1995. During this period the Indian security forces were on the defensive despite their massive numbers and firepower. Most neighborhoods of Srinagar, a sprawling city of about 1.5 million people, teemed with heavily armed rebels. Agha Shahid Ali captured the brutal atmosphere of a paradise lost:

> Srinagar hunches like a wild cat; lonely sentries, wretched in bunkers at the city's bridges, far from their homes in the plains, licensed to kill . . . while the Jhelum flows under them, sometimes with a dismembered body. On Zero Bridge the jeeps rush by . . . Guns shoot stars into the sky, the storm . . . rages on . . . night after night . . . Son after son taken away, never to return from the night of torture.[34]

After 1995, however, the insurgency waned to some extent. This was partly due to the ruthlessness and tenacity of the Indian counterinsurgency effort—the Indians operated a policy known as "catch and kill" against suspects—and partly because of problems within the insurgent ranks. In 1994–1995 the Pakistan-backed Hizb-ul Mujahideen group tried to consolidate its dominance by killing large numbers of members and supporters of the JKLF and other insurgent groups, as well as prominent religious, social, and political figures who opposed the JKHM and its pro-Pakistan stance. This campaign of murder produced a backlash—both among the public, who began to tire of internecine fighting and criminality among the mujahideen, and among former and active insurgents targeted by the JKHM, who sought protection, financial reward, and revenge through collaboration with the Indian counterinsurgency apparatus. By 1996 significant groups of ex-guerrillas who had metamorphosed into pro-India gunmen emerged in the Kashmir Valley, and these elements helped the Indians reassert control over Srinagar and other urban centers, as well as sizable rural areas.

The insurgency did not die out but changed in two ways. First, its locus moved out of population centers into remote rural areas that afforded the cover of forested and mountainous terrain to guerrillas. Concurrently, the insurgency spread from its initial bastion, the Kashmir Valley, to large tracts of the Jammu region (the Jammu region has almost five million people and is multireligious, unlike the overwhelmingly Muslim Kashmir Valley of almost six million people, which lies to its north). By the late 1990s topographically rugged areas of the Jammu region with predominantly Muslim or mixed Muslim-Hindu populations emerged as the new strongholds of insurgency. The second change was the growing presence of nonlocal fighters in the insurgency. Until the mid-1990s the guerrilla ranks were composed overwhelmingly of residents of Indian-controlled Kashmir. But from the mid-1990s growing numbers of radical Islamists from Pakistan, patronized by the ISI's department dedicated to operations in Kashmir, began to infiltrate across the LOC. By the late 1990s the insurgents were a mix of local and nonlocal elements, and this continues to be the case.

The *jehadi* volunteers who arrived from across the LOC introduced a new tactic into the insurgency from 1999 onward. This was *fidayeen,* or suicidal warfare. Typically, two-man fidayeen units armed with automatic rifles and grenades would launch frontal attacks on military camps, police stations, and government offices, as well as on such targets as airports, railway stations, and Hindu civilians. The most deadly jehadi groups of Pakistani provenance,

Lashkar-e-Taiba (responsible for the majority of fidayeen assaults) and Jaish-e-Mohammad, gradually recruited some locals to their cause, and the two-man fidayeen squads frequently consist of one local and one nonlocal militant. Apart from being psychologically unnerving for the security forces, fidayeen warfare posed potentially great dangers. The jehadis began to practice this form of warfare shortly after Pakistani regular forces who had infiltrated into a remote part of Indian-controlled Kashmir's sparsely populated Ladakh region around the small town of Kargil in early 1999, sparking fierce fighting with the Indians that summer, were compelled to withdraw after U.S. president Clinton talked tough in Washington to Pakistan's prime minister, Nawaz Sharif. The peak of the fidayeen campaign occurred in 2001–2002, when bloody fidayeen raids against India's parliament in New Delhi (December 2001) and against families of Indian soldiers near the city of Jammu (May 2002) triggered a massive Indian military mobilization and standoff with Pakistan that threatened to escalate into the fourth India-Pakistan war.

The ratcheting up of tension in the subcontinent caused serious alarm in Western capitals and around the world, especially because both India and Pakistan had successfully tested nuclear weapons in 1998. The war clouds eventually dissipated, partly as a result of effective American crisis diplomacy with the leaderships of both countries, but the episode was a warning of the risks inherent in an unresolved, festering Kashmir conflict. As the political activist and writer Prem Nath Bazaz noted presciently in 1967:

> It is an irony of history that by a combination of fortuitous circumstances a tiny nation of Kashmiris has been placed in a position of great importance, where it can be instrumental in making or marring the future of so many.[35]

The stakes have only become higher four decades later.

The Forging of Peace

The Kashmiri poet Agha Shahid Ali wrote poignantly in the 1990s
about the violence engulfing his homeland. But he was not devoid
of hope. In one of his most powerful poems—inspired by Osip
Mandelstam's untitled poem "We shall meet again, in Petersburg"
and dedicated to a Kashmiri Hindu friend—Ali expressed a vision
of peace:

> We shall meet again, in Srinagar,
> By the gates of the Villa of Peace,
> Our hands blossoming into fists
> till the soldiers return the keys
> and disappear. Again we'll enter
> our last world, the first that vanished
> in our absence from the broken city.
> We'll tear our shirts for tourniquets
> and bind the open thorns, warm the ivy
> into roses . . .
> Humankind can bear everything.[36]

A Kashmir settlement is attainable, but it faces three daunting
hurdles:

- The contentious history of the India–Pakistan relationship.
- The severely troubled relationship between Indian political authority and a large section of the population of Indian-controlled
  Kashmir.
- The diversity of political allegiances *within* Indian-controlled
  Kashmir, where pro-independence, pro-India, and pro-Pakistan
  population segments uneasily coexist (and to a lesser extent also
  in Pakistani-controlled Kashmir, where pro-Pakistan and pro-
  independence segments coexist).

The hurdles are not insurmountable, provided a settlement is built on four essential pillars:

- The (re)institutionalization of substantial self-rule in Indian-controlled Kashmir, with provision for "autonomy within autonomy" for the Jammu region, which has an overall Hindu (and pro-India) majority, and for Ladakh, almost half of whose population consists of (pro-India) Buddhists.
- Power sharing in Indian-controlled Kashmir's institutions between representatives of the three segments.
- The development of ties of cross-border cooperation between Indian-controlled and Pakistani-controlled Kashmir with the objective of gradually transforming the Line of Control from a forbidding iron curtain to a porous linen curtain.
- The embedding of a Kashmir settlement in a broader framework of regional cooperation across South Asia that renders sovereignties and borders less rigid.

Low-key and discreet forms of international, particularly U.S., engagement have a role to play in supporting a sustained peace process along these lines.

Since their last full-fledged war in December 1971 India and Pakistan have agreed upon two declarations of principles that could and should guide a peace process aimed at fundamentally improving their relationship and settling the Kashmir dispute. Meeting in Simla, a resort town in the hills of northern India, in July 1972, the prime ministers Indira Gandhi and Zulfiqar Ali Bhutto signed an agreement that "resolved that the two countries put an end to the conflict and confrontation that have hitherto marred their relations and work for . . . a friendly and harmonious relationship and . . . durable peace on the subcontinent . . . reconciliation [and] good neighborliness." They further agreed, in an implicit but obvious reference to Kashmir, that "the basic issues and causes of conflicts which have bedeviled relations . . . for the past twenty-five years shall be resolved by peaceful means . . . through bilateral negotiations or by other peaceful means mutually agreed." The Simla agreement stipulated that "in Jammu & Kashmir, the Line of Control resulting from the cease-fire of 17 December 1971 shall be respected by both sides without prejudice to the recognized position of either side [on the Kashmir conflict]. Neither side shall seek to alter it unilaterally, irrespective of mutual differences and legal interpretations. Both sides . . . undertake to refrain from the threat or use of force in violation of this Line." The agreement's concluding clause stated that "both Governments agree that their Heads will meet again at a mutually convenient time in the future and that, in the meanwhile, the representatives of the two sides will meet to discuss the modalities and arrangements for the establishment of durable peace and normalization of relations."[37]

The Simla agreement contained two significant concessions by defeated, dismembered Pakistan. The first was the characterization of the Kashmir dispute as a problem to be settled by *bilateral* negotiations, rather than through the intervention of an international third party such as the UN. The second was the rechristening of the cease-fire line running through Kashmir as the line of *control,* which both countries undertook not to violate. Since the mid-1950s Indian leaders had both dismissed the idea of an UN-administered plebiscite and expressed a preference for converting the cease-fire line in Kashmir into a part of the India-Pakistan international border, so these elements of the agreement represented movement in the direction of the Indian stance. On the other hand, the agreement clearly referred to Kashmir as a "basic" issue that had bedeviled India-Pakistan relations since 1947 and repeatedly jeopardized peace on the subcontinent, and unambiguously suggested that a negotiated settlement was a sine qua non for a new era of normalcy and lasting peace.

The Simla agreement never resulted in a structured, sustained peace process—for several reasons. A concerted intergovernmental peace process requires political will as well as institutional mechanisms, and both were lacking. The agreement was identified with its signatories, Indira Gandhi and Bhutto. Both charismatic leaders became mired in deep political trouble by the mid-1970s. In 1975–1976 Indira Gandhi suspended India's democratic institutions and civil liberties and attempted to impose an authoritarian regime. She badly lost a national election in a public backlash in 1977. Bhutto was deposed by a military coup in 1977 and then hanged in 1979 by the coup leader, General Zia-ul Haq. In the intervening years, India tested its first atomic bomb in 1974, spurring Pakistan to launch its own nuclear weapons program, and Indira Gandhi's government concluded an internal political deal with Sheikh Abdullah in 1975. Moreover there was no concerted international pressure on the two countries to follow up on the agreement. This was largely because of the global Cold War in which India and Pakistan occupied different sides—India as a pro-Soviet country and Pakistan as an ally of the United States and secondarily also of China, a country with which India had poor relations since an India-China border war in late 1962.[38]

The threads were picked up more than a quarter century later when in February 1999 India's prime minister Atal Behari Vajpayee—a Hindu nationalist, albeit a moderate—made a sensational diplomatic trip to Pakistan on the first run of a bus service connecting Delhi with the Pakistani city of Lahore, which is close to the border with India. The bus diplomacy resulted in a "Lahore declaration" signed by Vajpayee and Pakistan's prime minister, Nawaz Sharif. The Lahore declaration was a ray of hope in an unpromising regional context. India and Pakistan had both tested nuclear weapons in May 1998, and throughout the 1990s relations between the two countries had been characterized by antagonism and recrimination because of the armed conflict in Indian-controlled Kashmir, with India blaming Pakistan for abetting the insurgents and Pakistan accusing India of heavy-handed repression.

The Lahore declaration swam against the tide by bluntly asserting that "an environment of peace and security is in the supreme
national interest of both countries and the resolution of all out-
standing issues, including Jammu & Kashmir, is essential for this
purpose." "Recognizing that the nuclear dimension of the security
environment of the two countries adds to their responsibility for
the avoidance of conflict" and "reiterating the determination of
both countries to implement the Simla Agreement in letter and
in spirit," the governments agreed to "intensify efforts to resolve all
issues, including . . . Jammu & Kashmir" and to "intensify their
composite and integrated dialogue process"—meaning intergovernmental talks on all major and minor contentious issues, not just
Kashmir—on the basis of an "agreed bilateral agenda." The declaration contains two other significant points of principle. The governments "affirm[ed] their commitment to the goals and objectives
of SAARC [the South Asian Association of Regional Cooperation,
which has remained largely undeveloped compared to other regional blocs such as the EU and ASEAN] . . . with a view to pro-
moting the welfare of [all] the peoples of South Asia," and undertook to "promote and protect all human rights and fundamental
freedoms."[39]

The emerging thaw dissolved within a few months on the barren mountains of the Kargil district of Indian-controlled Kashmir's
high-altitude Ladakh region. Pakistani military units had already
infiltrated the LOC in Kargil when the Lahore declaration was being signed, and the Indians, once they discovered the infiltration in
May 1999 after winter snows melted, launched a massive land and
air campaign to evict the infiltrators. The fighting was fierce and
claimed the lives of 519 Indian military personnel (Pakistani casualties are not precisely known but were probably higher).[40] The hostilities ended only after President Clinton talked tough to Nawaz
Sharif in Washington in early July and the Pakistani military subsequently withdrew.[41] The Pakistani incursion—apparently intended

to bring the Kashmir dispute to global attention and apparently masterminded by the army chief, General Pervez Musharraf—was ill-advised and politically counterproductive. It roused global alarm and precipitated calls from major international players, including Pakistan's traditional allies, the United States and China, to respect the LOC and refrain from reckless escalations of the Kashmir conflict.

In October 1999 the unpopular Nawaz Sharif was deposed by a military coup and Musharraf seized power. Vajpayee subsequently tried to repair the damage by inviting Musharraf to a summit in Delhi in July 2001 (he presaged this move with a temporary cease-fire by Indian forces against insurgents, unless attacked first, in Indian-controlled Kashmir in the winter of 2000–2001). But the summit proved inconclusive and was regarded as a disappointment by both sides. Following the ill-timed summit, relations frayed further as fidayeen terrorism surged in Indian-controlled Kashmir, and after a fidayeen attack on India's parliament complex in New Delhi in December 2001 tensions escalated to a dangerous level. A renewed thaw emerged in late 2003 and was cemented by Vajpayee and Musharraf when they met during a SAARC summit in Islamabad in early 2004.

This turbulent history notwithstanding, the will and capacity for sustained intergovernmental cooperation between India and Pakistan is the prerequisite and bedrock of any process that may produce a settlement to the Kashmir conflict. The principles enunciated in Simla in 1972 and Lahore in 1999 provide abidingly relevant starting points and guidelines for such a process. They are a reminder that the history of the India-Pakistan relationship is not all about acrimony and war but also about moments in which the respective leaderships committed in principle to pursue lasting peace.

Making progress toward a Kashmir settlement requires jettisoning much conventional thinking—and posturing—about how to solve the Kashmir conflict. The route of the plebiscite, for example, is not just obsolete but an inappropriate, even dangerous, formula for addressing sovereignty disputes. Kofi Annan, the UN secretary-general, admitted on a visit to the subcontinent in 2000 that the old Security Council resolutions calling for a plebiscite were unenforceable and essentially defunct. India has squarely opposed the plebiscite for the past fifty years (the Indian argument is that the plebiscite could not be held during the first decade of the dispute because Pakistani forces failed to vacate the parts of Kashmir under Pakistani control, a condition for the referendum to take place, while Pakistanis as well as pro-independence and pro-Pakistan people in Kashmir feel that India never intended to honor its commitment to a plebiscite in any case). The Pakistani conception of the plebiscite limits the choice to the two options of the late 1940s and early 1950s—India or Pakistan. Such an exercise would *a priori* exclude the first preference—independence—of millions on both sides of the LOC. In fact, the Pakistanis have for decades used the plebiscite demand simply as a tactical weapon against India in the propaganda war over Kashmir. In 2004 Musharraf became the first leader in Pakistan's history to publicly acknowledge that it is pointless to flog the dead horse of the plebiscite and that an alternative path to settling Kashmir must be found.

Even if a plebiscite were feasible it would be inadvisable. As the experience of Bosnia recounted in Chapter 3 shows, sovereignty referendums in societies deeply divided on questions of allegiance and identity have a polarizing effect and dangerously inflame differences between population segments that harbor conflictual notions of national self-determination. Plebiscites represent an intrinsically winner-take-all approach and reduce sovereignty conflicts to a zero-sum game between fundamentally opposed preferences. A conflict as complex and incendiary as Kashmir calls for sophisticated tools of surgical precision, not the blunt instrument of a plebiscite decided by simple majority.

Indeed, a hypothetical three-way plebiscite may not produce a clear majority for any of the three positions. It would be likely to expose a vertical split between pro-Pakistan and pro-independence viewpoints in Pakistani-controlled Kashmir. In Indian-controlled Kashmir, which is socially and politically diverse, the picture is likely to be even more complicated. The Kashmir Valley would be likely to return a strong pro-independence majority, but even there a substantial minority of Muslims would vote for Pakistan while a smaller but not insignificant number of Hindus, Sikhs, and Muslims would vote for India. The highly heterogeneous Jammu region would be prone to complex fractures. Its Hindu-majority districts would go with India while its Muslim-majority districts would probably be divided between the three viewpoints, with independence supporters outnumbering the partisans of Pakistan and India. Furthermore, Hindu-majority towns within Muslim-majority districts would vote for India, while mixed Hindu-Muslim towns might become split three ways. The Buddhists who dominate the Ladakh region's Leh district would certainly opt for India, while the Shia Muslims who comprise a majority in the Kargil district may not. The Muslim minority in the Leh district may vote differently from the Buddhist majority, while the Buddhist minority in Kargil may be at loggerheads with the district's Muslim majority.

In short, the social and demographic complexity and political heterogeneity of Kashmir means that the fault lines would run through Kashmir's regions, districts, towns, villages, and even families. The imposition of any one political stance on such a complex and fractured society is a recipe for conflict and chaos, not peace and stability. The unitary-sounding concept of "self-determination" is inadequate when the "self" is deeply divided, even fractured.[42] A transition from war to peace requires the crafting of a delicate compromise that enables the contending preferences on self-determination and sovereignty among the people of Kashmir to coexist, however uneasily.

Perspectives that foreground territorial claims and ambitions are equally bankrupt. The long-standing Indian fixation with converting the LOC into a permanent, de jure international border is infeasible because no Pakistani regime or leader can agree to such a settlement of the territorial dispute on India's terms. The status of contested borders cannot be determined unilaterally on the basis of one party's preferences (the current Israeli government's preference for unilaterally drawing its border with a future Palestinian state is untenable for the same reason). But even if such a formalization of the territorial status quo *were* feasible, it would not solve India's fundamental problem in Kashmir—the presence of millions of people in Indian-controlled Kashmir, mostly pro-independence but also a pro-Pakistan segment, who do not accept the legitimacy of Indian rule.

Pakistan's restless revisionism vis-à-vis the LOC—which inspired the ill-fated cross-border incursions of 1965 and 1999—is equally unrealistic because no Indian government and leadership can agree to ceding any Indian-controlled territory to Pakistan. Indian public opinion would not tolerate any such scenario, and the determination with which the Indians confronted infiltration even in Kargil's remote, barren mountains in 1999 should have been a lesson to Pakistanis that any redrawing of the LOC in Pakistan's favor is not going to happen. But even if such a redrawing of borders were to be feasible—for example, if India were to be willing to hand over the Kashmir Valley, the most coveted piece of real estate in the Kashmir dispute, to Pakistan—it would be likely to aggravate problems rather than resolve them. The pro-independence majority in the Kashmir Valley is unlikely to welcome Pakistani rule, its pro-India minority even less so.

The Kashmir independentists' ideal scenario is the erasure of the LOC and the reunification of the pre-1948 princely state of Kashmir as a sovereign entity. In practical terms this is a fantasy since India and Pakistan are tacitly united in their absolute opposition to the emergence of a sovereign authority in all or any part of Kashmir's territory. But even if this scenario were to be permitted by the two countries, it would be extremely problematic. The Kashmir independentists' sacred geography, the territory of the former princely state of Kashmir, is a patchwork of diverse regions and communities that existed under a tin-pot monarchy for barely one hundred years, 1846–1947.[43] It is not clear why this territory should be a natural, timeless, and sacrosanct unit of sovereignty in the manner the rhetoric of the independentist JKLF seems to take for granted: "Jammu & Kashmir State as it existed on 14 August 1947—including Indian-occupied areas, "Azad Kashmir" ["Free Kashmir," the more populated and nominally self-governing part of Pakistani-controlled Kashmir] and Gilgit and Baltistan [remote and sparsely populated mountainous parts of Pakistani-controlled Kashmir directly governed by Islamabad as the "Northern Areas"]—is an indivisible political entity. No solution not approved by a majority of the people of the entire State as a single unit will be accepted."[44]

A sovereign Kashmir encompassing the former princely state's territory, *even if* approved by a 50-percent-plus-one simple majority of the population (which is possible but by no means definite), would have to be imposed on very large pro-Pakistan and pro-India segments of the population who disagree with its existence. If the territory of the independent state were to be truncated to just the Kashmir Valley—an idea that is occasionally circulated—it would still include minorities of pro-Pakistan and pro-India citizens who do not wish to be in such an entity, and *exclude* significant numbers of pro-independence people who live in Indian-controlled Kashmir's other regions and in Pakistani-controlled Kashmir. And if the "Azad Kashmir" region of Pakistani-controlled Kashmir were to be appended to a sovereign Kashmir Valley, the enlarged independent state would include large numbers of "Azad Kashmir" residents whose primary loyalty is to the idea and state of

Pakistan, not Kashmir. Territorially fixated approaches to the Kashmir conflict come in different variants. All are nonstarters and represent a dead end.

The architecture of a viable Kashmir settlement consists of several interlocking elements. The most important of these building blocks is self-rule. An honorable compromise between the power of the Indian state and the aspiration to azaadi that resonates with much of Indian-controlled Kashmir's population will be actualized only by the restoration of substantial powers of self-government to Indian-controlled Kashmir. The pre-1954 division of powers—in which Indian-controlled Kashmir was responsible for all matters of governance except external defense, the conduct of foreign affairs, and currency and communications, subjects that were under the jurisdiction of the Union government in New Delhi—can and should serve as an approximate benchmark for the reinstitutionalization of an autonomous regime. Indeed, Article 370 of the Indian constitution, which enshrines the autonomous status of Indian-controlled Kashmir, continues to exist but only on paper. It needs to be brought to life and given real meaning. It is likely that some aspects of Indian-controlled Kashmir's post-1953 integration—even if under authoritarian conditions—into the Indian Union will endure, for instance in economic, financial, fiscal and judicial matters. But this is ultimately a matter of detail. The *principle* of autonomy—*khudmukhtari* (which literally means being the master of one's own affairs) defined as substantial self-rule short of sovereignty—must form a pillar of any serious peace process and any durable settlement.

All pro-independence and most pro-Pakistan political groups in Indian-controlled Kashmir know that sovereignty is unattainable but correctly regard the recognition and institutionalization of the right to self-rule as indispensable, given Kashmir's history since 1947 and especially since 1990. Across the LOC "Azad Kashmir" has a range of autonomous institutions, including its own president, prime minister, legislative assembly, supreme court, high court, election commission, and public service commission. Yet intrusive interventions and heavy-handed control by the Pakistani center have endured in "Azad Kashmir," causing serious discontent among parts of the population. This situation too needs to be reformed. The sense of alienation from the Pakistani state that affects many in "Azad Kashmir" is likely to have intensified in the aftermath of the October 2005 earthquake, which devastated the northern part of "Azad Kashmir." The initial response of the Pakistani central authorities—particularly the otherwise omnipresent and domineering armed forces—to the calamity was slow and incompetent. The basic norm that must be respected is minimal interference by the central governments of India and Pakistan in the self-rule regimes of their respective parts of Kashmir—over which the countries retain sovereignty—so that statutory autonomy is actually translated into practice.

Such a self-rule regime in Indian-controlled Kashmir would generate apprehensions among the pro-India segment of its population, concentrated largely in the Hindu-dominated southern areas of the Jammu region. These apprehensions, which can be exploited by sectarian spoiler elements unless addressed constructively, stem from the perception that a self-rule regime represents a reward to Muslim secessionist claims emanating mainly from the Kashmir Valley at the expense of the rights of those whose allegiance lies with India. The tension between the political proclivities of the Valley's Muslims and the Hindus who are a majority in the Jammu region has a long lineage, dating back to struggles in the late 1940s and early 1950s.

The concerns about the implications of self-rule can be alleviated by emphasizing the fact that there is no change of sovereignty involved—Indian-controlled Kashmir remains under Indian sovereignty. The reassurance needs to be institutionally reinforced by a multitiered, cascading structure of devolution in Indian-controlled Kashmir, in which the Jammu and Ladakh regions enjoy their own autonomous status and powers—including elected regional legislative bodies—within the self-rule framework of Indian-controlled Kashmir. Such a structure would effectively protect the interests of the Jammu region's Hindu majority and the Buddhists who make up almost half of Ladakh's population against any possibility of centralized domination from Srinagar, a city most of them regard as a stronghold of insurgents and subversives. A piecemeal version of the "autonomy within autonomy" formula already exists in Ladakh's Buddhist-dominated Leh district, which has its own elected legislature and executive organ vested with statutory powers of local self-government. In another classic application of the federal principle, an upper chamber of Indian-controlled Kashmir's legislature can and should be constituted as a "house of the regions," and a constitutional court may be established to arbitrate relations between the three regions. Such a political structure may seem complex but is in fact already a working reality in several units of the Indian Union in which issues of multilayered diversity and intra-unit conflicts exist. The conflicting political allegiances within Indian-controlled Kashmir can be made to cohabit in an appropriately designed institutional space. Some of the most seasoned observers of the Kashmir conflict have been arguing for decades that the heterogeneity of Kashmir's society calls for such a structure of governance.[45]

During a transitional period lasting several years Indian-controlled Kashmir would benefit from an inclusive, power-sharing government in which the most significant representatives of all three segments of allegiance—pro-independence, pro-India, and pro-Pakistan—are accommodated. This would be anomalous in India's political system, which is strongly oriented to the adversarial patterns of competitive politics. But Kashmir is a special case, and the experience of peacebuilding in societies with deep internal schisms that are emerging from armed conflict suggests the need for broad-based transitional governments. Such arrangements also have the beneficial effect of minimizing the number of potential spoilers, the bane of peace processes. The establishment of an all-party forum of dialogue in Indian-controlled Kashmir would in any case be a necessary element of a peace process (such a roundtable was convened by the government of India in 2006 but shunned by all pro-independence and pro-Pakistan parties, who distrust the government's intentions). Similarly inclusive transitional arrangements should be set up in Pakistani-controlled Kashmir, where pro-independence parties have a long history of suffering persecution and being excluded from representation and participation in political institutions.

The best compromise between the contradictory positions on the LOC is to transform the character of the line—into a soft border between self-governing entities in Indian and Pakistani Kashmir, a bridge of cooperation rather than an iron wall of antagonism. The challenge here is "to make a virtue of porous borders and inter-twined economies and cultures" so that "self-determination can flourish without requiring the proliferation of micro-states or encouraging irredentist conflict."[46] The free movement of people and goods across the line is only the first step in this direction. The autonomous governments of Indian-controlled Kashmir and Pakistani-controlled Kashmir should be encouraged to develop intergovernmental cooperation in the range of subjects under their jurisdiction wherever such cooperation is sensible and mutually beneficial—in fields such as intra-Kashmir trade and commerce, intra-Kashmir waterways, cross-border transport, the protection and enhancement of environmental assets such as forests, the promotion of agriculture, cultural and religious matters, and tourism. Other cross-border institutions could include an interparliamentary body to bring together legislators of the two sides of Kashmir for regular meetings and consultations.

The institutionalized cross-border cooperation between the autonomous, power-sharing government of Northern Ireland and
the government of the Republic of Ireland mandated by the Good
Friday Agreement of 1998 provides a model to emulate in Kashmir.[47] The development of an array of cross-border linkages between the two parts of Kashmir will have the effect of connecting
the large pro-independence population on the Indian side of the
line to the sizable pro-independence population on the Pakistani
side, and the pro-Pakistan segment on the Indian side to their like-
minded brethren on the Pakistani side as well as to the country
they identify with (and vice versa). The systematic development of
cross-border ties transcending the LOC constitutes an essential pillar of a Kashmir settlement. The tragedy of the LOC as a hard, im-
permeable frontier was underscored in the aftermath of the October 2005 earthquake in Kashmir. The nature of the de facto border
made it impossible for Indian resources and personnel to be deployed to rescue survivors and provide succor to the hundreds of
thousands on the Pakistani side of the LOC whose lives and communities were ruined by the disaster, or for the anguished people of
Indian-controlled Kashmir, especially in the Kashmir Valley—some
of whose peripheral areas abutting the LOC were also severely affected—to go to the aid of their stricken compatriots in Pakistani-
controlled Kashmir. The lacerating experience of the earthquake
has strengthened cross-LOC empathy, solidarity, and a sense of
Kashmiri patriotism opposed to both India and Pakistan, adding
further urgency to the imperative of transforming the character of
the border dividing Kashmir.

A Kashmir settlement built on the pillars of self-rule, power
sharing, and cross-border cooperation can emerge only in the context of, and must be embedded in, the development of cross-border
ties across the subcontinent. A comprehensive security pact between the nuclear-weapon states of India and Pakistan must accompany and reinforce a settlement of the Kashmir conflict. More

broadly, a Kashmir settlement as outlined above can emerge and be sustained only in a regional environment where rigid notions of sovereignty and borders that divide have given ground to norms of transnational cooperation and solidarity across borders, driven as much by shared economic and security interests as by cultural bonds.

Almost sixty years after its inception the Kashmir conflict may be more amenable to a serious peace process than at any time in its history. This is because both India and Pakistan have compelling incentives to seek a modus vivendi, although for different reasons. India in the early twenty-first century has aspirations of emerging as a country that counts on the global stage. That aspiration is impeded by an unresolved, festering dispute that causes diplomatic embarrassment and consumes enormous human and financial resources. A Kashmir settlement would remove that thorn from India's side, liberate the bulk of the resources deployed year after year in a giant security and counterinsurgency apparatus, and most importantly, demonstrate to the world India's maturity and confidence as a vibrant democracy and growing economic power.

If the Kashmir conflict is a thorn in India's side, it is more like a millstone around Pakistan's neck. Pakistan is an unstable polity with weak institutions that is precariously held together by a military regime, and its economic prospects are at best uncertain. An indefinite confrontation with India over Kashmir is not a serious strategic option for Pakistan. The policy of supporting insurgency in Kashmir by radical Islamist factions based in Pakistan is not only difficult to sustain in a regional and international context altered by the events of 11 September 2001—in which the Pakistani regime is a principal U.S. ally in the "war on terror"—but has concrete and dangerous blowbacks. In December 2003 General Musharraf narrowly escaped two assassination attempts in the space of a fortnight. Members of Jaish-e-Mohammad, a radical Pakistani Islamist group active in the war against India in Kashmir, were implicated in these attacks, which were plotted by an alleged al-Qaeda network in Pakistan with the connivance of several junior officers in the Pakistani armed forces.

Within Kashmir, bled dry by seventeen years of low-intensity war, the dominant mood among political actors and the public is one of exhaustion—and pragmatism. Leaders once known as hardliners—such as Sardar Abdul Qayyum Khan, a veteran political figure in Pakistani-controlled Kashmir, and Yasin Malik, a pioneer of the insurgency that erupted in 1990 in Indian-controlled Kashmir—are advocates of an honorable compromise. Malik's organization, the Jammu and Kashmir Liberation Front—which introduced the gun into the Kashmir Valley in the end-1980s—collected 1.5 million signatures from the Valley's citizens in a grassroots campaign during 2004–2005, asking that the people of Kashmir be given adequate voice and representation in deciding the terms of a settlement.

For the incentives of all parties to the conflict to escape the zero-sum trap of antagonism to crystallize into a serious and sustained peace process, a greater degree of international engagement would be beneficial. The UN long ago became irrelevant to the resolution of the Kashmir dispute.[48] The sole global superpower, the United States, is the most plausible "third party" with the reach and clout to contribute to the prospects of a settlement, since it has direct leverage over Musharraf's Pakistan and considerable influence with India, which has since the end of the bipolar world order been interested and invested in building a wide-ranging strategic and economic relationship with the United States. There is no space for a direct third-party mediating role in a Kashmir peace process. India continues to be firmly opposed to any third-party intervention, and the perception of interference by the United States would not go down well in overwhelmingly Muslim Pakistan and Muslim-majority Kashmir either. Yet United States foreign policy *does* have a role to play vis-à-vis both India and Pakistan, albeit discreetly and largely behind the scenes, in ensuring that the nascent peace process does not fizzle out yet again. A contact-group-like body that includes the United States, Russia, China, and the European Union—all of which have substantial economic and/or strategic stakes in South Asia—could also play a role in encouraging India and Pakistan to keep moving forward on the road to peace. It is neither sufficient nor well advised for the international community to become actively engaged only when crises erupt, as in 1999 and 2002.

The peace process between India and Pakistan under way since 2004 is based on an incremental approach to making peace. This approach reflects the Indian preference, conceded reluctantly by the Pakistanis, for a very gradual, step-by-step process—conducted mainly by bureaucrats with occasional meetings between the political leaderships—that discusses all contentious issues with no precedence or priority given to particular issues over others. The Pakistanis like to emphasize and the Indians to de-emphasize the centrality of the Kashmir conflict to the India-Pakistan relationship and the peace process. This is consistent with their respective status since the late 1940s as the revisionist and the status quo power in the territorial dispute.

There is a rationale and logic to the incremental approach. A Kashmir settlement certainly cannot be hammered out overnight, contrary to what Musharraf's impatient utterances appear to presume. The India-Pakistan détente began in 2004 from a very low baseline with the normalization of diplomatic relations and travel links, which had been badly disrupted by the crisis of 2002. In violence-scarred Kashmir, as in any society that has experienced protracted armed conflict, step-by-step improvements on the ground are necessary through such measures as creating more sensitive and humane policing arrangements, releasing political detainees, reducing military and semimilitary forces' deployment in population centers, and fostering conditions that facilitate the return of people who have been displaced by the post-1989 conflict, such as the bulk of the Kashmir Valley's Hindu minority. Were a substantive settlement along the lines suggested in this chapter to materialize, its implementation would take several years.

But at the same time the incremental approach to making peace has its limitations, even perils. The postponement of direct engagement with the ultimate challenge—negotiating the framework of a Kashmir settlement—in favor of a gradualist and piecemeal approach runs the risk of generating a peace process that is little more than a series of disconnected loose ends. Postponing the basic task may simply stack up the odds of eventual failure. Some of the items on the agenda of intergovernmental talks during 2005 and 2006 were components of the Kashmir conflict—the standoff between the two armed forces on the Siachen glacier was discussed, as was the future of a major Indian hydroelectric project in Indian-controlled Kashmir about which the Pakistanis have serious reservations.[49] The talks on these issues were deadlocked—in other words, there was none of the tangible piecemeal progress that the incrementalist approach assumes will add up to a successful peace process in the longer run. The change of government in India following national elections in May 2004, when the coalition led by Vajpayee lost power to an alliance led by the Congress Party, has been a factor in stultifying the talks. The Congress, the emasculated dinosaur of Indian politics now led by Rajiv Gandhi's Italian widow Sonia, has a deeply conservative approach to India-Pakistan relations and the Kashmir question.

Moreover, while the intergovernmental process moves at a glacial pace there is no cessation of armed hostilities in the theater of low-intensity war, Indian-controlled Kashmir. Indian and Pakistani troops positioned on the LOC have been holding their fire since November 2003, but insurgency and counterinsurgency continue on a daily basis inside Indian-controlled Kashmir. Ambushes and car bombings targeted at Indian forces by the Hizb-ul Mujahideen and the Lashkar-e-Taiba occur regularly, as do fidayeen attacks by the Lashkar, which is a maverick and exceptionally violent Pakistan-based jehadi group. The continuation of violence between the state and insurgent factions has the potential to derail the halting progress of the peace caravan—as demonstrated by the experience of the post-1993 peace process between Israel and the Palestinians, which also followed a piecemeal, step-by-step approach and postponed negotiations on the major contentious issues. A mutual cease-fire is necessary in Indian-controlled Kashmir. Pakistan must prevail on the Muttahida (United) Jehad Council (MJC)—a coordination body of a dozen guerrilla groups chaired by the Hizb-ul Mujahideen and based in Pakistani-controlled Kashmir—to suspend armed operations. That would leave the Lashkar-e-Taiba, which is outside the MJC umbrella, isolated.

In mid-2006 Kashmir remains in limbo between war and peace. While there is some movement in developing cross-LOC links (a second bus route started in June 2006 between the border town of Poonch in Indian-controlled Kashmir's Jammu region and Rawalakote, a town forty kilometers away in Pakistani-controlled Kashmir), the key New Delhi–Islamabad track is stalled and concurrently there is little, if any, progress on the other vital front—mending and reconstituting the New Delhi–Srinagar relationship. There is a case for standing incrementalism on its head, taking the bull by the horns, and fast-tracking the negotiation of a framework settlement to the dispute in *all* its dimensions, with the understanding that details will remain to be sorted out later at various levels of engagement—New Delhi–Islamabad, New Delhi–Srinagar, Srinagar-Jammu, Islamabad-Muzaffarabad, and Srinagar-Muzaffarabad—and that implementation will of necessity be staggered over a number of years. A substantive and workable framework for such a settlement has been presented in the preceding pages. When the destination beckons, it makes compelling sense to embark boldly and purposefully on the journey.

· FIVE ·

Israel &
Palestine

In August 2005 Israel evacuated all twenty-one Jewish settlements and their nine thousand residents from the Gaza Strip. In early September all Israel Defense Forces (IDF) units withdrew from the Strip and the Israeli government announced the end of its military government in Gaza.

A few months prior to the "disengagement," in mid-May, tens of thousands of Jewish Israelis journeyed to Gaza to join the residents of the settlements in celebrating Israel's independence day. The celebration was held in Gush Katif, a cluster of fifteen settlements in the southwestern part of the Strip, separated from Palestinian-populated areas by a forbidding concrete wall ten meters high, watchtowers with machine-gun emplacements, and a buffer zone strewn with mines and the rubble of dozens of bulldozed Palestinian homes. At least forty-five thousand Israelis joined several thousand Gush Katif residents in a somewhat surreal "last celebration" dominated by flag-waving triumphalism. In the settlement of Kfar Darom, "hundreds of people, most . . . dressed in white, attended the dedication ceremony of a new and opulent synagogue . . . The residents never tired of relating that it was none other than Prime Minister Ariel Sharon, the architect of the disengagement plan, who laid the cornerstone of the synagogue."[1] In the Katif settlement children clambered over tanks at an IDF exhibition of weaponry and vehicles, while in the Ganei Tal settlement an exhibition memorialized Gush Katif settlers who had lost their lives over the years during their IDF service or in Palestinian terror attacks. The events culminated in a mass rally at Katif's artificial lake, where Holocaust survivors, a host of rabbis, and even an Israeli parliamentarian from a community of Druze (who are of Arab extraction) in Israel's northern Galilee region joined the soon-to-be-evacuated settlers in an emotional show of solidarity.

In the Palestinian town of Beit Lahia, in the northern Gaza Strip, the Raban family also coped with grief. The Rabans are strawberry farmers who make a living by selling their produce to a company in Israel, which then exports the product to Europe. One morning in January 2005 twelve of the Raban children, boys aged 11 to 17, were picnicking in the family's strawberry grove, playing marbles and eating the fruit on the first day of their school vacation, when an IDF tank shell landed in the grove and exploded. In a moment the children's playground was transformed into a scene of carnage. Seven of the children were killed instantly, "their limbs scattered in all directions." The other five were seriously injured—four also lost limbs and will remain "severely disabled for the rest of their lives." The oldest, Mohammad Raban, 17, lost both his legs, an eye, and one hand, and had to be kept alive by artificial respirator in Gaza's Shifa hospital. In the immediate aftermath of the incident the strawberry grove was not only "a terrible sight" but the scene of "a great silence." Only one of the twelve boys moaned weakly for help.

Mohammad Raban's mother, Maryam, lost three of her other sons in the strawberry grove—Hani, 16, Bassam, 15, and Mahmoud, 14. As her only surviving son, firstborn Mohammad, lay comatose in intensive care, she traveled to a polling station the weekend after the incident—which happened on a Tuesday—to vote in the Pal-

estinian presidential election for her favored candidate, Mahmoud
Abbas, better known by his Palestine Liberation Organization (PLO)
nom de guerre, Abu Mazen. She then spoke to an Israeli journalist
who visited her home: "I am calling on Sharon and [Israeli Defense
Minister] Mofaz . . . I have nobody to help me. I still have the child
in the hospital. I ask that they take him to a hospital in Israel . . . We
are looking to God and to the State of Israel [for succor]. We grew
up with the State of Israel."

Meanwhile, the mutilated Mohammad lay in the Shifa hospital's
intensive care unit. *Haaretz* reported that he "from time to time
open[ed] his remaining eye . . . from time to time he also smile[d] a
nervous smile, perhaps an involuntary, meaningless tic. Less than
half of his body is left . . . it's not clear whether he is aware of
that." In the hospital's orthopedic department his cousins Issa, 13,
Ibrahim, 14, and Imad, 16, recuperated, each "with both legs ampu-
tated above the knee."

The IDF issued the following statement on the incident:

> On January 4, 2005, two mortars were fired at the Erez indus-
> trial zone [on northern Gaza's border with Israel]. One of
> them fell near Israeli territory and injured an Israeli citizen. At
> about the same time, in the area of Beit Lahia, an IDF force
> identified a band with mortar launchers, some of whose mem-
> bers belong to Hamas. The force opened fire at the band. It
> should be mentioned that the terrorist band was operating
> from populated Palestinian territory. The IDF is investigating
> the incident; at its conclusion the findings will be presented.

Gideon Levy, the Israeli journalist, noted that the statement contained "not a word of regret for the killing of the children, [and]
not a word . . . [for] the bereaved families." He also wrote that he
felt obliged to record the incident and its aftermath "for the information of the soldier who fired, the commander who gave him

permission, and the spokesman who isn't sorry and isn't apologizing for anything."[2]

In the week after the Beit Lahia incident two suicide attacks occurred in Gaza. In the first incident, on 12 January, two Islamic Jihad members on a suicide mission penetrated the outlying Gush Katif settlement of Morag, located in a wedge of land between the large Palestinian refugee camps of Rafah and Khan Yunis. They killed a prominent settler and seriously wounded an IDF officer before being gunned down. In the second attack a day later, two suicide bombers in a car, probably from Hamas, struck at the Karni crossing point between central Gaza and Israel, killing three Israelis and injuring five others.

The Israeli withdrawal in 2005 from Gaza—which had been occupied briefly by the IDF during the 1956 Suez war and then for thirty-eight years from June 1967—is not surprising. The puzzle is that it took so long, because long-term control of Gaza defied strategic logic and rational considerations from the Israeli perspective. A few months before the eruption of the first Palestinian intifada, which began in northern Gaza's Jebalya refugee camp in December 1987, the IDF completed a classified study titled "The Gaza District up to the Year 2000." It was "one of the grimmest documents ever submitted to the Israeli defense establishment." It projected that "the Gaza Strip would break every known record of population density before [the end of] the twentieth century." Combined with scarcity of water for Gaza's Palestinians under the occupation regime, as well as an acute shortage of land—"whether for housing or for agriculture, roads, schools and hospitals," while areas designated as "state lands" were generously allocated to Jewish settlement blocs—this added up to "a human time-bomb ticking away at Israel's ear." In their study of the first Palestinian intifada, published in 1989, the Israeli analysts Zeev Schiff and Ehud Yaari wrote that "the Gaza Strip is a cancer that . . . will steadily drain the State

THE GAZA STRIP BEFORE ISRAEL'S 2005 DISENGAGEMENT

Mediterranean Sea

Erez Crossing

Jabalya RC

Shati RC

Beit Lahia

Gaza

Passageway to West Bank

Karni Crossing

An-Nuseirat RC

Bureij RC

Deir Al Balah RC

Al-Maghazi RC

Kfar Darom

I S R A E L

Katif Bloc

Kissufim Crossing

Khan Yunis

Morag

Rafah

Sufa Crossing

GAZA AIRPORT

EGYPT

Palestinian cities, localities, and refugee camps (RC)

Palestinian Autonomous Area

Israeli settlements

Settlement access road patrolled by Israel

Green Line

0   5   10 miles

of Israel," and predicted that "Israel will soon be on its knees begging all and sundry to do it the mercy of taking Gaza off its hands."[3]

That prophecy took another fifteen years to come to fruition, although the signs were unmistakable in the intervening years. During secret talks between Israeli and PLO representatives in Norway in early 1993—which led to the "declaration of principles" on an Israeli-Palestinian peace process signed in the White House in September 1993—the first point of agreement to emerge concerned the necessity, indeed inevitability, of Israeli withdrawal from Gaza. In the words of Dennis Ross, the chief American mediator for the Middle East between 1989 and early 2001: "In Israeli eyes, this was a promising beginning. The Israelis wanted out of Gaza." In 1994 most of the Strip—with the significant exclusion of a number of zones centered on the Jewish settlements, above all the Gush Katif bloc—were turned over by Yitzhak Rabin's government to interim self-administration under Arafat's Palestinian Authority (PA), along with the Judean desert town of Jericho on the West Bank, near the border with Jordan. In mid-2005 Prime Minister Ariel Sharon, the fallen idol of ideologically motivated settlers in the West Bank and Gaza, justified his decision to proceed with disengagement from Gaza in realist and strategic terms: "I am not prepared to accept the claim that leaving Gaza is the trampling of Zionism. It is in fact strengthening Zionism in areas that are much more important." He went on to refer specifically to the Galilee region of northern Israel, which has a large Arab population who are the majority in parts of the region, to the Negev desert region of southern Israel, which has a considerable Arab Bedouin community, and to the city and environs of Jerusalem as the areas that, unlike Gaza, were crucial to the Jewish state.[4]

The Israeli withdrawal from Gaza, for which each family evacuated received $200,000 to $400,000 in compensation, was broadly welcomed by the international community as an unusually decisive move that might just resuscitate the collapsed peace process between Israel and the Palestinians. In New York the UN's Middle East peace envoy Alvaro de Soto, who led the abortive UN effort to mediate a solution to the Cyprus conflict between 1999 and 2004, told the Security Council that "the Palestinians have experienced the joy of the departure of the occupier" and "the Israelis are no longer saddled with the unrewarding, Sisyphus-like grind of securing the Gaza Strip." Other voices were more circumspect. The liberal Israeli commentator Zvi Barel noted that "all the potential components of the explosion [in Gaza] are yet to be neutralized—the highest population density in the world, terrible poverty, a huge collection of arms, and a radical leadership [Hamas]." A cartoon in the Egyptian newspaper *Al-Ahram,* which is controlled by that country's authoritarian government, depicted Sharon contemptuously tossing a lean bone labeled "Gaza" on to an outstretched plate held by the Palestinian leader Mahmoud Abbas, while Abbas gazed longingly at the fat leg of lamb, labeled "West Bank," grasped firmly in Sharon's other hand.[5]

Indeed, almost concurrently with the dismantling of Gush Katif and the other Gaza Strip settlements, the IDF issued expropriation orders for Palestinian lands around Maaleh Adumim—the largest Jewish settlement on the West Bank, located just east of Jerusalem—which originated as a trailer park in the mid-1970s and now has at least thirty-one thousand residents. These orders acted upon an Israeli cabinet decision of February 2005 that approved the extension of Israel's "security barrier" with the West Bank to run in a wide arc around Maaleh Adumim, taking in a large adjacent "industrial zone" and several satellite settlements, a route that would "bite off a sizeable portion of the area between Jerusalem and Jericho."[6] Also in August 2005, the Sharon government announced its intention to locate the headquarters of the "Samaria and Judea District Police"—Samaria and Judea are the biblical Jewish names for what are today the northern and southern parts of the West Bank—in an area known as E-1, wedged between the Palestinian neighborhoods of East Jerusalem and Maaleh Adumim. An Israeli plan to construct thirty-five hundred new housing units for Jewish settlers in E-1 has been stayed for more than a decade by the opposition of successive U.S. administrations. As the Israeli lawyer and activist Daniel Seidemann put it in August 2004, if this route for the security barrier, "dovetailed with [expanded] settlement activity," were to go ahead, the ramifications . . . could hardly be starker. E-1 will cut East Jerusalem off from its environs in the West Bank, virtually ruling out the possibility of East Jerusalem becoming the national capital of [a sovereign state of] Palestine. Given the topography, it will dismember the West Bank into two cantons [centered on Nablus in the north and Hebron in the south] with no natural connection between them. If implemented, E-1 will create a critical mass of facts on the ground that will render the creation of a sustainable Palestinian state, with any semblance of geographical integrity, a virtual impossibility.[7]

On the other hand, opinion surveys in Israel in the wake of the Israeli withdrawal from the Gaza Strip revealed that 72 percent "of the Jewish public think that the unilateral disengagement from Gaza is not the end of the story, but only the first step toward an extensive evacuation of West Bank settlements in the context of a final agreement" with the Palestinians.[8] The prospects of an Israeli-Palestinian modus vivendi hang in the balance. The stance and policies of the United States, the crucial third party in the dispute, will be decisive in determining the future of a land contested between Arabs and Jews since the early twentieth century.

The Making of War

The history of Arab-Jewish conflict in Palestine until 1948, and of the Israeli-Palestinian conflict since then, is also the history of Zionism as an ideology and movement. Zionism—"Zion" is one of the biblical names of Jerusalem—arose in response to "the precarious situation of central and east European Jewry in the second half of the nineteenth century."[9] The experience of pogroms on the territories of the tsarist empire in the late nineteenth and early twentieth centuries, in particular, made a section of Central and East European Jews receptive to the salvationist appeal of Zionism, which argued that the solution to the Jewish predicament in much of Europe lay in returning to and reclaiming their ancient homeland in Palestine. The progenitor of the Zionist idea was Theodor Herzl, of Hungarian origin but settled in Vienna, who published a volume titled *Der Judenstaat—The Jewish State*—in 1896. The first Zionist congress was convened by Herzl in Basel, Switzerland, in 1897. *The Jewish State* did not specifically refer to Palestine as the site of the proposed state, but the program adopted by the first Zionist congress was explicit that "the aim of Zionism is to create for the Jewish people a home in Palestine."

The historian Avi Shlaim argues that "from the Basel congress onward the clear and consistent aim of the Zionist movement was to create a state in Palestine for the Jewish people."[10] Walter Laqueur concurs that "the Zionists believed . . . that without a country . . . [Jews] were bound to remain the bastards of humanity." Like many prophets of destiny, Herzl was convinced of the historical inexorability of his vision. He wrote in his diary: "At Basel, I founded the Jewish State. If I said this out loud today, I would be greeted with universal laughter. Perhaps in five years, and certainly in fifty, everyone will know it." A century later, as Israel celebrated the fiftieth anniversary of its founding in May 1998, Shlaim wrote that "in its central aim of providing . . . Jews with a haven, instilling in them a sense of nationhood, and forging a modern nation-state, Zionism has been a brilliant success." But Zionism's success in realizing its vision of self-determination and sovereignty for Jews in the land of Palestine also led to an explosive ethnonational conflict that has bedeviled the Middle East and the world. The root cause of this outcome was pithily expressed in a cable sent to Europe by a group of Viennese rabbis who visited Palestine after the Basel congress to investigate the feasibility of Herzl's vision: "The bride is beautiful," they wrote, "but she is married to another man."[11]

Walter Laqueur's sympathetic, indeed empathetic, account of the movement born of the Zionist idea, published in 1972, and Edward Said's eloquent critique of "Zionism from the standpoint of its victims," published in 1980, share important common ground. Laqueur emphasizes that "Zionism is a response to anti-semitism" in Central and Eastern Europe and "one cannot stress too strongly the force of circumstances"—without European anti-Semitism "Zionism would not have flourished" and "with the rise of Hitler it became a question of life and death" for much of the Jewish population of interwar Europe. In short, by the 1930s the agenda of Zionism was no longer an ideological choice but a practical compulsion for increasing numbers of European Jews. Said has written, "We cannot fail to connect the horrific history of anti-Semitic massacres [in Europe] to the establishment of Israel, nor can we fail to understand the depths, the extent and the overpowering legacy of suffering and despair that informed the post–World War II Zionist movement . . . Israelis are not white Afrikaners, nor are they like French settlers in Algeria. They have a history of suffering and persecution that has made the State of Israel a compellingly attractive resolution to that history." At the same time, Laqueur writes, "the Arab-Jewish conflict was inevitable, given that Zionism wanted to build more than a cultural center in Palestine" and that the movement's program involved "the transplantation of hundreds of thousands of Jews," the vast majority from Europe, into Palestine. "It was not the Arabs' fault that Jews were persecuted in Europe," Laqueur says, and it was quite logical that "from the Arab point of view Zionism was an aggressive movement, [and] Jewish immigration an invasion" of their homeland. This is entirely consistent with and indeed identical to Said's view that the "Palestinians . . . are the victims of the victims."[12]

The Laqueur and Said perspectives on Zionism do diverge, however. Laqueur argues that the Zionist movement's "intellectual origins go back to the French Revolution and the romantic wave of national revivals that followed it. As a political movement it was part of the liberal-humanist tradition of the [Italian] *risorgimento,* of

[Lajos] Kossuth and [Tomas] Masaryk."[13] Said's view is strikingly
different:

> Zionism was of European provenance: its institutions [in Pales-
> tine] referred to and identified themselves as colonizing un-
> dertakings in the manner of the European colonization of Af-
> rica and Asia, and its whole rhetoric and ideological language
> borrowed heavily not only from Jewish theology but from the
> rhetoric and language of the British in Africa and India, or the
> French in Algeria. Later interpretations of Zionism as a "liber-
> ation movement" are retrospective fantasy . . . Central to the
> enterprise was the qualitative distinction between incoming
> Jews from Europe and natives who were variously depicted as
> absent altogether or, in the words of [David] Ben-Gurion, like
> red Indians . . . a negligible quantity altogether.[14]

This is the divergence that separates even liberal Israeli views of
history and of the Israeli-Palestinian conflict from the Palestinian
understanding. Both versions make eminent sense when their dia-
metrically different vantage points are taken into consideration.
Michael Tarazi, an Arab-American adviser to the Palestinian Authority, has recently argued that "in theory, Zionism is the movement of Jewish national liberation. In practice, it has been a movement of Jewish supremacy." The fulfillment of the Zionist
conception of Jewish national self-determination has entailed first
the mass dispossession, in 1948, and then the occupation, since
1967, of the Palestinian nation, in a grim zero-sum conflict that
is yet to be broken. One people's quest for emancipation has gen-
erated the other's unending oppression; they are two sides of the
same coin, just as the Palestinians' "freedom fighter" is Israel's "terrorist." The British scholar Jacqueline Rose, who is Jewish, believes
that "messianism colors Zionism, including secular Zionism, at every turn" and asks: "How did one of the most persecuted peoples of the world come to embody some of the worst cruelties of

the modern nation-state?"[15] But perhaps there is not a puzzle or contradiction here after all. The nineteenth-century and early twentieth-century national self-determination movements identified with figures like Kossuth and Masaryk proved to be exceedingly callous and intolerant toward the rights of other peoples, particularly those who got in the way of the realization of their own aims. The intensity and magnitude of Jewish suffering in Europe, culminating in the Holocaust, steadily intensified the longing of many European Jews for the homeland in Palestine promised by Zionism. That posed a mortal threat to the basic interests, and eventually the very existence, of the Arab community of Palestine. In such circumstances, the distinction between an originally humanist movement of ethnonational liberation and a ruthless drive for ethnonational supremacy achieved by the force of arms proved to be a very fine one.

Between 1881 and 1914 the Jewish population of Palestine, then a province of the Ottoman empire, increased from twenty-four thousand to eighty-five thousand. Much of this immigration occurred after 1903, precipitated by a spate of pogroms in Eastern Europe between 1903—when a major pogrom took place in Kishinev—and 1906. The arrival of growing numbers of Jews intent on settling in Palestine roused alarm in the local Arabic press, such as the Haifa weekly *al-Karmil,* founded in 1908, and sparked sporadic clashes between Arab peasants and the Jewish settlers over farming and livestock-grazing rights.[16] But during World War I the Jewish population of Palestine declined to about fifty-five thousand and "by 1918 the viability of the *Yishuv* [the pre-Israel Jewish community of Palestine] had been placed in doubt." It was in this context that the beleaguered Zionist movement won a major breakthrough with the November 1917 "Balfour declaration." This was in fact a letter written by the British foreign secretary Arthur Balfour to the British peer Lord Rothschild, which stated that

His Majesty's Government views with favor the establishment
in Palestine of a national home for the Jewish people, and will
use its best endeavors to facilitate the achievement of this ob-
ject, it being clearly understood that nothing shall be done
which may prejudice the civil and religious rights of existing
non-Jewish communities in Palestine, or the rights and political status enjoyed by Jews in any other country.[17]

The Balfour declaration was the fruit of intense lobbying of the
British government by the Zionists, especially Chaim Weizmann,
one of the movement's most prominent figures. At the 1919 Paris
peace conference Weizmann announced that the movement's goal
was "to make Palestine as Jewish as England is English." Shlaim argues that from its formative phase Zionism acquired two enduring traits—"non-recognition" and "by-passing" of the Arab population, then the overwhelming majority in Palestine, and "the
quest for an alliance with a great power external to the Middle
East," making "reliance on a great power a central element of Zionist strategy."[18] Indeed, the support of the world's greatest imperial
power was to prove vital to the prospects of the Zionist project. In
1919 Balfour followed up his declaration with a memorandum,
which asserted that

. . . In Palestine we do not propose to even go through the
form of consulting the wishes of the present inhabitants of the
country . . . The four great powers are committed to Zionism
[which] be it right or wrong, good or bad, is rooted in age-old
tradition, present needs and future hopes of far profounder import than the desires and prejudices of the 700,000 Arabs who
now inhabit that ancient land. In my opinion that is right.[19]

In 1920 the League of Nations awarded the "mandate" over Palestine—a cross between a colony and a protectorate—to Britain.

The first British high commissioner of Mandate Palestine, Sir Herbert Samuel, who served until 1925, was a Jew and a Zionist who had been personally favored by Weizmann for the post. Jewish immigration to Palestine numbered 1,806 persons in 1919; it rose to 8,223 in 1920. Key Zionist institutions—the Jewish National Fund (JNF), dedicated to acquisition of land and its settlement by Jews, the Haganah, the Jewish armed force that would lead Israel's war of independence in 1948 and become the IDF, and the Jewish Agency—were established during the first decade of the Mandate. In the two decades from 1919 to 1939 a total of 364,519 Jews immigrated to Palestine, providing the Yishuv with more than the critical mass needed to pursue its ultimate goal of statehood. At the start of the Mandate period Arabs constituted about 92 percent of Palestine's population. By the time the Mandate ended in 1948, the Arab majority had been drastically reduced, to just over two-thirds of the population.

The growing tension between Arabs and Jews that resulted made Mandate Palestine a most unstable place, prone to frequent outbreaks of violence. In March 1920 fighting erupted at Tel Hai, a remote Jewish settlement in the upper reaches of the Galilee. Five Jews and an equal number of Arabs were killed. The Jewish dead included Yosef Trumpeldor, a well-known figure of Russian origin, who in death became a Zionist icon. In April 1920 violence broke out in Jerusalem, centered on its walled old city. Five Jews and 4 Arabs died; more than 200 Jews received injuries. Musa Kazim Pasha al-Husseini, the mayor of Jerusalem and a strong opponent of Zionist immigration, was removed from his post by the British authorities after the violence and replaced by a more pliable mayor from a rival Jerusalem Arab family. In May 1921 violence flared in Jaffa, the largely Arab port city just south of Tel Aviv (founded by Jews in 1909), starting with an attack by Arabs on a Zionist-run hostel for new immigrants. Forty-seven Jews and 48 Arabs were killed, the latter mostly by the British police and military. In addition, 146 Jews and 73 Arabs were injured. Herbert Samuel, who was deeply shaken by the scale and intensity of the violence, ordered that Arab rioters be bombed from the air. The disturbances spread from Jaffa to other locations abutting Jewish settlements in Petah Tikva, Rehovot, Kfar Saba, and Hadera. In November 1921 the old city of Jerusalem saw further violence, with 5 Jews and 3 Arabs killed.

The British authorities gradually realized that a policy of virtually untrammeled support for the Zionist "national home" program and its engine, immigration, risked aggravating fear and discontent among the Arabs to the extent that a large-scale conflagration would become inevitable. The Mandate regime accordingly toned down its permissiveness toward the Zionists, particularly after Samuel's departure in 1925. In 1927, for example, the number of Jewish immigrants entering Palestine fell sharply to 3,034 (from 34,386 in 1925 and 13,855 in 1926); in 1928 the figure was even lower at 2,178. But the problem remained. From the autumn of 1928 onward a controversy over Jewish access to the Western Wall in Jerusalem's old city gathered momentum. The outer side of the Wall, a remnant of the Temple of Herod, which was constructed on the site of the Temple of Solomon, is Judaism's single holiest site, while the inner side is part of the Haram al-Sharif, or "noble sanctuary" (usually referred to as the Temple Mount by Jews), a rectangular compound that includes the Dome of the Rock and al-Aqsa mosques and whose sanctity in Islam rivals that of Mecca and Medina. According to Islamic faith the Prophet Mohammad ascended to heaven from here and had tethered his steed, *al-Buraq,* to the wall.

In August 1929 the dispute came to a boil when several thousand Revisionist Zionists, a militant wing of Zionism led by Vladimir Zeev Jabotinsky, a Pole who settled in Jerusalem after World War I, held a demonstration at the Western Wall. Unlike the dominant socialist or labor version of Zionism, the Revisionists claimed not only Palestine but also the eastern bank of the Jordan river as ancestral Jewish patrimony, and accorded top priority to military organization and armed action, not just immigration and settlement of land. Jabotinsky, who died in 1940, became the spiritual inspiration for the Herut Party and its later incarnation, the Likud, in Israel, and one of his foremost disciples and fellow-Pole, Menachem Begin, who would become the first Likud prime minister of Israel in 1977, headed the Irgun, the deadly paramilitary organization spawned by the Revisionist movement, from 1944 until the climactic denouement of 1948. The Revisionist march of August 1929 touched off an orgy of violence, in a manner eerily similar to Ariel Sharon's visit to the Temple Mount in late September 2000, which sparked the second Palestinian intifada. The worst carnage in 1929 occurred in Hebron, where 67 Jews belonging to the city's mostly non-Zionist Jewish community were murdered by Arabs. Another 26 Jews died in Safad in northern Palestine. Arabs were killed by Jews in Jerusalem, Haifa and Jaffa. In all 133 Jews and 116 Arabs were killed, the latter again mostly by the British police and military, while 339 Jews and 232 Arabs were injured. Gory incidents such as the Hebron killings reminded Jews of the pogroms that many had come to Palestine to escape. The British high commissioner, Sir John Chancellor, who had replaced Lord Plumer in December 1928, was so depressed after visiting Hebron that he wrote to his son: "I am so tired and disgusted with this country and everything connected with it that I only want to leave as soon as I can."[20]

The second decade of the Mandate proved to be even more turbulent than the first. After a temporary decline between 1927 and 1931, Jewish immigration, especially from Poland and its adjacent areas, picked up significantly from 1932. Immigrants numbered 37,337 in 1933 and 45,267 in 1934, peaking at 66,472 in 1935. During 1933, large Arab demonstrations in Jerusalem and Jaffa protesting the growing tide of Jewish immigration were suppressed by British police action. By late 1935 Arab patience was running out and calls for radical action against the perceived British-Zionist alliance proliferated. The trigger to revolt came in November 1935. Sheikh Izz al-Din al-Qassam, a religious preacher from Haifa, had been calling for armed rebellion. In November 1935 he was killed in a skirmish with a British police detachment near the town of Jenin. The "news of al-Qassam's death sent a wave of grief and rage across Palestine. He became a symbol of martyrdom and self-sacrifice . . . Indeed, al-Qassam achieved more in death than during fifteen years of preaching." The slain sheikh's "funeral was an occasion for passionate expressions of militant nationalism." Decades later the Hamas military wing, formally established in 1991, would be named in honor of al-Qassam, as would Hamas's homemade arsenal of short-range rockets fired from Gaza since the outbreak of the second Palestinian intifada at nearby towns in Israel.[21]

The Palestinian Arab revolt commenced in 1936 with shooting incidents between Jews and Arabs and the proclamation of a general strike across Palestine. A nine-member Arab Higher Committee was formed under the chairmanship of the most important Palestinian religious figure, Haj Amin al-Husseini, the mufti of Jerusalem, to guide and coordinate the agitation. All of the major Palestinian Arab political factions were represented on the Committee, which included Christian as well as Muslim representatives. The revolt, which continued for three years before being ground down by British repression, exhaustion, and internecine feuding among the Palestinians, has been an important reference point for Palestinian nationalist politics and mobilization ever since, both during the PLO's armed struggle, which crystallized in the late 1960s, and the first and second Palestinian intifadas in the occupied territories, which erupted in late 1987 and the autumn of 2000. It rapidly assumed the dimensions of a large-scale armed insurgency. The Zionist leader Chaim Weizmann declared that "the forces of destruction, the forces of the desert, have risen, and on the other side stand firm the forces of civilization and building."[22] In June 1936, British forces demolished large parts of the old city of Jaffa as a punitive measure, the same month that all senior Arab civil servants of the Mandate government submitted a memorandum to the British high commissioner supporting their compatriots' sense of grievance and calling for redress. By autumn, however, the first phase of the uprising neared its end. The strike was difficult to sustain indefinitely, and by October almost a thousand Arab Palestinians had been killed in armed clashes, along with eighty Jews and thirty-seven British police and military personnel. A lull of sorts ensued from November 1936 with the arrival in Palestine from London of a commission appointed by the British government to inquire into the causes of the crisis in Palestine and suggest remedies—this was the Royal Commission, often referred to as the Peel Commission after its chairman, Lord Peel.

The Peel Commission stayed in Palestine for two months and submitted its report in July 1937. It had concluded that differences between Jews and Arabs in Palestine were irreconcilable and proposed the partition of Palestine into an Arab state, which would be attached to Transjordan, and a Jewish state. Under its formula the British would retain residual mandatory areas, most importantly a large swath of territory in the center of Palestine stretching from Jaffa on the coast to encapsulate Jerusalem and Bethlehem, and incorporating the towns of Lydda and Ramleh. The proposed Jewish state would cover about one-third of Palestine but would include most of Palestine's best arable land, particularly in the coastal plain region running from Haifa to the south of Tel Aviv, and also in the Galilee. Indeed, the Commission's recommendations of the borders of the Jewish state closely shadowed Zionist land-acquisition and settlement strategies: "Since the early 1930s," writes Bernard Wasserstein, "the Zionists had been buying land strategically with the objective of building large contiguous blocks . . . particularly in

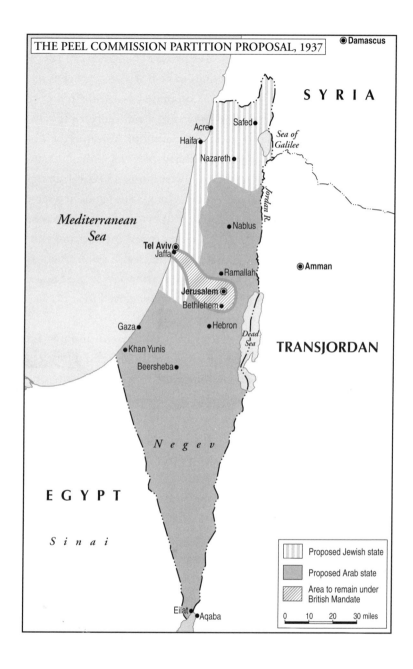

THE PEEL COMMISSION PARTITION PROPOSAL, 1937

◉ Damascus

S Y R I A

Acre ●   Safed ●

Haifa ●

        Nazareth ●

*Sea of
Galilee*

*Mediterranean
Sea*

● Nablus

Jordan R.

Tel Aviv ◉
Jaffa ●

◉ **Amman**

● Ramallah

Jerusalem ◉
Bethlehem ●

Gaza ●   ● Hebron

*Dead
Sea*

● Khan Yunis

TRANSJORDAN

Beersheba ●

N e g e v

E G Y P T

S i n a i

Eilat ● ● Aqaba

Proposed Jewish state

Proposed Arab state

Area to remain under
British Mandate

0   10   20   30 miles

the coastal plain, the valley of Jezreel, and the upper reaches of the River Jordan."[23]

This partition plan was unacceptable to the entire spectrum of Palestinian Arab society and political opinion. Apart from the proposed award of one-third of Palestine, including the bulk of its most desirable lands, to a community composed overwhelmingly of recently arrived immigrants, the proposal had another implication of grave import to Arab Palestinians. The partition boundaries suggested by the Peel Commission meant that while the proposed Arab state would contain a negligible minority of about 1,250 Jews, the Jewish state would contain at least 225,000 Arabs. To deal with this complication, the Commission suggested a population exchange modeled on a 1923 agreement between Greece and Turkey, and recommended that "it should be part of the agreement that in the last resort the exchange would be compulsory." This suggestion was naturally anathema to Palestinian Arabs, given the grossly unequal numbers involved. On the Jewish side the Peel proposals were rejected by the Revisionist Zionists on ideological grounds. The mainstream Zionist movement was split, but eventually a majority assented to qualified acceptance, at least as a basis for further negotiation. The Peel Commission had validated the idea of a Jewish state across a substantial part of Palestine, even if its borders did not meet maximalist Zionist aspirations and Jerusalem was excluded. The two top Zionist figures, David Ben-Gurion and Chaim Weizmann, both favored the thrust of the Peel proposals without necessarily agreeing with all of its content. Weizmann told a British official that the Zionists were prepared to assist the British transfer the Arab population of the Galilee to Transjordan. Ben-Gurion wrote in his diary that the transfer proposal "if . . . put into effect . . . would be of tremendous advantage to us . . . For every transferred Arab, we could settle four Jews on the land." The Arab Higher Committee, by contrast, called for independence for a united state of Palestine "with protection of all legitimate Jewish and other minority rights and safeguarding of reasonable British interests."[24]

The Palestinian Arab revolt intensified with a vengeance from the autumn of 1937, as did the draconian counterinsurgency measures of the British. In October the British outlawed the Arab Higher Committee and exiled most of its members to the Seychelles islands—they would do the same to the Greek Cypriot leader Makarios in response to insurgency on Cyprus almost two decades later. In 1937, 816 Arab Palestinians were held in detention camps in Palestine. That number climbed to 2,463 in 1938 and 5,679 in 1939. Between late 1937 and 1939, 112 suspected insurgents were executed by hanging. The British introduced the practice of razing insurgents' houses to rubble, a punitive method that would be liberally used by Israeli forces in the occupied territories decades later. The outnumbered and outgunned insurgents, lightly armed and fighting on foot or on horseback, nonetheless put up a fierce fight against numerically superior British forces equipped with armored combat vehicles and an array of powerful weaponry. They sabotaged oil pipelines and train lines, and in 1938 stamps issued in the name of the rebel movement appeared emblazoned with the slogan "Palestine for the Arabs!" and depicting Jerusalem's Dome of the Rock mosque and the Church of the Holy Sepulcher side by side. During the summer of 1938, guerrilla forces took partial control of some cities, including Haifa, Nablus, and even the symbolic prize, the old city of Jerusalem, from where they were only ousted by a major British counteroffensive in the autumn. By 1939, however, the rebellion was worn down by losses—at least three thousand and perhaps as many as five thousand insurgents had been killed over three years, of a Palestinian Arab population of about one million—as well as by counterproductive brutal tactics employed by some rebels against fellow Arabs who would not side with them.

The fighting during the 1936–1939 revolt was principally between British forces and Palestinian Arab fighters, overwhelmingly Muslim and drawn largely from rural areas (the vast majority of the rebel ranks were local Palestinians, joined by a small force of volunteers from neighboring Arab countries led by Fawzi al-Qawukji, a Lebanese-born commander). But the root cause driving the revolt was never far from the surface. The Israeli scholar Yehoshua Porath has found that "the rebellion was strongest in locations adjacent to the main areas of Jewish settlement, notably the central coastal plain, the Haifa-Acre Bay region and the Jezreel Valley."[25] There were instances of armed rebels committing atrocities against Jews, while militant Zionist elements, particularly the Irgun, conducted a sporadic campaign of bombings and other attacks of a terrorist nature against Arabs. The gulf separating Jews and Arabs was deepened further by the British practice of recruiting Jewish auxiliaries in the war against the insurgents, much as the British used Turkish Cypriots in the fight against Greek Cypriot insurgents on Cyprus in the late 1950s, with similar consequences for already troubled intergroup relations. The numbers of such Jewish auxiliary police have been estimated at between six thousand and fourteen thousand by Palestinian scholars.[26] Smaller numbers of Jews were recruited in 1938–1939 into a special counterinsurgency unit called the Special Night Squads (SNS), which conducted raids against Arab villages. The SNS were led by Orde Wingate, a ruthless and eccentric commander who attained fame during World War II for commando exploits in Ethiopia and particularly Burma. Moshe Dayan, later a redoubtable IDF chief of staff and Israeli defense minister, gained his first and invaluable combat experience as a member of the SNS. During World War II, the British again used Jewish fighting units in Libya, Syria, and Lebanon. These units developed into the Palmach, the crack assault force of the Haganah. The Palmach would play a pivotal role during the fighting of 1948.

Although the Palestinian Arab revolt was eventually crushed, the British were shaken by its fury and tenacity. The political response to the crisis came in May 1939, when the British government in London published a White Paper on the Palestine question. This document envisaged a united, independent state of Palestine in ten years' time in which power would be shared between Jews and Arabs. In the interim, Jewish immigration was not to exceed 75,000 over the next five years—after which any further immigration would require "the Arabs of Palestine . . . to acquiesce"—and restrictions were to be placed with immediate effect on Zionist land acquisition to protect the Arab population. The White Paper represented a virtual *volte-face* on the Peel Commission's recommendations of just two years earlier. It was now the turn of the Zionists to feel outraged and betrayed (the embittered Palestinians did not react favorably either). The Jewish Agency responded that "in the darkest hour of Jewish history . . . the British Government proposes to deprive Jews of their last hope and close the road back to their Homeland." Ben-Gurion denounced the Paper's "evil, foolish and short-sighted policy." In fact, legal Jewish immigration into Palestine dropped sharply during World War II and the quota of 75,000 was not used up. But legal and illegal immigration still combined to bring the Jewish population of Palestine to over 550,000 by the end of World War II and at least another 70,000 arrived, despite British opposition, between 1945 and the creation of Israel in 1948. The more radical tendencies of Zionism never forgot or forgave what they saw as British perfidy. From 1944 onward the Irgun and its even more militant offshoot, the Stern Gang, carried out an escalating wave of bombings and assassinations against British officials and personnel, climaxing in 1946 and 1947. For the duration of World War II the Palestine question remained in limbo, awaiting resolution.[27]

That resolution was to be based once again on partition. In the autumn of 1947 a majority of the eleven members of the United Nations Special Commission on Palestine (UNSCOP), constituted earlier that year, recommended a partition plan, which was passed with minor modifications by two-thirds majority in the UN General Assembly—thirty-three countries voted in favor, thirteen against, and ten abstained—on 29 November 1947. The United States and the Soviet Union both voted for partition, while Britain abstained. The plan assigned 56 percent of Palestine to the putative Jewish state. The plan recommended that the two states sign an agreement on economic union, and the borders drawn "created a criss-cross territorial arrangement with 'kissing points' between the proposed states that would, in the judgment of the Commission, compel the two to cooperate." That was wishful thinking, given ground realities and the history of the conflict. In fact "the overall territorial pattern, which allowed each state to intersect, and separate the provinces of the other," was more aptly described "as two fighting serpents entwined in an inimical embrace." Jerusalem and its environs, including Bethlehem, would have special status as a neutral zone under UN control, according to the plan.[28]

The Zionist leadership accepted the plan, which was in all respects superior from their viewpoint to the Peel recommendations of 1937. The Palestinian Arab response was one of shock and outrage. Their indignation was widely shared in the Arab world—Cairo, for example, saw a massive demonstration in December against the plan. It is probable that Arab opinion within and outside Palestine was hostile to *any* Jewish state in Palestine—in their view such recognition represented the ultimate legitimation of a program of land-grabbing colonization. But it is difficult to resist the conclusion that the *terms* of the partition plan could be reasonably regarded by Palestinian Arabs and by Arabs elsewhere as deeply unfair. Arabs, Muslim and Christian, still constituted a solid two-thirds majority of Palestine's population of slightly under two million. Of Mandate Palestine's sixteen administrative districts, Jews were a majority, 71 percent, in only one—the Jaffa district, which included Tel Aviv. Jews were almost half the population, 47 percent, in the

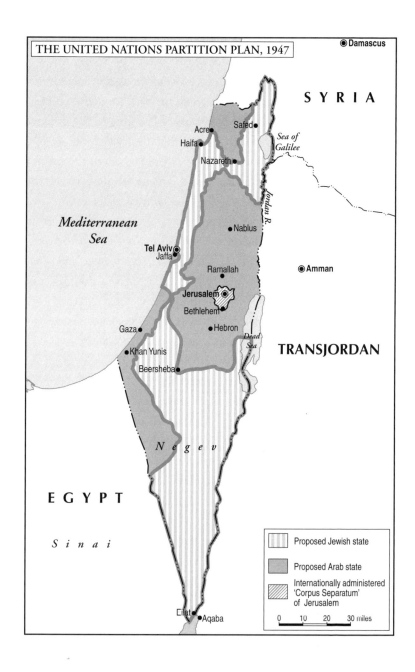

Haifa district and a very substantial minority of 38 percent in the
Jerusalem district. In all other districts the Jewish proportion of the
population varied from negligible to a maximum of one-third (in
the Tiberias and Beisan districts). The borders demarcated for the
Jewish state enveloped the vast majority of the Jewish population—
over 500,000 Jews—along with at least 400,000 Arabs.[29]

Later criticism of Palestinians for having missed a golden opportunity to protect their rights and preserve their community is based
on retrospective knowledge of subsequent events. In late 1947 or
early 1948 the Palestinians could not have been reasonably expected to quietly acquiesce to the international community's solution to the Palestine problem. This had been foreseen by Zeev
Jabotinsky as early as 1923:

> Every indigenous people will resist alien settlers as long as they
> see any hope of ridding themselves of the dangers of foreign
> settlement. As long as the Arabs preserve a gleam of hope that
> they will succeed in getting rid of us nothing in the world can
> cause them to relinquish this hope, precisely because they are
> not a rabble but a living people.[30]

Laqueur's history of Zionism holds that "[Palestinian] Arab intransigence was the natural reaction of a people . . . whichever way one
looks at it the conflict could not have been avoided because the basis for a compromise did not exist."[31] And David Ben-Gurion, Israel's first premier, apparently said as much in private conversation:

> Why should the Arabs make peace? If I were an Arab leader I
> would never make terms with Israel. That is natural; we have
> taken their country. Sure, God promised it to us, but what does
> that matter to them? Our God is not theirs. We came from Is-
> rael, true, but 2,000 years ago, and what is that to them? There
> has been anti-Semitism, the Nazis, Hitler, Auschwitz, but was

that their fault? They see only one thing: We have come here
and stolen their country. Why should they accept that?[32]

As in India in 1947 and Yugoslavia in 1991–1992, once partition
became a virtual certainty—the UN plan envisioned the end of the
British mandate on 1 May 1948—it proved to be the catalyst that
ignited all-out war between Palestine's ethnonational communities. Between December 1947 and March 1948 numerous deadly
bombings—often using car bombs—and other terror attacks were
perpetrated by both Jews (especially the Irgun) and Arabs against
civilian targets and populations of the other community. Even a
snapshot from the catalog of escalating violence makes grim read-
ing. On 29 December 1947, Irgun men hurled grenades into an
Arab crowd gathered at the Nablus Gate to Jerusalem's old city,
killing seventeen; on 7 January 1948 another Irgun bomb attack at
the Jaffa Gate killed twenty-five Arabs. On 30 December an Irgun
group threw bombs from a speeding car at a crowd of Arab workers
waiting outside the Haifa oil refinery in the hope of being hired
as day labor, killing six. Forty-one Jewish refinery workers were
lynched in retaliation. The Haganah's elite Palmach unit raided the
nearby Arab village of Balad al-Sheikh—the burial-place of Sheikh
Izz al-Din al-Qassam—in a revenge attack the next day, killing seventeen villagers. On 4 January an Irgun car bomb destroyed Jaffa's
grand serai (government complex) killing twenty-six Arabs, and on
5 January Haganah members blew up the Semiramis hotel in west
Jerusalem, killing twenty Arabs. On 3 March a Stern Gang car
bombing in Haifa killed eleven Arabs, and on 22 March another car
bomb in the same city killed twenty-three Arabs. Arabs bombed
the office of the *Palestine Post* newspaper in Jerusalem on 1 February 1948, killing twenty Jews. A massive blast on Jerusalem's Ben-
Yehuda Street killed fifty-seven Jews on 22 February, and on 11
March a bombing of the Jewish Agency's headquarters in Jerusalem
killed twelve Jews. Arabs also bombed the Haifa post office on 14

January, killing six Jews, and a car bombing in Haifa on 21 March left twenty Jews dead. In the words of the Israeli writer Meron Benvenisti, this was "by nature a total war. Such a war does not distinguish between combatants and non-combatants, and is fought over every plot of land, every house and every road."[33]

The U.S. administration was sufficiently alarmed by the horror unfolding in Palestine for President Truman, on 25 March, to call for an immediate Arab-Jewish truce and commit the United States to sharing responsibility for temporary international trusteeship over Palestine. Yet Truman subsequently extended American recognition to Israel immediately upon its declaration of independence on 15 May, overruling objections from some administration officials: "I'm sorry, gentlemen, but I have to answer to hundreds of thousands who are anxious for the success of Zionism; I do not have hundreds of thousands of Arabs among my constituents."[34] Israel's declaration of independence asserted that the Jews had "reclaimed the wilderness" of Palestine.

In March and April 1948, as the date of the British departure drew closer, the Jewish-Arab conflict in Palestine moved into the phase of actual fighting for control of territory. By the time the war wound down in November 1948, the Jews/Israelis had achieved an overwhelming military victory. The Israeli forces had won control of 77 percent of Palestine rather than the 56 percent allocated to the Jewish state by the UN's plan. Israel had captured the bulk of Jerusalem with the notable exception of the old city, where they were held at bay by the soldiers of the Jordanian Arab Legion. The Arabs/Palestinians, on the other hand, had truly suffered a *nakba,* or collective catastrophe. About seven hundred thousand of their number—well over half of the Arab population of Palestine and more than 80 percent of the Arab inhabitants of the three-quarters of Palestine that became Israel—had become refugees. Several hundred Arab villages—according to the Palestinian scholar Walid Khalidi at least 290 and perhaps as many as 472 villages—had become abandoned, ghostly ruins. The vibrant, sophisticated class of highly educated and prosperous Arabs who had resided in Palestine's urban centers—above all the cities of Jerusalem, Jaffa, and Haifa—had all but vanished. Between the establishment of Israel and the end of 1951 almost seven hundred thousand Jewish immigrants—in this wave mostly from the Middle East and North Africa—arrived in Israel. This figure was nearly identical to the number of displaced Palestinians, and slightly greater than the entire Jewish population of Palestine prior to Israel's emergence. In short, the landscape of Palestine had been utterly transformed. In 1946 the Haganah command in Jerusalem had confidently asserted to a British-American delegation:

> As far as the strength of the Arabs in Palestine is concerned, we are in possession of well-founded information. There is no doubt that the Jewish [military] force is superior in organization, training, planning and equipment, and that we will be able to handle any attack or rebellion from the Arab side . . . If you accept the Zionist solution but are unable or unwilling to enforce it please do not interfere, and we will secure its implementation.

There are several reasons why this prediction was borne out during 1948. The Haganah, and more generally the Yishuv, did in fact have significantly, and perhaps vastly, superior organizational structures, leadership caliber, and strategic acumen. "[Palestine's] Jewish community was accustomed to total mobilization and was united around its decision-making bodies. It generally displayed discipline and obedience . . . and despite intense differences of interpretation the entire community identified with Zionist ideology and loyally followed the strategies formulated." In addition, Zionist arms-procurement efforts in Europe since 1945 had been efficient and successful. The Haganah/IDF of 1948 had also developed its own basic armaments-manufacturing infrastructure, a rudimentary air force, and formidable intelligence-gathering operations, including access to dossiers about six hundred Palestinian Arab communities systematically compiled in the 1940s by agents posing as geographers and botanists. The Palestinians were by comparison weak and disorganized. They did not have the institutional strength and cohesion of the Jewish community, were poorly armed, and had not recovered from the strain and trauma inflicted by the 1936–1939 revolt. In December 1947 its educated urban class began to leave Palestine for the sanctuaries of Cairo, Beirut, Damascus, and Amman, leaving the community leaderless. Several thousand non-Palestinian volunteers of the Arab Liberation Army (ALA), who entered the country starting in early March and were active mainly in northern Palestine, proved largely ineffective.[35]

But for all these disadvantages the Palestinians had tactical battlefield skills, close knowledge of terrain, and until April and May of 1948 an overall numerical superiority, in population although not in combatants. Palestinian guerrilla groups concentrated on disrupting the major communication routes essential to the Jewish military effort, through often lethal ambushes that inflicted heavy casualties. Thus "in late March 1948 the Jewish population of Jerusalem was in dire straits. The approximately 100,000 Jews [in the city] were suffering from a severe shortage of food, since the Palestinian forces commanded by Abd al-Qadir al-Husseini had essentially succeeded in blocking the road from Tel Aviv."[36] Husseini, the son of a former mayor of Jerusalem—and the father of Faisal Husseini, many years later the key Palestinian figure in Israeli-occupied East Jerusalem until his death in mid-2001—had been a guerrilla commander during the 1936–1939 revolt and had returned to Palestine from exile in January 1948. But after Husseini was killed on 8 April during a battle for Qastal, a hilltop village overlooking the western approach to Jerusalem, the resistance unraveled. In early April the Haganah put its multipronged, phased

war strategy—Plan Dalet—into operation, and the Palestinians
crumbled. The collapse of one Palestinian urban stronghold after
another—Arab Haifa on 23 April, Arab west Jerusalem including
the neighborhoods of Talbiyeh, Qatamon, and the German Colony
on 30 April, Jaffa on 10 May, Safad on 11 May, and Acre on 17
May—induced not only mass flight from these cities and towns but
the emptying out of numerous villages in their rural hinterlands.
The pattern was repeated in Lydda and Ramleh in central Palestine—part of the territory allocated to the Arab state in the UN
plan, along with Jaffa and Acre—in July and in the Galilee in October and November of 1948.

But if it has been relatively easy to explain *why* Zionism tri-
umphed militarily in 1948, forming an understanding of *how* the
Palestinian catastrophe unfolded on the ground—with its obvious
implications for questions of culpability, restitution, and future reconciliation and coexistence, all central to the Israeli-Palestinian
conflict—has been more difficult. Painstaking research, based primarily on Israeli archival sources, by Israeli historian Benny Morris
has shed a great deal of light on the birth of the Palestinian question. His work is largely a mass of empirical evidence, but the con-
clusions are clear and instructive:

> The *Yishuv* did not enter the war with a plan or policy of ex-
> pulsion . . . But if a measure of ambivalence and confusion at-
> tended Haganah/IDF treatment of Arab communities during
> and immediately after conquest, there was nothing ambiguous
> about Israeli policy from summer 1948 towards those who had
> been displaced and become refugees and those yet to be dis-
> placed in future operations. Generally applied with resolution
> and often brutality, the policy was to prevent a refugee return
> at all costs . . . *In this sense it may fairly be said that all 700,000 or
> so who ended up as refugees were compulsorily displaced or "ex-
> pelled"* . . . The [Palestinian] urban masses and the *fellahin*

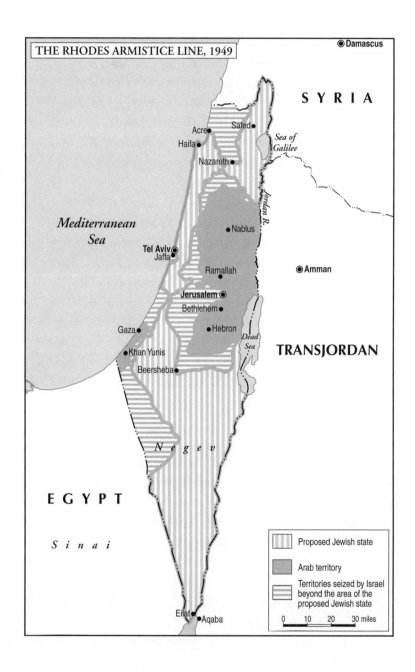

THE RHODES ARMISTICE LINE, 1949

Damascus

SYRIA

Acre
Safed
Haifa
Sea of
Galilee
Nazareth

Mediterranean
Sea

Nablus

Tel Aviv
Jaffa

Ramallah

Amman

Jerusalem
Bethlehem

Gaza
Hebron
Dead
Sea

Khan Yunis
TRANSJORDAN
Beersheba

Negev

EGYPT

Sinai

Proposed Jewish state

Arab territory

Territories seized by Israel
beyond the area of the
proposed Jewish state

0   10   20   30 miles

Eilat
Aqaba

[peasantry] had nowhere to go, certainly not in comfort. For most of them flight meant instant destitution; it was not a course readily adopted . . . In April–May and again in October–November the "atrocity factor" played a major role in flight from certain areas . . . Apart from the twenty or so cases of massacre, Jewish troops often randomly killed prisoners of war, farm hands in the fields and the occasional villagers who stayed behind . . . There were also several dozen cases of rape . . . Regarding April–May and the start of the main stage of the exodus, I have found no evidence to show that the [Palestinian] Arab Higher Committee or Arab leaders outside Palestine issued blanket instructions, by radio or otherwise, to inhabitants to flee . . . Ben-Gurion clearly wanted as few Arabs as possible in the Jewish state . . . He said so explicitly in meetings in August, September and October. But no expulsion policy was ever enunciated and Ben-Gurion always refrained from issuing clear or written expulsion orders . . . In early March the prospect of pan-Arab invasion gave rise to Plan Dalet. It accorded the Haganah brigade and battalion-level commanders *carte blanche* to completely clear vital areas of Arab populations.

Benvenisti concurs that "David Ben-Gurion did not have to give explicit orders. He knew he could depend on his military commanders to 'cleanse' the area, and on those in charge of land acquisition and the leaders of settlement movements [like Joseph Weitz, head of the JNF's land department] to press for the implementation of the [Zionist] doctrine of settlement." Walid Khalidi's research from the late 1950s is consistent with Morris's finding that the Palestinian exodus was not due to incitement to flee by local, national or international Arab leaderships.[37]

Eyewitness accounts of 1948 are invariably the most compelling way of understanding the making of the Israeli-Palestinian conflict. As a boy of fourteen living in Jerusalem, Meron Benvenisti, a Sephardic Jew who later became the city's deputy mayor, remembers the aftermath of the massacre in the nearby village of Deir Yassin, where a combined Irgun-Stern Gang force killed up to 254 villagers on 9 April 1948. "The surviving villagers were loaded on trucks and paraded in a 'victory march' through the main streets of Jerusalem," Benvenisti recalls, "escorted by cheering fighters, weapons in hand. [I] . . . along with thousands of the city's Jewish residents, still remember this disgusting spectacle." The Deir Yassin massacre, which occurred at a crucial stage of the war, was instrumental in generating a fear psychosis among the Palestinian population. Elias Srouji, a Nazareth physician, has written about his experiences during the IDF's "Operation Hiram" offensive to overrun yet-unconquered parts of the Galilee in the autumn of 1948. The village of Tarshiha was bombed from the air "and twenty-three people perished," while in the overrun village of Eilaboun "fifteen young men [were] arbitrarily picked . . . and shot at close range in two or three clusters in different parts of the village, to make it look like they had engaged in fighting." After Operation Hiram only twelve to fifteen thousand people remained of the captured area's population of fifty to sixty thousand—the rest had fled to Lebanon.[38]

The catalog of atrocities is unending. In early May 1948 the Palmach captured the village of Ein Zeitoun, close to the town of Safad in the north. "A few score young men" taken prisoner were executed, and all houses in the village blown up. The fate of the village was a warning to the residents of Safad—where twenty-six Jews had been killed by Arabs in the August 1929 disturbances—who fled before the Haganah days later. In the autumn of 1948, after capturing the village of al-Dawayima in the Hebron highlands, Israeli soldiers "killed between eighty and one hundred male villagers, blew up houses together with their occupants, murdered women and children, and committed rape." Around the same time

Israeli units captured the village of Safsaf in the north and "killed between fifty and seventy men. Four young women were taken to empty houses and raped. The [surviving] villagers fled to Lebanon." On 13 April, a few days after the Deir Yassin massacre, Palestinians ambushed a Jewish convoy en route to Hebrew University and Hadassah Hospital on Mount Scopus in East Jerusalem. Of the 112 people in the convoy, 78 were killed and 24 wounded. On 13 May, after overrunning the Kfar Etzion settlement—one of the four settlements composing the vulnerable Gush Etzion bloc south of Jerusalem—Jordanian soldiers and Palestinian irregulars killed 129 of its 133 inhabitants. Israel suffered more than six thousand dead—1 percent of its population—in its war of independence.[39]

There were those who had aspired against all odds to build a peaceful future of coexistence for Jews and Arabs in a shared land. One such person was Ephraim Krisher, a Haifa trade unionist "who had worked with Arab unionists for a decade and owed his life to their quick thinking and bravery on December 30, 1947" when forty-one Jews were lynched in Haifa after an Irgun bomb attack killed six Arabs. In the summer of 1948, Krisher, a railway worker,

> was busy trying to round up enough Jews who knew something about railway work to get what was now the Israel Railways up and running again. Some of his recruits were . . . survivors of the Nazi campaign to exterminate European Jewry who had only recently arrived in the new Jewish state. These, and Krisher's other recruits, filled jobs held until a few months earlier by Arabs, most of whom had lost their homes and homeland and were beginning bitter new lives as refugees.

Indeed, "the Zionist project of forging a link between the Jewish people and the land of Palestine was one of extraordinary remaking." Thus Prime Minister David Ben-Gurion, who arrived in Palestine in 1906 as an Eastern European youth called David Gruen, wrote in October 1949 to a committee of nine scholars he had commissioned to devise Hebrew names for places and topographical features in the Negev desert region, which was fully conquered by Israeli forces in early 1949: "We are obliged to remove the Arabic names for reasons of state. Just as we do not recognize the Arabs' political proprietorship of the land, so also we do not recognize their spiritual proprietorship and their names." Yet in 1969, shortly after Israel conquered the remaining 22 percent of Mandate Palestine creating up to 250,000 new refugees from the West Bank and 70,000 from the Gaza Strip and subjecting the rest to occupation, one of Israel's great warriors, Moshe Dayan, declared: "We came to this country that was populated by Arabs. There is not a single place in this country that did not have an Arab population." It was at approximately this time that the Palestinian national movement emerged around the PLO and its al-Fatah core led by Yasser Arafat, and Golda Meir, Israel's prime minister, asserted that there was no such thing as a Palestinian people.⁴⁰

The Forging of Peace

In 1978 the Palestinian scholar Walid Khalidi published an article in the journal *Foreign Affairs* titled "Thinking the Unthinkable: A Sovereign Palestinian State." There he argued, "The cornerstone [of Israeli-Palestinian peace] is . . . Palestinian sovereignty. Not half-sovereignty or quasi-sovereignty or ersatz sovereignty." He pointed to "the unique and anachronistic plight" of the Palestinians "with independence achieved by all Arab states and the process of decolonization almost completed in the Third World." He stressed that after thirty years the Palestinians needed to be liberated from "their anonymous, ghost-like existence as a non-people" and "their dependence on the mercy, charity or tolerance of other parties, whether Arab, Israeli or international." "Of all peoples," he wrote, "the Jewish people are historically qualified to understand this"—

the predicament of insecurity, nonrecognition, and discrimination tied to homelessness and statelessness. He warned, however, that such a solution to the Palestinian question would emerge neither via "a Bantustan 'federal' formula [for the West Bank] under a Hashemite [Jordanian] dressing" nor from the creation of an "Israeli [controlled] mosaic of Indian reserves and hen-runs" in the occupied territories, "criss-crossed by mechanized patrols and police dogs and under surveillance by searchlights, watchtowers and armed archaeologists." He also emphasized that a serious Israeli-Palestinian agreement could be neither negotiated nor implemented by "Quislings or Uncle Toms, present and future"—presumably meaning leaders of Arab regimes such as Egypt's Anwar Sadat, who concluded his own peace pact with Israel under America's stewardship in the late 1970s, as well as collaborators with Israeli occupation in the West Bank and Gaza—but "only [by] the representatives of the Palestinian people." "It is here that the PLO, if willing—which it is—can play a crucial role," he contended, arguing that under Israeli influence "the West—particularly the United States—is blind to the potentially constructive role of the PLO." He predicted "the likelihood that the centrist Fatah, the backbone of the PLO, will be the backbone of any Palestinian government."[41]

Khalidi went on to outline solutions to all the fundamental issues of the Israeli-Palestinian conflict. Regarding the borders of the Palestinian state, he held that "the frontiers of 1967 with minor and reciprocal adjustments are the most realistic under the circumstances." The two parts of the Palestinian state in the West Bank and the Gaza Strip would need to be connected via "guaranteed freedom of access along a specified route or routes." As the largest Palestinian urban center and one imbued with collective memory, historical significance, and religious meaning for Muslim as well as Christian Palestinians, East Jerusalem, he argued, was "the natural capital" of the sovereign Palestinian state. "To make it so," he wrote, "would involve the partition of the city along the [pre-] 1967 [armistice] lines . . . but not necessarily a return to the *status quo ante bellum* in all its details." He pointed out that "a partition solution does not mean the erection of a wall" and that "the frontiers could remain open between the capital of Israel in West Jerusalem and the capital of Arab Palestine in East Jerusalem." He proposed a joint, cross-border Israeli-Palestinian body in Jerusalem tasked with "certain essential common services" and "a grand inter-faith council" of Jewish, Muslim, and Christian representatives "under UN or rotating chairmanship" to administer a regime for the holy places in the old city, which would include "an irreversible right of access to the Wailing Wall" for Jews. On the question of the Palestinian refugee population, he noted that "as many refugees as possible need to be [re]settled in East Jerusalem, on the West Bank and in the Gaza Strip" and "given the need for every inch of territory in East Jerusalem, the West Bank and the Gaza Strip to solve the Palestinian refugee problem, it would not make sense to maintain the Israeli settlements established in these territories after 1967." Khalidi also criticized the notion that a weak, poor Palestinian state could pose a threat to Israel's security given the overwhelming preponderance of Israeli military power, and emphasized the need for close economic connections between Jordan and the Palestinian state, most of whose territory would be contiguous or close to Jordan.

Khalidi's ideas and prescriptions were prescient. Many of them would enter the discourse of the "Oslo" peace process between Israelis and Palestinians more than fifteen years later, in the 1990s. But the fact remains that "for the first 45 years of its independent existence Israel's leaders were unwilling to discuss the right of the Palestinians to national self-determination." Indeed, "the term 'the Palestinian people' appeared in Israeli official documents only in the 1990s." But like Banquo's ghost in Shakespeare's *Macbeth*, the Palestinian question refused to disappear. In the aftermath of Israel's crushing victory over Egypt, Syria, and Jordan in the six-day war of

June 1967—an exploit described as "the apogee of blitzkrieg" in
the Israeli military historian Martin van Creveld's study of the
IDF—the Palestinian dispossessed of 1948 rose like a phoenix to
torment and haunt Israel's existence. The Palestinians had been socially and politically shattered by the defeat and dispersal of 1948,
and it took two decades after the disaster for a Palestinian national
movement to emerge. Palestinian poet Mahmoud Darwish expressed the post-nakba sense of despair: "Where should we go after
the last frontiers; where should the birds fly after the last sky?" But
from the late 1960s, the emergence of the PLO—personified by
the distinctive pistol-packing, sunglass-wearing, olive-green-clad
and *kaffiyeh*-headscarfed figure of Yasser Arafat—put the Palestinian people and the Palestinian question back on the map of the
Middle East and the world. By the time Khalidi's article appeared,
the PLO—for all its shortcomings, internal fissures, and questionable strategic and tactical decisions—had developed into something
of a Palestinian national institution.[42]

Meanwhile, the euphoria and triumphalism that gripped Israel
and much of the Jewish diaspora, particularly in the United States,
after the June 1967 victory was badly jolted by the October 1973
"Yom Kippur war" in which the armed forces of Egypt and Syria
succeeded in giving Israel a bloody nose, regaining some of their
lost pride in the process. The lesson of October 1973 was that military might had its limits. The provisions for Palestinian autonomy
in the West Bank and Gaza incorporated in the September 1978
Camp David accord between Egypt's Sadat and Israel's Menachem
Begin, midwifed by the U.S. administration of Jimmy Carter, were
a nonstarter and went absolutely nowhere. "Each party had oppos-
ing interpretations" of these provisions "and their positions were
polarized"; despite an American third-party presence, the Egyptian-
Israeli dialogue on this issue "went into deep freeze" and by 1981
"all parties had basically given up on it." Jordan refused to join this
dialogue. The dead-end outcome highlighted the futility of the Is-

raeli insistence of bypassing the PLO and attempting halfhearted palliatives in the occupied territories in conjunction with non-Palestinian Arab parties. Much to Israel's relief the PLO was bloodily ejected from Jordan by King Hussein's army in 1970–1971, but the movement relocated to Lebanon, another country bordering Israel, where it established the infrastructure of an embryonic state during the 1970s. Israel's large-scale invasion of Lebanon in 1982, masterminded by then defense minister Ariel Sharon, was successful in driving the PLO's leadership and its main armed forces out of Lebanon, albeit at a tremendous cost of Lebanese and Palestinian lives. But that success proved to be ephemeral in two ways. Israel became bogged down in the Lebanese quagmire for the next eighteen years and its Lebanese adventure gave rise to a new and formidable enemy—the Shiite Hezbollah movement. But more importantly, Israel's eviction of the PLO's state-within-a-state from Lebanon did not provide long-term relief from its Palestinian problem. Within a few years of the exiling of Arafat and his compatriots to Tunis that problem flared on the "home front" in the form of the first Palestinian intifada in the occupied territories.[43]

The first Palestinian intifada is the decisive development that led to the peace process of the 1990s. Between December 1987 and June 1991, 983 Palestinians were killed by Israeli forces in the occupied territories, 120,000 suffered injuries, beatings, and other abuse, more than 15,000 were arrested, and at least 1,882 homes were demolished by the Israelis as punishment. The intifada was not simply "a political uprising against the occupation." It was also, in the words of a Palestinian participant-observer, "a social and psychological phenomenon internal to Palestinian society; an awakening, a self-cleansing and a breaking away from the Palestinians' own past and inherited social structures." Edward Said noted in 1991 that "as part of the intifada Palestinian men and women have taken their difficult lives under Israeli military occupation into their own hands; they have tried to construct a system of self-help and relative independence from the occupation . . . [and] a model for communal life that is not based on the exclusive authority of one party and one sultan." The image of the Palestinian changed very significantly in the Western world, including the United States, as a result of the intifada, as the masked gunman (and occasionally, gunwoman) hijacking civilian airliners and executing Israeli Olympics athletes yielded to the slingshot-armed, stone-throwing teenager being shot by the enforcers of a repressive regime of occupation.[44]

When the intifada began, Yitzhak Rabin, then Israel's defense minister in a "national unity" coalition government, famously ordered the IDF's soldiers to break the protesters' bones. Five years later Prime Minister Rabin dourly shook Arafat's hand at the White House to signal the beginning of an Israeli-Palestinian rapprochement. As the American scholar Ian Lustick has pointed out, there was something approaching a consensus among Israel's political elite, and to a relatively lesser degree its public, during the 1970s and 1980s on three points: "The PLO was a terrorist organization with which Israel could never negotiate, a Palestinian state of any kind in the West Bank and Gaza would mortally threaten the Jewish state, and Israel's sovereignty over Jerusalem, in the [expanded] boundaries [for the city] established after June 1967 [unilaterally by Israel after military conquest] was an immutable fact."[45] The near-consensus on the first two points—with implications also for the third shibboleth, the status of expanded Jerusalem as Israel's eternal, undivided capital—had by the early 1990s been seriously eroded in Israeli (and American) elite and public opinion by the intifada effect. In July 1988 King Hussein of Jordan renounced his country's legal claim to the West Bank, effectively eclipsing any prospect of an Israeli agreement with Jordan bypassing the Palestinians and the PLO. The intifada effect coincided with a renewed sense of urgency in the 1989–1992 George H. W. Bush administration to be seen as doing something to break the Israeli-Palestinian impasse in the wake of the successful campaign—which involved numerous Arab states, including Syria, and invoked international law—to eject Saddam Hussain's Iraqi forces from Kuwait in early 1991. The result was the Madrid peace conference of October 1991 convened at the initiative of the United States, which included Palestinian representatives and in which Israel's prime minister Yitzhak Shamir, a member of the Stern Gang in his youth, agreed only reluctantly to participate.

The PLO may have shed its anathema status in influential Israeli and American eyes by the early 1990s, and at least implicitly the idea of a Palestinian state in the occupied territories was no longer the "unthinkable" proposition of Walid Khalidi's 1978 essay but rather the intuitive and logical outcome of an Israeli-Palestinian peace process. But by the time the PLO entered the nascent peace process, the capacity of its dominant leadership, centered on Arafat, to advance fundamental Palestinian interests had been significantly weakened, and new obstacles and complications had arisen in the path of an Israeli-Palestinian modus vivendi. The PLO leadership stood politically isolated from Arab capitals after its misguided decision to support Saddam Hussain's Kuwait adventure, and it was in dire financial straits. In the occupied territories new forces outside the PLO umbrella had arisen from the intifada—notably Hamas (the Islamic Resistance Movement), which was formed in Gaza in the first days of the intifada as the militant arm of the Strip's long-established Muslim Brotherhood network and began developing its organization in the West Bank from early 1988 onward—and Islamic Jihad, which split off from the Brotherhood in 1980 and whose activists played a major role in igniting the intifada, particularly in Gaza, before the Unified National Leadership of the Uprising (UNLU), dominated by Fatah and the smaller left-wing PLO factions, asserted authority over the uprising. During the intifada a younger generation of Palestinians in the occupied territories came

into their own politically; by the early 1990s Arafat and his colleagues were already an "old guard" operating from a relatively distant Arab capital, Tunis.

The most significant change, however, had occurred on the demographic map of the occupied territories. The number of Jewish
settlements in the West Bank, as well as in Gaza, had mushroomed
after the Likud Party's ascendancy to power in Israel in 1977, and
the population of settlers had increased exponentially. The main
ideological settlers' movement, the Gush Emunim or Bloc of the
Faithful, closely aligned to Israel's long-established and influential
National Religious Party (NRP), was formed in 1974 and received
some backing in its first years from the Labor politician and future
dove Shimon Peres, who became Israel's defense minister in that
year.[46] Nonetheless in 1977 there were only about seven thousand
Jewish settlers in the West Bank and Gaza. Settlement activity
picked up dramatically after the Likud's rise to power in Israel, under the patronage of Begin and especially Ariel Sharon. By the time
the peace process came into being in the early 1990s about two
hundred thousand Jews—the hard core inspired by the ideological
view of "Samaria and Judea" (the northern and southern West
Bank) as integral parts of the Land of Israel but most attracted by
government-proffered incentives of cheap housing and generous
subsidies—were settled on land captured by Israel in June 1967, the
vast majority in the West Bank and the areas of East Jerusalem and
its environs declared by Israel as constituting part of the "reunified"
city in 1967. The formula for a two-state solution based on the
pre–June 1967 borders, advanced by Khalidi in 1978 and formally
adopted by the PLO a decade later at the November 1988 session
of the Palestine National Council (PNC), faced a new reality on
the ground by the time of the September 1993 handshake on the
White House lawn.

There was no question of formal PLO representation at the
U.S.-sponsored Madrid conference, in deference to Israeli wishes.

The Palestinian representatives, drawn only from the West Bank and Gaza—to the exclusion of Palestinians from East Jerusalem and the diaspora, another concession to Israeli strictures and conditions—were moreover subsumed into a joint Jordanian-Palestinian delegation. Said commented acidly on the oddity of a situation in which "Israel can pick the team both for itself and the other side" and warned that "the United States . . . has already incorporated too many Israeli designs into the structure of the agenda of the conference."[47] The conference nonetheless led to ten rounds of talks over a period of twenty months, from late 1991 to the summer of 1993, between Israeli and Palestinian delegations in Washington. The talks did not produce any significant progress, let alone a breakthrough. In 2002 Dr. Haidar Abd al-Shafi, a respected citizen of Gaza who headed the Palestinian team in the talks, said, "We went to Madrid in the hope that the American government—the sponsor—would adopt a balanced position [between Israeli and Palestinian interests and perceptions] . . . A second reason for going was not to give Israel the chance to make propaganda that we don't want peace, that we only want violence and terrorism." He further stated:

> Israel's [continued] settlement-building was a clear violation of the very terms of reference of the [post-Madrid] peace process—it made the process meaningless. It was over this issue that the Washington negotiations reached an impasse, while we pressed the Israelis to stop their settlement activity and they refused. Finally they said plainly: "Why are you asking this? We are settling on our own land." So we went to see [Secretary of State James] Baker. In fairness, he did try to get Israel to stop but they wouldn't budge, so he came back to us and said: "Why don't you set this issue aside?" I said: "How can it be delayed? It deprives the peace process of any meaning" . . . The Americans did not honor their commitments and responsibil-

ity as the [third] party that had called the negotiations . . . by allowing Israel to violate the ground rules . . . So after the second negotiating round in Washington, my advice to our leadership [the PLO, above all Arafat] was to suspend our participation. Our sitting at the table provided Israel with a cover for its violations on the ground. But the leadership did not take my advice.[48]

The ground rules that al-Shafi refers to, and which he says Israel flouted with the toleration and indeed the acquiescence of the United States, the broker of the talks, were contained in a "Letter of Assurance" the U.S. administration gave the Palestinians in October 1991. The letter said that the United States would oppose Israeli actions that were "prejudicial or precedential," that would "make negotiations more difficult or preempt their final outcome" and "predetermine" core issues of the conflict.[49]

The deadlocked Washington talks were suddenly superseded in August 1993 by the disclosure that PLO and Israeli representatives had been engaged since January 1993 in a series of secret meetings in Oslo and elsewhere in Norway—facilitated by, among others, Terje Larsen, the director of the Norwegian Institute of Applied Social Science, and the Norwegian foreign minister Johan-Jorgen Holst—and that this back channel, headed by senior PLO leader Ahmed Qurei (Abu Ala) and the director-general of the Israeli foreign ministry, Uri Savir, had reached agreement on a historic "declaration of principles" on an Israeli-Palestinian peace process with the assent of Arafat on the one hand and Rabin and Peres on the other.[50] The Oslo channel had been made possible by the victory of the Labor Party in Israel's June 1992 election, after which Rabin became prime minister and Peres foreign minister. On 13 September 1993 the declaration negotiated in Oslo was signed by Peres and Abu Mazen in the presence of Rabin and Arafat as their host,

President Bill Clinton, looked on. A new era had dawned in the Israeli-Palestinian conflict.

The declaration of principles made all the right noises about putting "an end to decades of confrontation and conflict" and achieving "peaceful coexistence" and "mutual dignity and security" through "a just, lasting and comprehensive settlement." It spoke of an "elected Council for the Palestinian people in the West Bank and Gaza Strip" and "a strong Palestinian police force" in these territories. It laid out a vision for Israeli-Palestinian cooperation in a variety of fields as well as the outlines of a broader program of regional cooperation involving Jordan and Egypt.[51]

The declaration sidestepped the substantive issues of the Israeli-Palestinian conflict. The sole reference to Jerusalem stated that the Palestinian population of the city would have the right to participate in elections to the envisaged Palestinian authority. There was no reference to the Palestinian refugee question. There was no reference to the future of Jewish settlements and settlers in the occupied territories, *except* in the context of references to a confidence-building Israeli military withdrawal from most of the Gaza Strip—excluding settlements and zones around them—and the West Bank town of Jericho. According to the timetable projected in the declaration, an agreement on this withdrawal would be concluded by December 1993 and the Palestinian authority would then be in charge of education and culture, health, social welfare, direct taxation, and tourism in the two areas. The declaration stipulated that "the withdrawal of the military government [in Gaza and Jericho] will not prevent Israel from exercising the powers and responsibilities not transferred," and in particular that "subsequent to the Israeli withdrawal Israel will continue to be responsible for external security, internal security and . . . settlements and Israelis. Israeli military forces and civilians may continue to use roads freely within the

Gaza Strip and the Jericho area." The declaration projected a "five-year transitional period" starting from the date of the Gaza-Jericho agreement for a final peace agreement to be reached, and specified that "permanent-status negotiations will commence as soon as possible, but not later than the beginning of the third year of the interim period" (so, according to the declaration's timetable, by late 1995 or early 1996). The declaration projected that elections to the Palestinian representative body in the West Bank and Gaza would be held by July 1994. It stipulated that "not later than the eve of [these] elections, a [further] redeployment of Israeli military forces in the West Bank and Gaza Strip will take place." The nature and extent of this redeployment was left open and vague, apart from the premise that "Israel will be guided by the principle that its military forces should be redeployed outside populated areas" and a clause that "further redeployments to specified locations will be gradually implemented commensurate with the assumption of responsibility for public order and internal security by the Palestinian police force."

An exchange of letters between Arafat and Rabin supplemented the declaration of principles. Arafat's letter, dated 9 September, stated that "the PLO recognizes the right of the State of Israel to exist in peace and security" and "accordingly, the PLO renounces the use of terrorism." It affirmed that "those articles of the Palestinian Covenant which deny Israel's right to exist . . . are now inoperative and no longer valid." In a terse reply dated 10 September Rabin responded that "in light of the PLO commitments included in your letter the Government of Israel has decided to recognize the PLO as the representative of the Palestinian people and commence negotiations with the PLO within the Middle East peace process." The upshot of this exchange was that while the PLO recognized Israel within its pre–June 1967 borders and affirmed its right to exist in peace and security within those borders, Israel, while recognizing the PLO as the representative of the Palestinian people, made no reciprocal acknowledgment of the Palestinian aspiration to sovereignty in an independent state on the remaining 22 percent of Mandate Palestine's territory. The principle of Palestinian self-determination was also not explicitly acknowledged in the declaration of principles, which referred in more general terms to "the legitimate rights of the Palestinian people and their just requirements." All of this was consistent with the slant of American policy. As American scholar William Quandt writes, "The Clinton administration until Oslo refused all contact with the PLO and even after Oslo refused to speak positively of a Palestinian state as an outcome; had it done so the transition to Israeli acceptance of the outcome that Rabin and his successor Peres privately acknowledged as inevitable might have been eased."[52]

The Gaza-Jericho agreement was eventually concluded only in May 1994 and Arafat arrived in the occupied territories two months later. The elections to the Palestinian Authority took place only in January 1996, a year and a half after the date projected in the declaration of principles. The elections were preceded by an agreement on interim Palestinian self-rule in the West Bank, usually referred to as Oslo II, signed in Washington on 28 September 1995. In the words of Dennis Ross, the chief American mediator, "The difficulty of crafting the Gaza-Jericho agreement paled in comparison to what would be involved [in finalizing the September 1995 interim agreement] . . . Exploratory work on the agreement did not even begin until the fall of 1994." Valuable time and crucial momentum were lost in the two years between Oslo I and II. Ross, who is candid about his personal affinity for Israel—he took up a position at the Washington Institute for Near East Policy, a think tank that engages in pro-Israel advocacy, after leaving government—expresses the central problem that bedeviled the peace process succinctly: "The Israelis envisioned a Palestinian Authority profoundly limited not only in its geography but in its powers, one in which, from security to economics, little could happen if the Israelis did not want it to happen."[53]

Oslo II established a "cartographic cheeseboard" on the West Bank. Three percent of the area of the West Bank, centered on the towns of Jenin, Nablus, Tulkarm, Qalqiliya, Ramallah, Jericho, Bethlehem, and Hebron, was designated as Area A; here the PA would exercise civil powers as well as security control. Another 24 percent, covering several hundred Palestinian villages, constituted Area B; over this area the PA would have civil powers but the Israelis would retain security control, in a somewhat diluted form of occupation. The remaining 73 percent, Area C, would remain under full-fledged Israeli occupation. Area C included the entire length of border between the West Bank and Jordan. The Area A enclaves were territorially completely disconnected from each other by vast Israeli-occupied areas, and the Area B zones were also mostly severed from each other and from the Area A towns. This arrangement has been described by the former Clinton administration Middle East official Robert Malley and the Palestinian academic Hussein Agha as "a quasi-state with incomplete powers over a crazy quilt of land" and by Edward Said as a "crazy patchwork [of] . . . municipal responsibilities in a series of Bantustans controlled from the outside by Israel."[54]

The scenario of "ersatz sovereignty" in a "mosaic of reservations and hen-runs" subject to constant Israeli control and surveillance that Walid Khalidi had warned against two decades earlier had come true. In a postmortem analysis of the peace process published in the autumn of 2001, Israeli academic Ron Pundak, who was intimately involved in the Oslo back channel, describes the consequences:

> The imbalance of power between occupier and occupied
> impeded negotiations. . . . The patronizing Israeli attitude to-

wards the Palestinians continued unabated . . . The average
Palestinian continued to experience daily humiliation, and
new settlements were established both off and on expropriated
land . . . For the average Palestinian the "fruits of peace" were
hardly encouraging: closures interpreted as collective punishment [for terror attacks], restrictions on movement, a permit-
issuing system for travel, mistreatment at IDF and Border Police checkpoints, water shortages in contrast to water abun-
dance in neighboring Israeli settlements, the destruction of
Palestinian homes while new houses were built in the settlements, the non-release of prisoners held for activities committed before Oslo, restrictions on building on Palestinian land
outside Areas A and B, and the establishment of Bantustan-like
enclaves controlled on the whims of the Israeli military and
dictated by the military's symbiotic relationship with the settlers' movement.[55]

Between the Madrid conference of 1991 and the eruption of the
second Palestinian intifada in the autumn of 2000, the number of
Jewish settlers in the occupied territories doubled from about two
hundred thousand to about four hundred thousand; the West Bank,
along with East Jerusalem, accounted for almost all of this increase.
Throughout the 1990s a vast network of "bypass roads" totaling
hundreds of miles, connecting settlements with one another and
with Israel, were built in the West Bank for the exclusive use of the
Israeli military, police, and settlers—"in March and April 2002,"
when Israel launched a massive military operation against PA areas
after a spate of terrorist attacks killed 133 Israelis in one month,
"these bypass roads proved to be the sinews of the re-occupation of
the West Bank and its division into dozens of isolated pockets by
more than 100 Israeli checkpoints."[56]

In early November 1995 Yitzhak Rabin was assassinated in Tel
Aviv by a Jewish extremist. In the months preceding the murder Is-

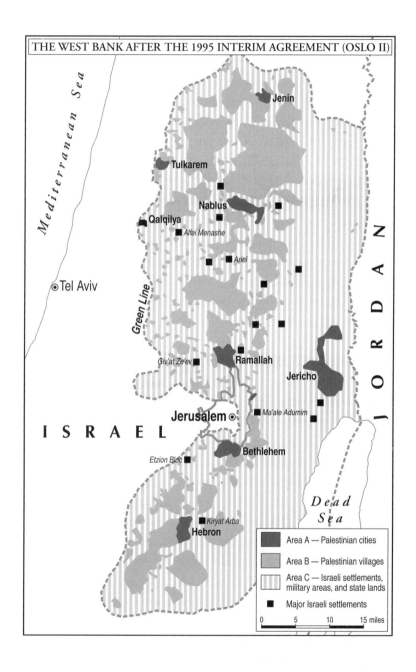

THE WEST BANK AFTER THE 1995 INTERIM AGREEMENT (OSLO II)

Mediterranean Sea

Jenin

Tulkarem

Nablus

Qalqilya

Alfei Menashe

Ariel

⊙Tel Aviv

Green Line

J O R D A N

Giv'at Ze'ev   Ramallah

Jericho

Jerusalem ⊙   Ma'ale Adumim

I S R A E L

Etzion Bloc   Bethlehem

Dead
Sea

Kiryat Arba
Hebron

- Area A — Palestinian cities
- Area B — Palestinian villages
- Area C — Israeli settlements, military areas, and state lands
- Major Israeli settlements

0   5   10   15 miles

rael was gripped by right-wing agitation against the peace process, as militant groups tried "to block traffic throughout the country" and West Bank settlers "seized hilltops and attacked Palestinian villages." The following May, Rabin's successor, Shimon Peres, lost elections to the Likud challenger Binyamin Netanyahu by a razor-thin margin. Netanyahu's narrow victory was almost certainly the result of four Palestinian suicide bombings in nine days during the spring of 1996, which hit both Jerusalem and Tel Aviv and killed fifty-nine Israelis. The bombings in turn resulted from the Israeli assassinations of Fathi Shikaki, a top Islamic Jihad figure, in Malta in late 1995 and of Yahya Ayyash, a Hamas operative known as "the engineer," in early 1996. The peace process went into "free fall," in Dennis Ross's phrase, during Netanyahu's term in office, which lasted until he lost elections in May 1999 to the Labor leader Ehud Barak. Avi Shlaim writes that "Netanyahu showed hatred and bitter animosity towards the Palestinians," and Pundak concurs that "Netanyahu sabotaged the peace process relentlessly and made every effort to de-legitimize his Palestinian partners." The Netanyahu years were marked by constant stonewalling and goalpost-moving. Thus "Israel did not implement the three stages of the second redeployment and did not leave [West Bank] territory supposed to be transferred to the Palestinians, completed only one section in four with regard to the freeing of Palestinian prisoners, did not undertake the implementation of the safe route supposed to connect the West Bank with Gaza [under the September 1995 interim agreement], repeatedly delayed the permit to build the airport and maritime port in Gaza, prevented the transfer of monies to the PA for extended periods, and continued to establish new settlements, to confiscate land for new settlements and to expand existing ones." Netanyahu was not just a hard-liner vis-à-vis the Palestinians but an inept leader more generally; the British ambassador to Israel privately described him as "a drunk who lurches from one lamppost to the next."[57]

It seems that the top echelons of the U.S. administration agreed that Netanyahu was a disaster for the peace process. Ross recalls that "both Madeleine [Albright, the secretary of state] and Sandy [Berger, the national security adviser] . . . feared that Bibi [Netanyahu] was trying deliberately to destroy the Oslo process; if that were the case, we needed to resist him now and confront him."[58] But the Americans did not confront Netanyahu. Instead, Ross became mired in an unfruitful dialogue with Netanyahu over the further redeployments of Israeli forces from the West Bank, and Netanyahu seized the opportunity to haggle with him for months on end over minute percentages of territory to be handed over to the Palestinians, while the peace process sank into deeper and deeper crisis. Netanyahu constantly resorted to obstructive tactics, such as demanding that the Palestinians revoke the entire PLO covenant. In October 1998, with the peace process running out of all steam, the U.S. administration sponsored and mediated a conference between the Israeli and Palestinian leaderships at the Wye River plantation in Maryland that produced an agreement enlarging Areas A and B from 27 percent to almost 40 percent of the West Bank. The Wye summit was the first time that President Clinton became personally involved in the details of the peace process. Netanyahu dragged his feet in implementing the agreement, robbing it of much of its value. The implementation of the Wye accord dragged into early 2000. In any case, it did nothing to address the fundamental problems with the piecemeal, incremental "Oslo" approach that had become increasingly evident since at least the September 1995 Oslo II agreement, if not even earlier.

A rare "advance" to the peace process during the Netanyahu years was the implementation of a considerably overdue partial IDF "redeployment" from the town of Hebron, the hub of the southern West Bank, which had been envisaged by Oslo II but not implemented until a protocol was signed between the Israeli government and the Palestinian Authority in January 1997. The nature of the

Hebron compromise and its consequences tellingly illustrates the built-in flaws of the peace process that led to its collapse. Hebron is a city of religious and historical significance to both Muslims and Jews. Hebron's Ibrahimi Mosque—the Tomb of the Patriarchs to Jews—was the site of a massacre of twenty-nine praying Palestinians by Dr. Baruch Goldstein, a settler from Brooklyn, New York, in late February 1994, the event that sparked five Palestinian suicide bombings during 1994, mostly by Hamas, which began in April and killed forty Israelis. Because, unlike in any other West Bank town, the city center of Hebron was home to four hundred to five hundred very militant settlers, Oslo II divided the city into two zones: H-1 and H-2. The IDF was to move out of H-1, which covered 80 percent of the city's municipal area, and let it be administered by the Palestinian Authority. But H-2, the other 20 percent of the city—which would include the city center, taking in the settler enclave and the Ibrahimi Mosque/Tomb of the Patriarchs—would remain under Israeli control, essentially under IDF occupation. The H-2 area enveloped 35,000 to 40,000 of Hebron's 140,000 Palestinians. The actual IDF redeployment was delayed "until after a bypass road for settlers [living in and around Hebron] was completed."[59]

When in July 1996 Edward Said visited Hebron's Palestinian mayor, the mayor told him that "he had pleaded with Yasser Arafat and his men during the summer 1995 negotiations that led up to Oslo II not to sign an agreement that would put a Palestinian seal of approval on the 450 illegal settlers, most of them fanatics." The 1997 Hebron protocol listed several Jewish holy sites in the PA-administered H-1 area, and guaranteed right of access of Jews to those sites, with the stipulation that they would be escorted by joint Palestinian-Israeli units. But "a similar right is not conferred on [Muslim] worshipers wishing to attend the Ibrahimi Mosque [in H-2] . . . Israeli guards control the gates to the mosque and subject all worshipers to security checks." In the autumn of 2005 an Israeli investigative journalist discovered that the H-2 area had been

largely depopulated of its Palestinian inhabitants by constant settler harassment, violence, and vandalism, perpetrated with the connivance of Israeli soldiers and police. "Hundreds of abandoned
[Palestinian] homes" and "dozens of destroyed stores, burned or
shuttered" littered the city center. "Every walk to school for a Palestinian child has become a journey of fear," he found, "every
shopping outing for a housewife a journey of humiliation." He
witnessed "settler children kicking old women, settlers setting their
dogs on elderly men, garbage, junk metal and excrement [being]
thrown from settlers' balconies into the courtyards of Palestinian homes, rocks thrown at passers-by," and lamented "the awful
mistake of Rabin, who lacked the courage to uproot this settlement immediately after the slaughter" perpetrated by Baruch
Goldstein.[60]

The January 1997 Hebron protocol was considered as progress in
the peace process at the time, especially because it followed a serious outbreak of Israeli-Palestinian violence the previous autumn—
in which, ominously, Palestinian police officers fired at Israeli soldiers for the first time—triggered by a dispute with Muslim-Jewish
religious connotations in the old city of Jerusalem. Scores of Palestinian demonstrators were killed by Israeli forces in the autumn
of 1996, while an entire platoon of fifteen IDF soldiers were killed
by Palestinians at the site of Joseph's Tomb in Nablus. Soon after the Hebron protocol was signed, Israeli-Palestinian relations de-
teriorated severely when in March 1997 the Netanyahu government authorized the building of a new settlement—in standard
Israeli parlance, a new "neighborhood"—in Har Homa, a hilltop in
southeastern Jerusalem overlooking Bethlehem. In November 1998,
Netanyahu extracted Bill Clinton's personal acquiescence to the
construction of thousands of housing units in Har Homa, built
partly on confiscated Palestinian land, as part of the "price" for pro-
ceeding with the Wye redeployment.[61] The Har Homa issue be-

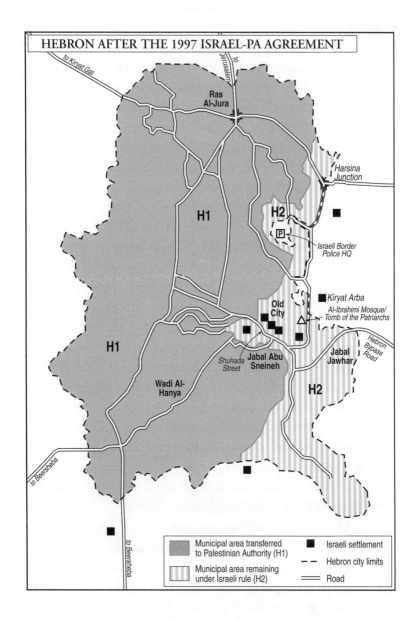

HEBRON AFTER THE 1997 ISRAEL-PA AGREEMENT

to Kiryat Gat

to Jerusalem

Ras
Al-Jura

Harsina
Junction

H1

H2

P

Israeli Border
Police HQ

Kiryat Arba

Old
City

Al-Ibrahimi Mosque/
Tomb of the Patriarchs

H1

Jabal Abu
Sneineh

Shuhada
Street

Jabal
Jawhar

Hebron
Bypass
Road

Wadi Al-
Hanya

H2

to Beersheba

to Beersheba

Municipal area transferred
to Palestinian Authority (H1)

Israeli settlement

Municipal area remaining
under Israeli rule (H2)

Hebron city limits

Road

came a symbol of the terminal illness of the peace process in the late 1990s.

The last nails were hammered into the coffin of the peace process during Ehud Barak's ill-starred term as Israel's prime minister from May 1999 to February 2001. Barak was imbued with a sense of urgency, but during the first year of his term he focused his energies on trying to reach an agreement with Syria that he hoped would smooth Israel's withdrawal from southern Lebanon, and he neglected the peace process with the Palestinians. This was a strategic misjudgment. Barak concentrated on the Syrian track— which ended in deadlock, an outcome that became clear following an abortive summit between President Clinton and Syria's leader Hafez al-Assad in Geneva in March 2000—at a time when the Oslo process was practically on its deathbed and needed urgent attention to survive. Although a September 1999 meeting between Israeli and Palestinian representatives in the resort town of Sharm al-Sheikh, on the southern tip of the Egyptian Sinai, fixed September 2000 as a new deadline for the conclusion of a permanent-status agreement between the two sides—the original deadline projected in Oslo I expired in May 1999—Barak delayed appointing an Israeli negotiator until the end of the year. Then for several months, until well into 2000, he resisted American efforts to establish an Oslo-type back channel to discuss substantive issues.

When during the first half of 2000 Barak gradually turned his attention to the Palestinians, his behavior was intransigent. He wished to put additional Israeli redeployments in the West Bank— as called for by the September 1995 interim agreement and reaffirmed by the Wye accord of October 1998—on hold, in anticipation of a breakthrough in the final-status negotiations to which he had not shown any serious commitment. This was unacceptable to Arafat, whose patience had been worn thin during the Netanyahu years. Barak initially confirmed to President Clinton a positive response to a request from Arafat that three Palestinian townships in

the Jerusalem suburbs—Abu Dis, Azariya, and Ram—be transferred from Area B to Area A (full PA control) under the redeployment plan, and then refused to follow through on this commitment. His attitude on other pending issues of importance to
Palestinians—the release of prisoners, the establishment of safe-
passage routes between the West Bank and Gaza, and the curbing
of settler violence against Palestinian civilians in the occupied territories—was as niggardly and uncompromising as his predecessor's.
And Barak almost called off a visit to Ramallah in March 2000—
the first-ever by an Israeli premier to the PA-controlled area of the
West Bank—on the grounds that the route, and the hotel in which
he was to meet with Arafat, had been decorated with the Palestinian national flag. The Palestinians were mystified by this churlish reaction to the grand welcome they had organized for Israel's
leader.[62]

They were not alone. Dennis Ross recalls that Secretary of State
Albright was also "mystified by Barak's behavior." Barak appeared
to be a prisoner of the rigid Israeli security paradigm to an even
greater extent than his role-model Yitzhak Rabin, in whose trail he
followed as a former IDF chief of staff. According to Ron Pundak,
Barak was "emotionally sympathetic to Gush Emunim, the settlers'
movement, and was mentally conditioned by his 35 years in the
military." He was also desperate to hold together his unwieldy
coalition government, which included right-wing parties like the
settler-affiliated NRP, the Sephardic religious Shas Party, and a
party led by Natan Sharansky. He did not succeed in doing so. The
three parties quit his coalition on the eve of his July 2000 Camp
David summit with President Clinton and Chairman Arafat, which
was held at Barak's insistence even though the groundwork and atmosphere for a successful summit that would deliver a final Israeli-
Palestinian agreement were conspicuously absent. But through his
errors, feebleness, and muddled policies Barak did succeed in con-
tributing fatal damage to any prospect of reviving the peace process.

Pundak comments that "under the circumstances Arafat's distrust of Barak was not surprising . . . [Arafat] . . . at one point said: 'Barak is worse than Netanyahu.'" Barak's behavior was all the more surprising—and eventually very costly—given that since late 1999 both the IDF and the Shin Bet, Israel's internal security organization, were convinced that frustration and anger among the Palestinian public were approaching dangerous levels and would result in an explosion sooner rather than later. Indeed, violence broke out in the occupied territories in mid-May 2000 as Palestinians observed the anniversary of the 1948 nakba—these disturbances paled in comparison to the second intifada, which erupted in the autumn. If Barak's place in history is marginal, his credibility among the Israeli public is even more derisory. An opinion survey in August 2005 found that Barak was the preferred leader for 3.8 percent of Jewish Israelis and had a support level of just 6.7 percent even among Labor voters.[63]

The Camp David summit took place in this unpropitious climate in July 2000. Palestinian-American scholar Rashid Khalidi argues that "at Camp David Barak made a stingy take-it-or-leave-it offer to Arafat that was predictably rejected. The offer . . . was ludicrously described in the ensuing mythology that grew up around Camp David as 'generous.'"[64] Khalidi's trenchant characterization is broadly supported by an analysis of the summit published in August 2001 by Hussein Agha and Robert Malley, who was closely involved with the summit as Clinton's special assistant for Arab-Israeli affairs.[65] Agha and Malley pinpoint several problems with the summit. It was organized on "Barak's timetable, imposed after his Syrian gambit had failed, and designed with his own strategy in mind. Arafat was not about to oblige." Barak had failed to act on prior agreements and commitments of even the most piecemeal nature, hardly a confidence-building step toward a final resolution of the Israeli-Palestinian conflict. Additionally, "strictly speaking there never was an Israeli offer . . . The ideas put forward at Camp

David were never stated in writing, but orally conveyed . . . Nor were the proposals detailed." Finally, the Palestinian participants saw the "proposals as inadequate; they were silent on the question of refugees, the land exchange was unbalanced [the final Israeli proposal, conveyed through the Americans, was that Israel would annex 9 percent of the West Bank to accommodate its settlements and the Palestinians would receive a 1 percent compensation of land from Israel proper in return] and both the Haram [al-Sharif] and much of Arab East Jerusalem would remain under Israeli sovereignty [while most suburban Palestinian neighborhoods would become part of the Palestinian state, the inner districts comprising the heart of Palestinian East Jerusalem would have 'autonomy' under Israeli rule]." Ross's account of Camp David recalls that the Palestinian delegation asked for clarifications on many aspects of the Israeli-American proposals:

> What was the meaning of "custodianship" of the Haram [offered to Arafat]; who would have sovereignty? Since the Palestinians would have sovereignty over 85 percent of the length of their border with Jordan, would Israel have control or sovereignty over the other 15 percent? What was meant by a "satisfactory solution" to the refugee problem? Why were only seven or eight of the outer [Palestinian] neighborhoods [of Jerusalem] to get sovereignty and not all nine? [Why] the 9 percent annexation and [only] 1 percent [compensation]?[66]

The clarifications asked for, especially the repeated emphasis on the issue of "sovereignty," suggest that Arafat and his circle were wary of signing on to any deal that might be perceived by Palestinians as delaying or, worse still, permanently compromising even the most minimalist definition of Palestinian sovereignty. After seven years of a peace process that had gone steadily downhill from at least the mid-1990s, Arafat, who won the Palestinian presidential election by a landslide in early 1996, had seen his popularity plummet among the elites as well as the masses of Palestinian society as he stood accused of repeatedly accepting crumbs from Israel's table. Pundak's and Agha and Malley's analyses of Camp David concur that the vast majority of Palestinians were so disillusioned with the Oslo process by July 2000 that it would have been extremely difficult for the weakened Arafat to assent to an unsatisfactory and incomplete Israeli proposal passed through an American filter. Pundak writes that the story of Israeli generosity and the Palestinians' seizing yet another opportunity to miss an opportunity at Camp David is "a version presented in retrospect by Israeli spokespersons . . . [and] an attempt at rewriting history" to evade culpability and blame the other side for the final collapse of the peace process.[67] Clinton added grist to this story by fulsomely praising Barak—who had behaved temperamentally throughout the summit—for showing flexibility and at least implicitly blaming Arafat for its failure, in probable violation of a presummit understanding between the Americans and the Palestinians that apportioning blame would be avoided should the summit fail. Two months later the "al-Aqsa intifada" erupted. By the autumn of 2005 about four thousand Palestinians and eleven hundred Israelis had been killed in the violence.

Why did the peace process fail?

Fixing the blame on particular individuals, as Dennis Ross's memoir ultimately does on Arafat, is shallow and unconvincing. Ross claims that "only one leader was unable or unwilling to confront history and mythology: Yasser Arafat." Apart from letting Israeli leaders from Rabin onward off the hook, and harking back to the Israeli-led demonology of Arafat and the PLO that was prevalent in the United States prior to the advent of the Oslo process and was revived from 2001, there are other serious questions about the veracity of singling out Arafat in this manner. There is no doubt that Arafat was a controlling, manipulative autocrat addicted to cronyism and that he failed to make the transition from being the icon of Palestinian nationalism to becoming the responsible, competent national leader the Palestinians sorely needed in the post-revolutionary phase. Haidar Abd al-Shafi noted with regret in 2002 that "the chairman insists on remaining the sole decision-maker," and Muhammad Dahlan, the prominent Gaza figure and onetime Arafat acolyte, said in 2005 that Arafat "was not interested in anything other than his own position" even during the crisis of 2002–2003. Yet Ross's own dense account is replete with episodes in which Arafat, having invested in the piecemeal, gradualist strategy of the peace process, was genuinely let down by Israeli leaders who would not fulfill their part of the bargain. For example, regarding Arafat's decision to suspend negotiations with the Israelis in early 2000 in response to Barak's obduracy, Ross writes that "this was not necessarily a case of Arafat playing games. He genuinely believed that Barak . . . was taking him for granted."[68]

Indeed, Arafat appears in many places in Ross's book as a figure more sinned against than sinning, material that provides ample fodder for contradicting the American mediator's eventual indictment of Arafat as the villain of the piece. Nor did Arafat exploit the terror option during the peace process in the facile manner suggested by some Israeli and other propaganda. Ross writes, for instance, that in the spring of 1996, "in the period following four [suicide] bombings in nine days [in Israel] Arafat directed the most severe crackdown on Hamas and Islamic Jihad . . . He replaced many of the imams in mosques and arrested many of the leaders of Hamas's military wing. He permitted real [PA] security cooperation with the Shin Bet to continue."[69]

If Arafat is partly culpable for the failure of the peace process, so is Rabin. Ross notes that when "during Rabin's time, the military administration in the [occupied] territories was supposed to be withdrawn and was not, we did not say so publicly out of concern

that Rabin was already under a great deal of pressure from the [Is-
raeli] right, and we did not need to compound his difficulties." Indeed, Rabin was "the intellectual father" of the concept of the se-
curity/separation barrier with the West Bank's Palestinians that
Israel has constructed since 2002 under Ariel Sharon's premier-
ship—eating into West Bank territory in the process and resulting
in land expropriations, hardship, and uncertainty for tens of thousands, if not hundreds of thousands, of West Bank and Jerusalem
Palestinians—mostly as a fence structure but also as an ugly wall in
Tulkarm, Qalqiliya, and above all extensive areas around Jerusalem.
After an Islamic Jihad suicide bombing in Israel in January 1995
killed twenty soldiers and one civilian, Rabin declared in a nationally televised address that he intended to "take Gaza out of Tel
Aviv" and that this would be achieved through "a separation between us and them . . . though not according to the borders prior
to 1967." At that time Sharon, the settlement movement's god-
father, poured scorn on the idea of a physical barrier in an op-ed
article titled "The Silliness of Separation": "Won't these fences
be sabotaged? Won't they be penetrated? Where will the forces
to secure this system come from? From what budgets? It is difficult
to fathom such silliness." On the eve of the tenth anniversary of
Rabin's assassination the Israeli commentator Gideon Levy described Rabin as "a cowardly statesman." Levy observed that Rabin
"did not dare to do what a much smaller 'man of peace,' Sharon,
did ten years later [in Gaza]. Rabin did not dare to put the evacuation of settlements on the agenda [of the peace process], even from
the Gaza Strip, despite his conviction that at least some of them
should be evacuated." Rabin "wanted peace," Levy writes, "but like
most Israelis did not agree to pay the price . . . He was assassinated
on the altar of peace, but what he did for peace was too little and
too late." In the autumn of 2005 a veteran activist of Israel's Peace
Now movement, who always considered Sharon "the embodiment

of the ugly Israeli," noted that unlike him "the Labor party never dared to move a single settler."[70]

Avi Shlaim identifies a different villain of the tragic drama. He argues that "the Oslo accords should not be adjudged a failure. They did not collapse under the weight of their own contradictions . . . the process was subverted by Netanyahu and his colleagues in the ultra-nationalist camp." While it is incontrovertible that Netanyahu inflicted severe damage on the prospects of the peace process, the process's problems both predate Netanyahu's term in power and are far deeper than this assignment of prime culpability suggests. Similarly, Ron Pundak's conclusion that "poor management of the process" led to its failure is inadequate and superficial and somewhat at odds with his robust critique of Israeli elites' attitudes and behavior during the 1990s.[71]

What of the role of spoilers in sabotaging the prospects of peace? A major risk of an incremental approach to making peace is that it allows spoilers the time to get their act together and prepare and implement destructive interventions. On the Palestinian side the identity of the spoilers is obvious—Hamas and Islamic Jihad, particularly the former. Hamas disapproved of the Oslo process but did not wish to have a full-blown confrontation with the PA for both ideological and strategic reasons. It continued to use terrorist tactics as an element of its multifaceted activities, however. Between September 1993 and September 2000, thirty-one suicide attacks were perpetrated by radical Palestinian groups—of which eighteen were claimed by Hamas, six by Islamic Jihad, and another two jointly by Hamas and Islamic Jihad—killing 137 Israelis and injuring 989. These attacks, particularly suicide bombings in Israel, undeniably had a corrosive effect on the peace process by undermining the Israeli public's confidence in the process. But there were also fallow periods when there were no Palestinian terror attacks at all, such as September 1997 to October 1998. In the two-year period from

October 1998 to September 2000 there were only five attempted
bombings, which in total killed one Israeli and injured 25 others.
The contrast with the period after the second intifada began is
stark. In the four-year period from October 2000 to September
2004 there were 219 Palestinian suicide attacks (beginning mostly
from March 2001), including 135 human bombs, which killed 650
Israelis and injured 3,277 others. It is implausible that Hamas (and
Islamic Jihad) violence destroyed the peace process.[72]

On the Israeli side the spoiler phenomenon is driven by the
competitive dynamics of Israel's plural political system. The fear of
being outflanked and upstaged from the right influenced and con-
strained Rabin's and Barak's behavior toward the Palestinians. The
decade of the peace process coincided with a diversification and
fracturing of Jewish Israeli society and the proliferation of political
parties in the Knesset representing a variety of mobilized identity
and interest groups. This added an additional complicating dimension to the prospects of the peace process—Israeli leaders' need
to maintain unwieldy and fractious coalition governments. This
compulsion affected both the rightist Netanyahu and the centrist Barak. The third party to the peace process—U.S. administrations—proved acutely, even extraordinarily, sensitive to the vicissi-
tudes of Israel's domestic politics and the constraints on Israeli
leaders stemming from these two factors. In somewhat different
ways, these constraints provided Netanyahu and Barak with alibis
for behavior damaging to the peace process, and U.S. officials and
mediators were too willing to entertain the alibis and tolerate such
behavior. Yet the irony is that while the peace process was progressively eroded, the political fortunes of Israel's leaders were not
saved. Rabin paid for Oslo with his life. Netanyahu's hard-line posturing and pandering to the demands and prejudices of his core
right-wing base did not save him from being solidly beaten by
Barak—by 56 percent to 44 percent in the direct election for prime
minister—three years into his term. Barak's strongman stance to-

ward the Palestinians did not save him from suffering even more ignoble humiliation—a 62.5 percent to 37.5 percent trouncing at the hands of Sharon—less than two years into his term. The logic of sacrificing Israeli-Palestinian peace to the compulsions and constraints of Israel's political arena is questionable at best.

The root cause of the peace process's failure lies in insufficient Israeli (and American) recognition of the fact that in Palestinian eyes "Oslo itself is the historic compromise—an agreement to concede 78 percent of mandatory Palestine to Israel." Indeed, as Shlaim points out, the dominant leadership of the PLO "had made their choice. They offered Israel peace in return for a minimal restitution of what had been taken away from [the Palestinians] by force." Yet as Pundak says, Israeli leaders "failed to grasp that . . . the Palestinians had already made the most important territorial concession. They had accepted . . . the principle of a Palestinian state on only 22 percent of mandatory Palestine." That is why, as Agha and Malley correctly put it, post-Oslo "the notion that Israel was 'offering' land, being 'generous,' or 'making concessions' seemed to them doubly wrong."[73]

The continuous establishment of new settlements, expansion of existing settlements, and building of bypass roads on the territory of the putative Palestinian state throughout the peace process went to the heart of the matter. The history of the Arab-Jewish conflict in and over Palestine until 1948 and subsequently of the Israeli-Palestinian conflict is one of life-and-death struggle for control of land—and the resources that come with such control, like water—and the right to live on that land. Walid Khalidi wrote in 1978 that Palestinians genuinely could not understand "why, after having acquired 77 percent of Palestine, Israelis should want to settle in yet more [of its] territory." Haidar Abd al-Shafi recalls that his experience of negotiating with the Israelis in the early 1990s convinced him that while the PLO had explicitly and irrevocably climbed down from its claim to all of Palestine—asserting only a claim to sovereignty over a fraction of historic Palestine in its stead—the Israelis had not, in a reciprocal quid pro quo, "given up their claims to all of Palestine." This was manifested above all in the continuation of settlement activity, the engine of the Zionist program since the early twentieth century. Eventually, as Pundak observes, the vast majority of Palestinians "came to the conclusion that Israel did not in fact want to end the occupation" and believed that they had been tricked, and their leadership co-opted, into a "barren process" and "historical trap."[74]

When a peace process is being conducted between two utterly unequal parties in the context of a deeply asymmetric power relationship, the role of the third party becomes critical. The United States failed to live up to the role it had to play if the Israeli-Palestinian peace process was to transform a deadly zero-sum conflict into some sort of positive-sum outcome. Ross writes that "our involvement [was] desired strongly by both sides, but especially by the Palestinians," and that "Arafat saw us as his equalizer with the Israelis." But when, "from the very beginning of the implementation process the Israelis felt no need to fulfil many of their obligations" (Ross's words), the United States did not use its leverage as Israel's essential and indispensable military, economic, and diplomatic patron to ensure that they did. Instead,

> We shied away from putting the onus on one side or the other because we feared we would disrupt a process that had great promise . . . We could always convince ourselves that it was never the right time to disrupt the process. It was never the right time to insist on freezing all discussions until a breached commitment had been corrected. It was never the right time to go public and say clearly why we had a problem and who was responsible . . . By never holding either side accountable . . . we contributed to an environment in which commitments

were rarely taken seriously by either side, knowing that there would never be any real consequences.

Ross seeks to both apportion blame evenhandedly and more important, convey an appearance of American impartiality. Both, especially the latter, have been convincingly challenged. Pundak, an Israeli, argues that "the Israeli breaches were both more numerous and more substantive in nature." He also says that "the American . . . approach was to adopt the position of the Israeli prime minister. This was demonstrated most extremely during the Netanyahu government, when the American government seemed sometimes to be working *for* the Israeli prime minister, as it tried to convince and pressure the Palestinian side to accept Israeli offers." At Camp David in July 2000, as William Quandt writes, "the Palestinian negotiators spoke openly of the need for the United States to leave aside its bias toward Israel in order to be an honest broker, asking that the US put forward compromise proposals of its own rather than [simply present] warmed-over Israeli ideas." Agha and Malley's assessment of Camp David concurs that "in the end . . . the US either gave up or gave in, reluctantly acquiescing in the way Barak did things" and "the US ended up . . . presenting Israeli negotiating positions [to the Palestinians] and couching them as rock-bottom red lines." The irony was that "the administration by and large shared Arafat's views . . . on matters of substance the US was much closer to the Palestinians' position than to Israel's . . . [and] the visible alignment between Israel and the United States obscured the real differences between them." The Palestinian representatives did bear a lesser share of responsibility for the summit's failure by failing "to present a cogent and specific counter-proposal" of their own. This was consistent with an established syndrome; Ross is right that "throughout the Oslo process Chairman Arafat was extremely passive. His style was to respond, not initiate ideas."[75]

Clinton did come up with a more equitable set of ideas to anchor a permanent Israeli–Palestinian accord in late December 2000, on which more below. But tragically, the timing was too late. The peace process and Israeli–Palestinian relations had irretrievably broken down, and 350 Palestinians, mostly demonstrators, had been killed in the preceding three months by deliberate Israeli use of overwhelming force against the second intifada. Clinton himself was about to leave office, and Sharon's assumption of power in Israel was imminent.

The post-Oslo peace process was premised on the logic and peacebuilding potential of incrementalism. Indeed, "Oslo was supposed to embody a process of living together. Israelis and Palestinians would build a web of cooperative relations [and] cooperation would take on a life of its own . . . so that the harder issues would become resolvable in a very different climate."[76] The peace process that actually unfolded convinced Palestinians that the piecemeal, gradualist approach was just a cover for the imposition of a parody of a solution based on Israel's power differential with the Palestinians—with the tolerance, if not the connivance, of Israel's superpower patron—which disregarded even the radically pared-down agenda of Palestinian national rights and self-determination. Over seven years the confidence-building process turned into a confidence-destroying morass.

The basis of a minimally equitable Israeli–Palestinian compromise is contained in the "Clinton parameters" of late 2000. These parameters visualized the Palestinian state as having about 95 percent of the West Bank (along with 100 percent of the Gaza Strip). The 5 percent or so of the West Bank that would be appended to Israel would cover the largest settlements—mostly contiguous or relatively close to the pre–June 1967 Green Line—including Ariel, Modin Illit, Maaleh Adumim, and the Etzion Bloc, and take in about three-quarters of the West Bank's settler population, and the

Palestinians would be compensated, substantially if not wholly, by a turnover of land from Israel to the Palestinian state. Although the location of that land was not specified, Palestinian representatives did refer, before the peace process broke down, to Israeli territory contiguous to Gaza, in order to enlarge the Strip and relieve its population density and attendant social problems. The Clinton parameters envisaged that the Israeli withdrawal from the West Bank would be phased over three years, and that the transition would be overseen by an international peacekeeping force. A small Israeli military presence would remain in specified locations in the Jordan Valley for another three years in deference to traditional Israeli security perceptions about the defense of Israel's eastern frontiers, but under the authority of the international force.

On the question of Palestinian refugees, the Clinton parameters called on Israel "to acknowledge the moral and material suffering caused to the Palestinian people as a result of the 1948 War and the need [for Israel] to assist the international community in addressing the problem."[77] However, in practical terms Palestinians would have an absolute and unfettered right to return to the Palestinian state (including areas transferred to it in the projected land exchange), with priority given to residents of refugee camps in Lebanon, while any return to Israel would be subject to Israel's consent. The implicit implication, not spelled out, was that Israel might agree to a very limited, virtually symbolic Palestinian right of return to Israel, perhaps under the humanitarian rubric of elderly person and/or family reunification criteria.

On the contentious issue of Jerusalem the parameters proposed a simple but persuasive formula for a complex but perfectly workable territorial division of sovereignty: "What is Arab in the city should be Palestinian and what is Jewish should be Israeli; this would apply to the old city as well." In effect, this meant that the Palestinian inner-city neighborhoods of East Jerusalem such as Sheikh Jarrah, Wadi al-Joz, Silwan, and Abu Tor would become part of the sovereign Palestinian state, as would the Muslim Quarter and the Christian Quarter of the old city and the Haram al-Sharif compound with its two holy mosques. Israel would have sovereignty over the districts of pre–June 1967 West Jerusalem, the Armenian Quarter, and the Jewish Quarter (which has been expanded since 1967) of the old city and the sacred Western Wall, along with eleven Jewish settlements (in Israeli parlance, "neighborhoods") established on lands captured by Israel in June 1967 in the former Jordanian sector of East Jerusalem and adjacent areas of the West Bank that were incorporated unilaterally by Israel into the "reunified" city's expanded municipal boundaries. By 2006 as much as 39 percent of Jerusalem's Jewish population resided in the areas captured in June 1967.

The Clinton parameters aimed to create a Palestinian state with borders closely approximating those between Israel and the occupied territories prior to June 1967, consistent with the PLO's watered-down formula of self-determination since the late 1980s and UN Security Council resolutions 242 and 338. It aimed at a human and moral acknowledgment of Palestinian dispossession and suffering since 1948 while regulating the Palestinian right of return in a way that would not be seen as fundamentally threatening by Israel. To Palestinians, such an acknowledgment of their exodus and subsequent exclusion from their historic homeland—in glaring contrast to the right since 1950 of Jews from anywhere in the world to enter and live as citizens in the 78 percent of Mandate Palestine that became Israel—is a *sine qua non* of any permanent compromise with Israel. The parameters also sought to break the logjam on Jerusalem by taking a decisive stance in favor of two capitals in the city. The parameters made it clear that the Palestinian state must have sovereignty over the overwhelmingly Palestinian-populated urban and historical heart of East Jerusalem as well as those parts of the old city that carry deep resonance for Palestinians, Christian as well as Muslim, and for the Arab and Muslim worlds.

In other words, the Palestinian claim to Jerusalem could not be marginalized to outer suburbs like Abu Dis—a neighborhood now cut in two by the separation/security wall—nor fobbed off with vague formulae of "autonomy" under continuing Israeli rule for inner-city Palestinian neighborhoods of East Jerusalem and/or parts of the old city. The creation of two capitals in Jerusalem in a meaningful and equitable sense must accompany any two-state solution to the Israeli-Palestinian conflict.

Ian Lustick argued during the first months of the Oslo process that "redefining Jerusalem" is essential to solving the tussle over the city. After capturing the walled old city, East Jerusalem, and the West Bank in June 1967, Israel declared not only the six square kilometers of Jordanian-held East Jerusalem but an additional 64 square kilometers, covering an area of the West Bank dotted with numerous Palestinian townships and villages, as comprising the "reunified" city that would, along with thirty-eight square kilometers of West Jerusalem, be its eternal, undivided capital. While Palestinians in the West Bank and Gaza were subjected to military occupation, those within Jerusalem's expanded boundaries were subjected to a different regime—they were ostensibly not under occupation, could claim some social benefits from Israel, and could vote in the city's municipal elections. This attempt to envelop expanded Jerusalem's Palestinian population under Israeli hegemony has proved to be a resounding failure. Benvenisti puts it bluntly: The slogan of "unified Jerusalem was nothing but a forcibly imposed fiction . . . [a mish-mash of] propaganda and wishful thinking." In fact Jerusalem is divided, broadly along a meandering seam separating west from east, into Jewish and Arab sectors between which there is little, if any, traffic, commerce, contact, or communication. Two parallel societies exist side by side but quite separately and very unequally in one urban environment. After the eruption of the first intifada this seam became the axis of a "geography of fear." Lustick noted in late 1993, "Most Jewish taxi drivers will not

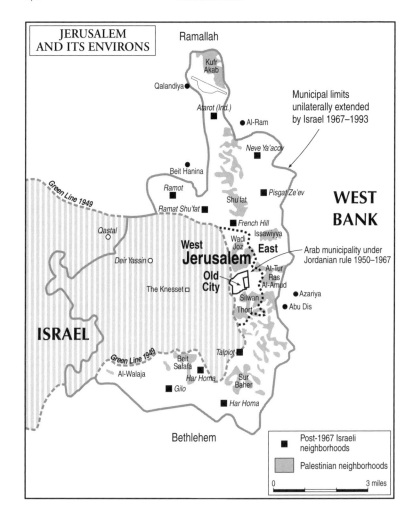

JERUSALEM AND ITS ENVIRONS

Ramallah

Kufr Akab

Qalandiya

Atarot (Ind.)

Al-Ram

Municipal limits unilaterally extended by Israel 1967–1993

Neve Ya'acov

Beit Hanina

Ramot

Pisgat Ze'ev

WEST BANK

Shu'fat

Ramat Shu'fat

French Hill

Qastal

Issawiyya

West

Wadi Joz

Jerusalem **East**

Arab municipality under Jordanian rule 1950–1967

Deir Yassin

Old City

At-Tur

Ras Al-Amud

The Knesset

Azariya

Silwan

Abu Dis

Thori

ISRAEL

Green Line 1949

Talpiot

Beit Safafa

Al-Walaja

Har Homa

Sur Baher

Gilo

Har Homa

Bethlehem

Green Line 1949

Deir Yassin

■ Post-1967 Israeli neighborhoods

▨ Palestinian neighborhoods

0   3 miles

accept fares to the Arab neighborhoods and villages within Greater East Jerusalem, except for one or two locations immediately accessible to Jewish Jerusalem. In their ordinary calculations Israelis consider those districts part of the West Bank," the official administrative distinction notwithstanding. The geography of fear dividing Jerusalem was entrenched by the second intifada. Menachem Klein noted in 2004, "West Jerusalem taxi drivers refuse to take passengers to the eastern city except for the American Colony Hotel, which is on the seam and considered neutral territory." Michael Dumper observed in 2002 that in the Palestinian parts of the divided city, "the only elements of the Israeli state that are visible are the restrictive planning laws and the security forces." In 1992 the last city budget submitted by the long-serving and relatively liberal mayor Teddy Kollek—he was defeated by the right-wing Likud challenger Ehud Olmert in November 1993—allocated just 6 percent to the Palestinian areas; per capita expenditure in the Palestinian areas was $150 compared to $900 in the Jewish areas.[78]

In the 1993 municipal election, held shortly after the beginning of the peace process, just 5 percent of Jerusalem's Palestinian electorate exercised their right to vote. The figure in 1989, during the first intifada, was even lower at 3 percent. In the autumn of 2005 the Jerusalem Institute for Israel Studies estimated Jerusalem's population at 706,000 residents, of whom 469,000 were Jews (one-third ultra-Orthodox) and 237,000 were Palestinians. Almost all of the Palestinians who are 34 percent of Jerusalem's population live in neighborhoods and townships where there are no Jews (or next to none), except for about two thousand ideologically motivated settlers who have established residence in enclaves in their midst, such as the Silwan neighborhood immediately southeast of the old city. In 1997 the old city of Jerusalem had 31,551 residents, most of whom—22,086—lived in the Muslim Quarter. The Muslim Quarter had an overwhelming majority of Muslim inhabitants, 20,653 of 22,086. Merely 140 Jews lived in the Christian Quarter, the second most populous, along with 3,830 Christians and 892 Muslims. Overall, the old city's 31,551 residents included 22,188 Muslims, 6,290 Christians, and just 3,073 Jews.[79]

The Clinton parameters responded to demographic and political realities on the ground and balanced religious sensitivities in a pragmatic formula that sought to solve the Jerusalem problem by redefining it, rejecting in the process both the maximalist Israeli

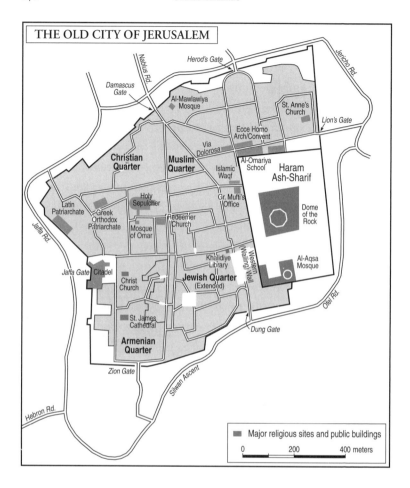

THE OLD CITY OF JERUSALEM

claim and a return to the pre–June 1967 situation. The Palestinians
would have a proper capital in Jerusalem encompassing its Palestinian areas and the Muslim and Christian Quarters of the old city together with the Haram al-Sharif, while Israel would acquire sovereignty recognized by the world over not just the old city's Jewish
Quarter and the Western Wall but also areas captured in 1967 that
have subsequently been populated with Jews. The latter would take
in such neighborhoods as Gilo in southern Jerusalem—which
overlooks the West Bank Palestinian town of Beit Jala and is home

to forty thousand Israelis—as well as, most likely, the large West Bank Jewish settlement of Maaleh Adumim, which lies just east of Palestinian East Jerusalem. The Oslo process's policy of putting the Jerusalem issue in cold storage, along with the other core issues of borders and refugees, almost certainly had the effect of exacerbating tension and conflict in and over the city in the 1990s and beyond. A solution whereby Palestine would gain a proper capital, al-Quds, and Israel world recognition—missing so far—of *its* Jerusalem as Israel's capital would be both a necessary condition for and an inevitable outcome of Israeli-Palestinian peace.

The prospects of that peace depend on four factors.

  1. Rashid Khalidi writes that "only a dispassionate, fair and impartial arbiter can help bring the two sides to mutually acceptable terms" and argues that "if there is to be peace between Palestinians and Israelis the US must begin to act in this fashion, or it must allow another [third] party to do so." It is indeed difficult to exaggerate the importance of such an evenhanded and assertive U.S. role to the prospects of Israeli-Palestinian rapprochement. The United States has not always been aligned with Israel, and the Israeli tail has not always wagged the American dog. As Khalidi observes, "Until the mid-1960s the United States acted more as an honest broker in the [Arab-Israeli] conflict than as a dedicated ally of Israel."[80] Palestinians recall that era with nostalgia. In the words of Haidar Abd al-Shafi:

> I remember Israel's occupation of Gaza during the Suez invasion in 1956. It was clear that they were engaged in long-term planning, that they intended to stay. When the UN passed resolutions calling for withdrawal France and Britain withdrew immediately from the canal area and Israel began slowly to withdraw from the parts of Sinai it had occupied. But they made no move to withdraw from Gaza and when President

Eisenhower sent a letter to Ben-Gurion asking why Israel did
not withdraw Ben-Gurion had the gall not to reply. But then
Eisenhower wrote a second letter threatening sanctions, and
Israel withdrew in one night. That night we went to bed to the
noise of armored cars roaming the streets, and woke up the
next morning to find no trace of the Israelis in the Strip. It
took a president with a moral fiber to get them out.[81]

There are those who argue that the Israeli-Palestinian conflict
and the Palestinian question are not central to peace and stability in
the Middle East.[82] But an important fact remains, and is well expressed by Dennis Ross:

Solving . . . the Arab-Israeli conflict would not make our
problems in the Middle East disappear. It would not suddenly
end terror . . . It would not be the panacea . . . But it would remove a cause [of unrest and violence] that remains more evo-
cative than any other in the region, and it would undo or miti-
gate one of the greatest sources of resentment easily exploited
by radical Islamists.[83]

That is a compelling incentive for U.S. policy.

2. Commenting on Israel's 2005 disengagement from the Gaza
Strip, columnist Rami Khouri wrote in Lebanon's *Daily Star* newspaper, "Israel is doing the right thing, but perhaps for the wrong
reasons. It is a shame that so few voices in Israel or among the Jewish community around the world come out and say in clear terms
that Israel is leaving because occupation is illegal, morally wrong
and politically counter-productive, or [because] the Palestinians
have the right to live in freedom, independence and national dignity."[84]

Israeli moves in the direction of a two-state solution are increasingly justified simply on the basis of two Israeli compulsions: en-

hancing the security of Israel's citizens from terror, and protecting the Jewish demographic majority in Israel. The latter concern stems from the fact that Arabs (Palestinians and Israel's Arab citizens combined) already account for at least 47 percent of the population of historic Palestine, the land between the Mediterranean Sea and the Jordan River, and according to most demographic projections will become a majority within the next decade.[85] So unless Israel separates itself from the occupied territories, a scenario of a Jewish minority oppressing an Arab majority is likely to materialize in the near future. Just before the July 2000 Camp David summit Barak argued that the "alternative . . . [to] physical separation [and an] independent Palestinian entity . . . is a bi-national state prone to conflicts and internal rifts as in Belfast [sic] and Bosnia, or an . . . ostracized apartheid state [run by a hegemonic Jewish minority]."[86] There is nothing inherently wrong with Israeli policy being driven by such perceptions about security and demographic "threats"; after all, each side's agenda in any peace process is driven by its own motives. Yet the extraordinary degree of self-absorption that has come to dominate even the thinking of many, if not most, pro-rapprochement Israelis implies a studied disregard and lack of acknowledgment of the powerful legitimacy of Palestinian national rights and aspirations, above all their right to self-determination in a sovereign state on minimally equitable terms. This breeds an Israeli attitude dominated by condescension and contempt toward the Palestinians, which is clearly detrimental to prospects of minimally equitable accommodation. Just as it takes two hands to clap, it takes two parties who acknowledge each other's claims in a spirit of equality and mutuality to make peace. The discourse of a successful peace process must be framed in terms of the acknowledgment and realization of inalienable Palestinian rights, not just Israeli fears and unavoidable compulsions that produce reluctant "concessions" to a weak and undeserving enemy despised and feared at the same time.

The as-yet unrealized Israeli longing to become a "normal"

country provides a compelling incentive for such an approach. It has always been "one of the professed aims of the Zionist movement that Israel should take its place alongside the other nations of the world, that it should become normal, 'like unto the nations' [in Ben-Gurion's phrase]."[87] One dimension of becoming "normal"— a society freed from the routinized but oppressive tension and fear caused by the undisarmed specter of terrorism—depends on a real peace with the Palestinians. But so does another vital dimension— becoming a normal member of the international community. In the autumn of 2003 the UN general assembly voted on two motions, calling on Israel not to deport or kill Arafat, and to suspend the construction of its security/separation barrier vis-à-vis the West Bank's Palestinians. The first motion was passed by 133 to 4 votes, the second by 141 to 4 votes. In both instances the naysayers were the United States and Israel itself, along with two tiny Pacific island entities that are U.S. dependencies, Micronesia and the Marshall Islands. Israel cannot become "normal" as long as this level of isolation continues, and as long as it does not command widespread support and respect anywhere in the world outside the United States.

3. It is important for the United States, Israel, and the formerly hegemonic Fatah officialdom of the Palestinian Authority to recognize that "a meaningful and inclusive Palestinian national unity is necessary for a negotiated [Israeli-Palestinian] peace." In practical terms this implies the co-optation of Hamas into the Palestinian political process and its institutions and at least indirectly into any resuscitated peace process with Israel. Many seasoned observers agreed even before Hamas won an absolute majority of seats in the Palestinian parliament in January 2006 that the movement, with its extensive activities conducted through its social welfare, political, and armed wings, had become too significant an actor among Palestinians—even as Fatah declined and fragmented—to be repressed, ignored, or wished away. Mahmoud Abbas (Abu Mazen), the PA's

president, who is recognized as well intentioned and moderate even by many hard-line Israelis, apparently agreed too. Through 2005 Hamas performed strongly in Palestinian local elections, not just in its stronghold in the Gaza Strip, the cradle of the movement, but also in the West Bank, where it won resoundingly in cities like Nablus and towns like Qalqiliya. In early 2006 it took 74 of the Palestinian parliament's 132 seats. The triumph was sweeping; Hamas won handsomely not just in places where it was expected to do well, like religious-minded Hebron, but also in Ramallah, regarded as a bastion of secularists and leftists. In a sense the Oslo process came full circle with the Hamas victory.[88]

Hamas contains hard-liners and pragmatists, and its leaders in the West Bank and Gaza usually speak in a more moderate tone than its officials based "outside," in other Arab countries. The movement's ideological stance—which holds that "the land of Palestine is an Islamic *waqf* [endowment held in trust] to all Muslim generations until the day of resurrection [and] it is not right to give up any part of it" and that "there is no solution to the Palestinian problem except by Jihad"—coexists with a stated strategic willingness to abide by a *hudna,* a long-term "interim" truce with Israel lasting up to fifty years, if a Palestinian state is created according to the pre–June 1967 borders with East Jerusalem as its capital. The *hudna* concept and its terms were reiterated in May 2006 by Ismail Haniyeh, the Hamas leader who is the PA's prime minister, in an interview granted to an Israeli newspaper. A former chief of Mossad, Ephraim Halevy, then broke ranks with the Israeli security and political establishment to suggest that Israel should not rule out negotiating such a long-term cease-fire with Hamas.[89]

The Hamas charter also asserts that the relationship of Hamas to the PLO "is that of a son toward his father, a brother toward his brother," emphasizing a spirit of solidarity and coexistence despite differences of ideology and strategy. As the one-party-dominant system presided over by Arafat has given way to two major move-

ments competing for popular support and the spoils of office, stable
power-sharing arrangements between Fatah and Hamas have become essential. After the Israeli withdrawal from Gaza it was reported that "Hamas' short-term confidence is coupled with a sense
of the Palestinians' strategic weakness . . . nervousness . . . and
a feeling that Palestinians would do better with a government of
national unity." Israel of course has a well-established tradition of
such national unity governments. Fatah rejected the idea of such a
formal coalition with Hamas after the latter's victory in the parliamentary election, but the negotiation of effective power-sharing
arrangements is both inevitable and urgent. The urgency was underscored by sporadic eruptions of violence in Gaza during the first
half of 2006 between Hamas and Fatah loyalists, sparked by stand-
offs over which side will control and administer the Palestinian police and security agencies.[90]

A Fatah-Hamas modus vivendi is also important to prospects
of an Israeli-Palestinian rapprochement. The pragmatist Hamas
perspective was expressed in the autumn of 2005 by Professor
Mohammed Ghazal, its political leader in the West Bank city of
Nablus, just before his arrest along with several hundred other West
Bank Islamist activists by Israel. "The [Hamas] charter is not the
Koran," he said, "[and while] we believe that all of Palestine belongs
to Palestinians, the reality is different and we are talking about reality, about political solutions." He added that it was premature to
recognize Israel when "Israel doesn't recognize me as the victim"
but asserted that Hamas was not in principle against negotiations
with Israel. Mahmoud al-Zahar, the top Hamas political leader in
the territories after the assassination of the movement's founder,
Sheikh Ahmad Yassin, and others like Abd al-Aziz Rantissi and
Ismail Abu Shanab by Israeli forces, said in the autumn of 2005 that
Hamas would not obstruct PA talks with Israel if they focused on
speedy Israeli withdrawal from the West Bank.[91]

In May 2006 it came to light that a group of prominent Palestinian political prisoners held by Israel had reached a consensus on Palestinian national aims and strategy. The document they negotiated was signed by members of five groups—including a representative of Islamic Jihad, who expressed "reservations." But the two key signatories were Fatah's most popular West Bank leader, Marwan Barghouti, and Sheikh Abdel-Khaliq Natsheh, a senior Hamas figure from Hebron. Barghouti, who as leader of Fatah's *tanzeem* militia was a key organizer of the second intifada, apparently drafted the document, which was revised during talks. The document defined the central Palestinian aim as the "establish[ment of] an independent state with holy Jerusalem as its capital on all the territories occupied in 1967" and asserted a strategy of "confining resistance [to] the territories occupied in 1967, in addition to political, negotiating and diplomatic action." Abbas then announced that he would call a national referendum on this document if Hamas's leadership did not accept it within ten days, to which the latter responded that they would not capitulate to ultimatums and pressure tactics.

Regardless of the significance of the "prisoners' initiative," peace processes benefit from, and peace settlements generally require, broad-based support on all sides of the divide, and co-optation is a sensible way of politically disarming potential spoilers in some circumstances. It is not possible to marginalize, repress, or ignore Hamas. There is a thus a compelling case for "seeking ways of adding Hamas to the peace equation" between Israel and the Palestinians.[92]

4. To be fruitful, a renewed quest for Israeli-Palestinian peace will require a decisive approach to resolving the core issues at some point in the near future. This means that the gradualist, indeed snail-like, approach of the international community's April 2003 "road map" will not suffice and will need to be superseded. In any case Israelis and Palestinians have very different interpretations of the fifty-two paragraphs of the roadmap, particularly regarding the

most divisive issues, such as Israeli settlement activity and Palestinian terrorism. Gradualism has had its day in the Israeli-Palestinian peace process. The fundamental issues will need to be decisively tackled and equitably resolved, even if implementation of agreed-upon solutions is somewhat staggered over time.

There is no alternative to a two-state solution to the Israeli-Palestinian conflict. The idea of a single, binational state in historic Palestine has articulate and even inspiring proponents. Meron Benvenisti has argued for a binational model based on confederation of predominantly Jewish and predominantly Arab regions and power sharing at the center, following the consociational approach. The late Edward Said wrote, "Israelis and Palestinians are too intertwined in history, experience and actuality to separate, even through each proclaims the need for separate statehood and will in fact have it. The challenge is to find a peaceful way to co-exist . . . as equal citizens in the same land." Rashid Khalidi writes more cautiously that "it may be . . . that a completely new approach will have to be found, since Israeli actions have rendered a two-state solution all but obsolete" (he refers above all to the 420,000 settlers in the West Bank and the areas in and around Jerusalem occupied by Israel since June 1967).[93]

The binational idea has a long lineage. It was advocated, even if halfheartedly, by some leaders of the Yishuv in the 1920s and by minority factions in the socialist Zionist movement in the 1930s and 1940s. Walter Laqueur's monumental history of Zionism concludes on the quixotic note that "the bi-national solution . . . would have been in every respect a better solution for the Palestine problem [than partition]." Yet as Benvenisti concedes, "turning Israel/Palestine into a bi-national state is unacceptable to both sides . . . [and] there is no chance of such an idea becoming the focus of concrete political discourse." The reasons are crystal clear. First, the history of conflict between the two peoples over the past one hundred years makes a binational state look like a fantasy. Second, the idea violates the core of the doctrine of self-determination of both peoples. The vast majority of Jews have striven for and remain absolutely committed to a *Jewish* state, while the mirror-image aspiration overwhelmingly dominant among Palestinians is to have their own state—territorially at least minimally coherent, internationally recognized, and with a foothold in Jerusalem. Much recent Palestinian and pro-Palestinian advocacy in favor of the binational idea smacks of posturing and tactical point-scoring.[94] The continuous settling of land occupied in June 1967 by Jews has made a two-state solution—the only feasible way of addressing the conflict—that does not yield a moth-eaten Palestinian state very difficult and complicated but not impossible. There is simply no alternative to salvaging the most equitable two-state solution that is possible from the ruins of the peace process.

Yet it is true that Israel and the occupied territories "share the same aquifers, the same highway network, the same electricity grid and the same international borders." And "there are both Jews and Palestinians who dream of Israel/Palestine undivided in its physical and human landscapes, pluralistic and open, a country in which cultural relations, human interaction, intimate coexistence and attachment to a common homeland will be stronger than militant tribalism and segregation in national ghettos." That points to the necessity, indeed inevitability, of cooperation cutting across the borders between Israel and Palestine. Such cooperation, embedded in broader cooperative ties across the region surrounding the contested land, was visualized in the September 1993 declaration of principles. The problem with the vision, as Benvenisti wrote in 1995, was that "'cooperation' based on the current power relationship is no more than Israeli domination in disguise, and Palestinian self-rule merely an euphemism for bantustanization." Building networks of cross-border and transregional cooperation provide the long-term anchor of stability for peace settlements, but are not a substitute for such settlements and can be fully realized only after a minimally equitable and mutually acceptable solution to the conflict.[95]

Such a solution will not be a panacea for the acute asymmetry of the Israeli-Palestinian relationship. In 1991 the economy of the West Bank and Gaza was just 5 percent of the size of Israel's economy, and occupied Palestinians were extremely dependent on access to the lower echelons of the Israeli labor market. Fifteen years and much water under the bridge later, the chic bars and cafes of West Jerusalem's German Colony neighborhood, popular with affluent young Israelis, are a short distance but a world apart from the poverty and squalor of the Qalandiya refugee camp on Jerusalem's outskirts, where young Palestinians struggle with despair. In 1999 Barak, Israel's prime minister, described the Palestinians' military capability in relation to Israel's as "ludicrous."[96]

Yet a minimally equitable peace agreement would represent a beginning to a new era in Israeli-Palestinian relations. The concept of a shared homeland, under two interlinked sovereignties, is likely to grow and not diminish in relevance in the future. That is not only because the more than 3.8 million Palestinians in the West Bank, Gaza, and East Jerusalem (2.3 million, 1.3 million, and 230,000-plus, respectively) and the 5.2 million-plus Jews of the State of Israel inhabit a compressed geographical space. It is also because the State of Israel contains a large minority of Arab citizens—a million and a quarter people, at least 18 percent of the population, the survivors and descendants of survivors of the nakba—who have faced a long and arduous struggle over the decades for their rights in the face of the repressive and discriminatory policies of the Jewish state. The vast majority of "Israeli Arabs" describe their national identity as "Palestinian." Some of these Palestinian citizens of Israel became peripherally involved in the first intifada in the occupied territories, and at the outset of the second intifada thirteen of them were killed by Israeli police while demonstrating in northern Israel in solidarity with their compatriots' uprising. Bernard Wasserstein is right when he predicts that despite the construction of the "anti-Arab dike"—the separation/security barrier, which he says is "dubious as a security device and a monstrous environmental scar across the landscape" of Israel/Palestine—"separation is unlikely to be hermetic or permanent . . . the self-interest of both sides is likely in the end to dictate a soft border rather than a new Berlin Wall in the Middle East."[97]

Benvenisti writes that "Israeli-Palestinian reconciliation is still a dream."[98] But then life—whether individual or collective—without dreams is just a barren emptiness.

Conclusion

Competing claims to territory lie at the heart of each of the ethnonational conflicts studied in this book. While the fixation with control of territory that characterizes deeply divided countries and regions may seem myopic and even anachronistic in the context of an increasingly interconnected world, devising broadly acceptable solutions to the territorial dispute is the central challenge of peace processes and the linchpin of peace settlements.

That is easier said than done. The drawing of stable borders between ethnonational communities through negotiation and compromise is rarely simple and almost always hotly contested between the parties to the conflict.

In Sri Lanka virtually the entire spectrum of Tamil opinion is united behind the Tamil Tigers in demanding very extensive powers of self-rule for the Tamil-dominated north and east of the country, the region defined by Tamil autonomy movements since the 1950s as the Tamils' "traditional homeland." The bulk of Sri Lanka's Sinhalese majority are either lukewarm or hostile to this demand even after two decades of debilitating and bloody civil war. They balk at the prospect of rewarding what they view as a relentless Tamil campaign of terrorism—which is regarded as a glorious

liberation struggle by most Tamils—and point to the existence of
sizable non-Tamil minorities on the territory of the Tamil "homeland" and of a significant Tamil minority outside the territory of
the putative self-rule region. Many Sinhalese are outright opposed
to the radical institutional surgery needed to transform Sri Lanka
into a federal polity, and even Sinhalese supporters of a federal-style
solution cringe at the scope of self-rule demanded by the Tiger-led
Tamils. The divide between the unitary and centralized state whose
continuation is favored, at most with cosmetic changes, by Sinhalese majoritarian nationalists and the decentralized state sought by
Tamils is conceptually unbridgeable; the divide between the moderately devolved state (of the type found in Spain or the United
Kingdom) favored by Sinhalese doves and the loose confederation
(on the lines of post-Dayton Bosnia or the blueprint proposed
for Cyprus by the UN's Annan Plan) sought by Tamils is conceptually bridgeable but prone to practical difficulties of negotiation and
implementation that could be fatal to the chances of peaceful resolution.

In Cyprus the Green Line that divides the northern Turkish
Cypriot entity from the Greek Cypriot south in a 37:63 ratio is
seen by most Greek Cypriots as an illegal and illegitimate border
erected by the Turkish military invasion of 1974 that led to the
uprooting of over one-third of the Greek Cypriot community,
165,000 people, from their homes in towns and villages occupied
by the invader. Turkish Cypriots, by contrast, see the 1974 Turkish
invasion as the inevitable culmination of Greek Cypriot attitudes
and actions that threatened not just the political status and rights
but the very existence of the Turkish Cypriot minority, and they
view the maintenance of a self-governing Turkish Cypriot statelet
over a part of the island's territory as the essential guarantee of security and political equality. The yawning chasm between the two
sides' perceptions of an equitable settlement was laid bare in 2004
when over three-fourths of Greek Cypriots voted down the UN-

engineered Annan Plan—which proposed a confederation of two ethnonational statelets on a loosely united island—while almost two-thirds of Turkish Cypriots approved the plan.

In Bosnia the nature of the Dayton settlement has been the focus of intense and often bitter controversy for over a decade. Bosnian Muslims, the single largest ethnonational group in the country, tend to view the November 1995 agreement's recognition of an autonomous "Serb Republic" covering almost one-half of Bosnia's territory as deeply unjust, a reward to the systematic "ethnic cleansing" of hundreds of thousands of non-Serbs, mainly Muslims, from those areas during the 1992–1995 war. Bosnian Serbs, by contrast, tend to regard their self-governing statelet within Bosnia as minimal restitution for the grave injustice inflicted on their community by the destruction of the federal, multinational state of Yugoslavia—primarily caused, according to them, by Croat, Slovene, and Muslim secessionism shortsightedly sanctioned by key Western countries and European and Euro-Atlantic institutions. The polarization between Bosnia's two largest ethnonational groups endures more than a decade after the war and is compounded by the sense of grievance felt by many Bosnian Croats, the third group, with the delicate compromise engineered by robust American diplomacy at Dayton, Ohio.

India and Pakistan have contested sovereignty over Kashmir since 1947. India regards the insurgency that has gripped Indian-controlled Kashmir since 1990 as primarily a problem of "cross-border terrorism" fomented from and by Pakistan, while Pakistan views the conflict as stemming from Indian occupation of a predominantly Muslim population since 1947 aggravated by India's repressive counterinsurgency policies since 1990. The sharply conflicting stances on the Line of Control that separates Indian-controlled Kashmir from the smaller and less populous Pakistani-controlled Kashmir illustrate the zero-sum character of the dispute. Since the mid-1950s Indian leaderships have, while not giving up the formal claim to "Pakistan-occupied Kashmir," expressed a preference for resolving the territorial dispute by converting the LOC into a de jure international border between India and Pakistan. Pakistani leaderships have flatly rejected the Indian preference for recognizing the territorial status quo and instead emphasized the need for an internationally administered plebiscite across disputed Kashmir to decide rightful sovereignty, the exercise to ascertain the "will of the people" that was supposed to be held during the first decade of the dispute but never materialized. Pakistani leaderships have always underscored that the choice presented to the people of Kashmir in any sovereignty referendum should be India or Pakistan, ruling out of the agenda the "third option" of independence that appeals to much of Kashmir's population. In reality, Pakistani leaders have known for several decades that any plebiscite is an extremely remote possibility, and their actual first preference has probably been a redrawing of the LOC in a way that would incorporate more of Kashmir's territory and population into Pakistan. This revisionist preference for altering borders in Kashmir has in turn always been and continues to be unacceptable to Indians. For its part the significant pro-independence segment of Kashmir's population, which exists on both sides of the LOC, regards the LOC as an imposition, an artificial border that divides their homeland. Their "pox on both your houses" stance cements a triangular impasse that is intractable and unstable at the same time.

The history of the Israeli-Palestinian conflict is that of a zero-sum struggle between Arabs and Jews for control of Palestine waged over the past one hundred years, ever since the birth of Zionism as an ideology among a segment of Central and Eastern European Jews. The program of the Zionist movement, based on the immigration of more and more Jewish settlers into Palestine with the aim of creating a "national home" there for Jews—thinly veiled code for a sovereign Jewish state—was quite understandably seen as a mortal threat by the Arabs who were a 92 percent majority in

Palestine at the end of World War I and a two-thirds majority in 1948, the year of reckoning between the incompatible visions and aspirations of the two communities. Since 1948 Palestinians have viewed the conflict through the lens of the nakba—the catastrophe of the Jews' victory and the fulfillment of the Zionist enterprise through the formation of the State of Israel on 77 percent of Palestine, which led to the permanent displacement of seven hundred thousand Arab Palestinians from their homeland. To Palestinians and other Arabs the injustice of 1948 has been compounded by the occupation since 1967 of the rest of Palestine and its population by Israel, and the implantation of several hundred thousand settlers in those occupied territories. Israel has viewed the conflict as an unending struggle first for survival and then for security—initially against the hostility of Arab states, then against the movement of the dispossessed of 1948 (and their descendants) represented by the PLO, and most recently against the suicide bombers produced by the occupied population.

This book has shown that the imperative of crafting peace necessitates that the borders drawn in blood through contested lands become the basis of compromise between antagonistic peoples—*but* with important caveats.

Thus Chapter 1 has demonstrated that in Sri Lanka the termination of armed conflict and the forging of durable peace require that the war zone, the north and east, become an autonomous region with extensive self-rule powers within a restructured Sri Lankan polity. But self-rule for Tamils must be accompanied and balanced by guaranteed representation and an effective voice in decision making in self-rule institutions for non-Tamils (principally Muslims) who live in the north and especially the east, *and* by the incorporation of Tamils into reconfigured Sri Lankan federal institutions in a meaningful and effective way through an upper chamber of the federal parliament constituted as a "house of peoples," following the principle of robust bicameralism characteristic of federal systems. In short, the imperative of encouraging coexistence and enabling cooperation must never be lost sight of. The principle of "shared rule," which along with self-rule is constitutive of federalism, is the key tool here and should be institutionalized at both federal and regional levels of government in Sri Lanka. Autonomy does not imply, let alone equal, segregation. Socioeconomic and other drivers make it inevitable that the border between the north and east and the rest of Sri Lanka will be thoroughly porous.

In Cyprus the UN's comprehensive peace plan proposed ethnically defined Greek Cypriot and Turkish Cypriot "constituent states" on an island reunified as a confederation, where the Greek Cypriot constituent state would cover 72 percent of the island and the Turkish Cypriot constituent state 28 percent (altering the post-1974 63:37 ratio in favor of the Greek Cypriots). The swath of territory north of the Green Line earmarked for transfer to the Greek Cypriot entity covered the hometowns and villages of almost three-quarters of the Greek Cypriots who became refugees as a result of the 1974 Turkish invasion, while the rest of the refugee population and their descendants were to be eligible for an elaborate compensation scheme. The UN's plan also proposed the establishment of common institutions—on the basis of consociational norms of shared decision making and equality between the ethnonational communities—for the limited central government of the umbrella state of Cyprus, which would be incorporated into the framework of the European Union as one country. As Chapter 2 explains, the plan failed to pass muster with the Greek Cypriots partly because of that community's mutually reinforcing syndromes of historic grievance and contemporary contentment and partly because the two tracks of international engagement with Cyprus—the UN and the EU—ended up working at cross-purposes and the Greek Cypriot south was assured of the benefits of EU membership without a settlement to the ethnonational conflict. Indeed, this latter factor gave Greek Cypriots a perverse incentive to block the settlement and "punish" both the Turkish Cypriots, who were eager to break their isolation, and their patron, Turkey, which was eager to advance its own EU prospects by getting the Cyprus problem out of the way. Yet any settlement to the imbroglio that may materialize during the next few years is very likely to be within the parameters established by the Annan Plan.

In Bosnia the Dayton settlement recognized a largely self-governing Bosnian Serb statelet across almost half of the war-torn country and also gave Bosnian Croats cantonal and municipal autonomy in some parts of the rest of Bosnia. The U.S.-sponsored settlement's confederal design was very probably a major influence—even if unacknowledged—on the architects of the UN's eerily similar Cyprus plan. The division of Bosnia into entities (and cantons) largely followed, with limited modifications, the maze of fracture lines drawn across Bosnia during the bloodbath of 1992–1995. Yet the Dayton settlement balanced the recognition of ethnonational autonomy with a vigorous affirmation of the right of all victims of "ethnic cleansing" to return to and reclaim their homes. In the decade since Dayton about 450,000 refugees and internally displaced persons of all three nationalities have, with the essential assistance of the large international peacebuilding operation in postwar Bosnia, returned to places that are now dominated demographically and politically by members of another ethnonational community. This figure, substantial for a small country of about 3.5 million people, includes 160,000 Bosnian Muslim returnees to the Bosnian Serb entity. Under international supervision, the precarious confederation engineered in late 1995 has made significant, if difficult, progress toward becoming a viable tri-national federal state. The competencies and capacities of institutions at the level of the umbrella state, threadbare in the immediate aftermath of the war, have been expanded and strengthened, and a decade after Dayton Bosnia is poised to embark on its journey to the EU, membership in which is an aspiration shared across Bosnia's ethno-national divides. That journey to long-term security and relative prosperity will take the best part of another decade, but as Chapter 3 concludes, Bosnia is in some ways a relatively successful case of international peacebuilding.

In Kashmir the establishment of self-rule regimes in both Indian-controlled and Pakistani-controlled Kashmir—particularly in Indian-controlled Kashmir, the arena of armed conflict—is the basis of any serious settlement. Both sets of self-rule authorities and the regions they govern will remain under the respective sovereignties of India and Pakistan. So the Line of Control will endure (although most probably with a different name) but its character must be transformed—from an iron curtain to a linen curtain, from a barrier to a bridge. This implies not just the free movement of people across a soft border but the institutionalization of wide-ranging ties of cross-border cooperation between the autonomous governments of Indian-controlled Kashmir and Pakistani-controlled Kashmir. In short, the LOC must be transcended without being abolished. Such a combination of robust autonomy and systematic cross-border linkages is the only way of reconciling, however uneasily, the three contending nation-state perspectives on Kashmir and their adherents within the disputed territory. As Chapter 4 argues, these arrangements must be complemented by devolution of power to regions within Indian-controlled Kashmir, given its social and political diversity, as well as by power sharing in Indian-controlled Kashmir's government during a transitional period between representatives of the pro-independence, pro-Indian, and pro-Pakistani segments of identity and allegiance (and between pro-Pakistan and pro-independence segments in Pakistani-controlled Kashmir).

The Israeli-Palestinian conflict can be defused only by the establishment of a sovereign Palestinian state alongside Israel. In Chapter 5, where I lay out the historical context of the conflict and chart the fate of the 1993–2000 peace process, I conclude that a minimally equitable two-state solution represents the sole viable formula for a settlement. To be consistent with norms of international legality as well as of minimal equity, the borders of the Palestinian state must approximate the pre–June 1967 borders between Israel and the subsequently occupied territories. Any land in the West Bank and Jerusalem annexed to Israel as part of a final-status agreement in order to accommodate Jewish settlements and their inhabitants must be substantially compensated by a reciprocal transfer of Israeli territory to the Palestinian state. Sovereignty over 22 percent of pre-1948 Palestine is the least owed by Israel and the international community to Palestinians after nearly six decades of statelessness. The settlement must ensure that Jerusalem is split equitably between the two states in order to accommodate two national capitals in the city, in the manner explained in Chapter 5. And Israel must acknowledge in principle the suffering caused by the Palestinians' 1948 dispossession, without accepting anything more than a very limited actual Palestinian right of return to the State of Israel. A settlement along these lines was suggested by the Clinton parameters of December 2000 and would be acceptable to the vast majority of Palestinians. In the aftermath of such a settlement the September 1993 Israeli-PLO declaration's vision of Israeli-Palestinian and broader regional cooperation in a variety of fields will become a vision built on some foundation rather than wishful thinking. The states of Israel and Palestine will hardly become substantive equals even after such a settlement, given their enormous military and economic disparities, but a vital step toward a more stable Middle East will still be accomplished. It is very true that Israelis and Palestinians are in many ways "intimate enemies"—the well-chosen title of a book on the conflict—and that a compelling case for cooperative links exists.

Because the cases studied in this book are of a generic type—ethnonational conflicts rooted in clashing ideologies and agendas of collective "self-determination"—it is logical that the nature of the solutions also conform to a pattern. Those solutions involve in varying combinations territorial autonomy (in the specific case of the Palestinians, full sovereignty) and federal and consociational structures as the bedrock of peace settlements. The longer-term guarantee for such settlements lies in anchoring them in a web of cooperative relationships that unite the antagonistic peoples and the wider regions they inhabit. The first building block of that web is cooperation across the dividing lines forged by war and institutionalized by peace. Wider transnational networks of cooperation and integration that enshrine regional economic and security alliances are a further bulwark.

So war-torn Sri Lanka and divided Kashmir need to be enveloped within a framework of South Asian regional cooperation, fractured Bosnia and its neighbors Serbia and Croatia as well as a reunified Cyprus (and in the future Turkey) within the EU, and the states of Israel and Palestine within a cooperative regional framework that encompasses the neighboring states of Jordan and Egypt. The borders, at once political and psychological, that divide the contested lands of Sri Lanka, Cyprus, Bosnia, Kashmir, and Israel-Palestine will become attenuated over time as their internal borders as well the borders in their wider regions become bridges rather than barriers. But substantive and durable settlements to these cancerous conflicts are a condition for cooperation across borders to flourish.

That is what this book reveals about the substantive nature of the settlements needed to make the transition from war to peace. The question of how to get there remains, and the range of challenging cases covered in this book has yielded two important lessons on the process of making peace. The first is about the necessity of third-party engagement, and the second is about the limits and pitfalls of incrementalism as a peacebuilding strategy.

As I asserted in the introduction to this book, peace processes will not emerge and peace settlements will not materialize in eth-nonational sovereignty disputes without external, third-party engagement. Third-party engagement is in itself no guarantee of a successful outcome, but in its absence the chances of bridging the gulf that separates sworn antagonists are virtually nonexistent. Even countries with mature democratic credentials, such as India and Israel—albeit an "ethnic democracy" in the case of Israel—are unable on their own to reach the compromises that are in their fundamental national interest. Indeed, as the cases of Sri Lanka, Cyprus, Israel, and India demonstrate, the competitive dynamics of democracy complicate and frequently impede the prospects of peace, because the peace process presents a tempting target for domestic political players keen to advance their particular interests against rivals by assuming a hard-line stance and acting as spoilers.

These spoilers seek to exploit deeply entrenched belief systems of majoritarian domination among Sinhalese in Sri Lanka and Greek Cypriots in Cyprus, and of hegemonic power based primarily on military might in India (vis-à-vis Kashmir) and Israel (vis-à-vis Palestinians). These belief systems are antithetical to the logic and objectives of peace processes, which are premised on equality and mutual recognition between the parties. Peace processes to end protracted, polarized conflicts are necessarily uphill struggles because they have to contend with the burden of deep-seated distrust and animosity between the parties to the conflict and there are constituencies—particularly in ethnonational communities and/or states in which ideologies of hegemony hold sway—that can be readily mobilized by the politics of intransigence and extremism. The intensity of antagonism appears immune even to the impact of major natural disasters. The Asian tsunami of 26 December 2004, which took a heavy toll of all of Sri Lanka's ethnonational communities, failed to breathe new life into the country's moribund peace process; instead the process's stagnation deepened during 2005 and slipped into crisis in 2006. The Himalayan earthquake of 8 October

2005 that ravaged parts of Kashmir similarly did not bring India and Pakistan closer in the quest for a negotiated settlement of that dispute.

The identity of the principal third party varies across the cases explored in this book, from the United States in the Israeli–Palestinian process and in the brokering of the peace pact in Bosnia (although the American role there has been gradually but surely superseded by the EU during the protracted implementation process that has followed the settlement), to Norway in Sri Lanka and the United Nations in Cyprus. The form and extent of the third-party role is also variable depending on the specific features of the conflict and the position of the external party in relation to the belligerents. The third-party role can range from being merely a "communicator" carrying messages between the belligerents through being a "formulator" of general ideas or concrete proposals regarding the substance of a settlement to being a strategic "manipulator" deploying purposeful diplomatic endeavor involving a variable mix of tactics to secure a settlement.[1] Of course, third-party engagement in any particular context can be a hybrid of these roles, and can also shift over time between them.

This book has argued that the United States holds unique leverage and influence, globally and in particular world regions, that equip it to play the role of a constructive third party with decisive results. If played well, such a role can significantly enhance American interests and American prestige across the world. The prospects of an Israeli–Palestinian rapprochement hinge crucially on an assertive and evenhanded American intervention. It took a decisive American intervention to terminate the war in Bosnia and secure a peace agreement (after three years of failed efforts by European nations and institutions), and a low-key, discreet, but continuously involved American role would be extremely helpful to prospects of peace between India and Pakistan over Kashmir. Even in the "lesser" conflicts of Cyprus and Sri Lanka, concerted American support for the efforts of third parties such as the UN and Norway can make a vital difference to prospects of peace.

The other major lesson for the process of peacemaking that has recurred throughout this book is that the prospects of peace are not necessarily well served by the incremental approach that emphasizes gradual, piecemeal progress and prioritizes less contentious issues over the more fundamental issues that divide the antagonists. Protracted and complex conflicts do call for gradual de-escalation and confidence building between the parties, and the spirit of recognizing the other side as equally human and acknowledging that their grievances and claims are not outrageous or illegitimate takes root only gradually even in relatively propitious circumstances. Yet incrementalism has its risks, even perils. Time is not necessarily on the side of peace. If the steady progress envisaged by the incrementalist paradigm fails to materialize, and if the precious momentum that normally accompanies the onset and early stages of a peace process is lost, the tide can turn rapidly and the window of opportunity may close. Incrementalism by its nature provides spoiler elements on all sides with the time and opportunity to mobilize, and a faltering peace process can be pounced upon by spoilers eager to destroy it altogether. There is no clear and simple formula for combating spoilers—the options range from politically confronting and marginalizing groups such as the Sinhalese ultranationalist JVP in Sri Lanka to possibly co-opting others such as the Palestinian Hamas. Another option may be to narrow the time and political opportunity available to spoilers by accelerating the drive to peace.

That would mean adopting a relatively fast track, rather than a deliberately slow one, to the ultimate goal of a substantive settlement. The Israeli-Palestinian peace process, premised on incrementalism, turned over seven fateful years from a confidence-building exercise into a confidence-destroying morass. Any resuscitated peace process between Israelis and Palestinians requires a decisive, purposeful approach to tackling the core issues. The incremental process currently under way between India and Pakistan will not deliver a Kashmir settlement, and a more ambitious, audacious strategy is called for. In Sri Lanka the steady unraveling of the peace process can be reversed only by decisive moves toward the negotiation of a settlement. The principle that guided the UN's determined effort toward the crafting of a comprehensive Cyprus settlement—"nothing is agreed until everything is agreed"—was fundamentally sound. The effort failed primarily because it was unwittingly undermined by the parallel EU track of engagement with Cyprus. And the Bosnian example shows that once that elusive target—a settlement—has been achieved, it can be implemented over a period of time to meet logistical and practical compulsions and also modified to iron out the rough edges.

Contested lands do not have to remain contested. The challenge is immense but the dividends are so great and the alternative is so grim that the quest for peace is worth every ounce of sweat and toil.

Notes

Chapter 1 • Sri Lanka

1. John Lancaster, "Tamil Tiger Guerrillas Direct Relief Effort: In Ruined Town, Rebels Outperform Officials," *Washington Post*, 4 Jan. 2005; "All Mullaithivu Tsunami-Affected Are in Transit Camps: Maran," *TamilNet*, 16 Apr. 2005.

2. Robert A. Pape, "Blowing Up an Assumption," *New York Times*, 18 May 2005.

3. See Stephen Hopgood, "Tamil Tigers," in Diego Gambetta, ed., *Making Sense of Suicide Missions* (Oxford: Oxford University Press, 2005).

4. According to the United Nations Children's Fund (UNICEF), more than thirteen hundred children were serving in the LTTE's military formations as of September 2004 (*Daily Mirror* [Colombo], 10 Sept. 2004, 1).

5. On the challenges of building nations and states, see Clifford Geertz, *Old Societies and New States: The Quest for Modernity in Asia and Africa* (New York: Free Press, 1963), 105–157.

6. On the violence in 1947, see Mushirul Hasan, ed., *India's Partition: Process, Strategy and Mobilization* (Delhi: Oxford University Press, 1993).

7. Stanley J. Tambiah, *Sri Lanka: Ethnic Fratricide and the Dismantling of Democracy* (Chicago: University of Chicago Press, 1986), 5.

8. Gananath Obeyesekere, letter to the *New York Times*, 24 Apr. 1984.

9. The "Cleghorn Minute" of 1799 is reproduced in the *Journal of the Royal Asiatic Society* 3 (1954): 125–152.

10. D. C. Wijewardena, *The Revolt in the Temple*, 3, cited in Alfred Jeyaratnam Wilson, *The Break-Up of Sri Lanka: The Sinhalese-Tamil Conflict* (London: Hurst, 1988), 52.

11. Wilson, *Break-Up of Sri Lanka*, 24.

12. See Tarzie Vittachi, *Emergency 1958: The Story of the Ceylon Race Riots* (London: A. Deutsch, 1958).

13. Ben H. Farmer, *Ceylon: A Divided Nation* (Oxford: Oxford University Press, 1963).

14. See R. A. L. H. Gunawardena, "The People of the Lion: Sinhalese Identity and Ideology in History and Historiography," in Jonathan Spencer, ed., *Sri*

Lanka: History and the Roots of Conflict (London: Routledge and Kegan Paul, 1990).

15. See Sammy Smooha, "Minority Status in an Ethnic Democracy: The Status of the Arab Minority in Israel," *Ethnic and Racial Studies* 13 (1990): 389–413; and Yoav Peled, "Ethnic Democracy and the Legal Construction of Citizenship: Arab Citizens of the Jewish State," *American Political Science Review* 86, 2 (June 1992): 432–443.

16. Satchi Ponnambalam, *Sri Lanka: The National Question and the Tamil Liberation Struggle* (London: Zed Books, 1983), 257–258.

17. See Donald Horowitz, "Incentives and Behavior in the Ethnic Politics of Sri Lanka and Malaysia," *Third World Quarterly* 11, 4 (Oct. 1989): 18–35.

18. Quoted in Sumantra Bose, *States, Nations, Sovereignty: Sri Lanka, India and the Tamil Eelam Movement* (Thousand Oaks: Sage, 1994), 73.

19. By 2006, Trincomalee was a tinderbox as the cease-fire between the government and the LTTE unraveled on the ground. See Somini Sengupta, "Sri Lankan City Mired in Ethnic Violence," *New York Times*, 15 May 2006.

20. Jonathan Spencer, "Popular Perceptions of the July 1983 Violence: A Provincial View," in James Manor, ed., *Sri Lanka in Change and Crisis* (London: Croom Helm, 1984), 191–192.

21. Quoted in Bose, *States, Nations, Sovereignty*, 135.

22. Cited in ibid., 149.

23. The Sri Lankan Tamil jurist Nadesan Satyendra, quoted in Sumantra Bose, "Flawed Mediation, Chaotic Implementation: The 1987 Indo-Sri Lanka Peace Agreement," in Stephen John Stedman, Donald Rothchild, and Elizabeth Cousens, eds., *Ending Civil Wars: The Implementation of Peace Agreements* (Boulder: Lynne Rienner, 2002), 642.

24. Quoted in Bose, "Flawed Mediation," 644.

25. Quoted in Sumantra Bose, "Tamil Self-Determination in Sri Lanka: Challenges and Prospects," *Economic and Political Weekly* 29, 39 (24 Sept. 1994): 2537–39.

26. In May 1991, India's former prime minister Rajiv Gandhi, who was responsible for the July 1987 agreement between India and Sri Lanka and the subsequent Indian military intervention until 1990 against the LTTE insurgents, was assassinated by a young female suicide-bomber wearing a high-explosive belt while he was on an election campaign in the Tamil province in south India. Indian investigations have pointed to an LTTE network being behind the assassination. The modus operandi is very suggestive of the Tigers.

27. For the full text, see www.slmm.lk/documents/cfa.htm.

28. Scott McDonald, "Tigers Say They Will Change Stripes, Give Up Eelam: Substantial Autonomy Rather than Statehood," *Indian Express*, 19 Sept. 2002,

1; "LTTE Leader Calls for Autonomy and Self-Government for Tamil Homeland," LTTE press release, 27 Nov. 2002.

29. "LTTE Suspends Negotiations with Sri Lanka pending Implementation of Agreements Reached," *TamilNet,* 21 Apr. 2003.

30. Author's personal information from a senior LTTE source who participated in the talks.

31. See Sumantra Bose, "War and Peace in Sri Lanka: The Government's Reform Proposals and Beyond," *Economic and Political Weekly* 30, 39 (30 Sept. 1995): 2423–26.

32. "Tamil National Alliance: Election Manifesto, 2004," *TamilNet,* 13 Mar. 2004.

33. "Embrace Reforms, End Conflict, Rocca Tells Sri Lanka," *TamilNet,* 21 Apr. 2005. The Tigers continued killing Tamil paramilitaries working with the Sri Lankan security forces after the cease-fire, and since 2004 they have been involved in a tit-for-tat series of killings with followers of Karuna, a top LTTE commander in the east who defected from the organization. In August 2005, Sri Lanka's foreign minister Lakshman Kadirgamar, an ethnic Tamil and one of the most protected persons in the country, was assassinated at his Colombo home in a daring sniper attack. The Tigers, who regarded him as a despicable traitor, are the prime suspects.

34. "Bring LTTE into Democratic Mainstream, Says Chandrika," *The Hindu* (Chennai), 17 June 2005.

35. Daniel Elazar, *Exploring Federalism* (Tuscaloosa: University of Alabama Press, 1987).

36. "Ceasefire in Sri Lanka Boosts Economic Recovery," *Hindustan Times,* 10 Aug. 2003.

37. "India, Sri Lanka Move towards Comprehensive Economic Pact," *Hindustan Times,* 10 Sept. 2003.

Chapter 2 • Cyprus

1. "Report of the Secretary-General on the United Nations Operation in Cyprus," UN Security Council document S/2004/427 (26 May 2004), 2. On the opening of the Green Line, see "Crossing the Divide," *Guardian,* 23 Apr. 2003; "False Dawn?" *Guardian,* 3 May 2003; "The People Respond," *Al-Ahram Weekly,* 1–7 May 2003; and "Crossing the Green Line," *Irish Times,* 16 Aug. 2003.

2. Yiannis Papadakis, *Echoes from the Dead Zone: Across the Cyprus Divide* (London: Tauris, 2005), 244.

3. Ibid., 243.

4. Some Turkish Cypriots focused on the near-term and immediate, by, for example, looking for jobs in the better-paying south, just as some Greek Cypri-

ots have tried to do their shopping in the north, where prices are much cheaper. Several thousand Turkish Cypriots have been working in the south since 2003, mostly as construction workers. Greek Cypriot police regard as contraband, and will confiscate, items that Greek Cypriots purchase in the north.

5. Yiannis Papadakis, "Nicosia: The National Struggle Museums of a Divided City," *Ethnic and Racial Studies* 17, 3 (July 1994): 409.

6. Ibid., 412.

7. Rolandos Katsiaounis, *Labor, Society and Politics in Cyprus during the Second Half of the Nineteenth Century* (Nicosia: Cyprus Research Center, 1996), 210–214.

8. Richard Patrick, *Political Geography and the Cyprus Conflict, 1963–1971* (Waterloo: University of Waterloo Press, 1976), 27.

9. See Bruce Clark, *Twice a Stranger: How Mass Expulsion Forged Modern Greece and Turkey* (London: Granta Books, 2006).

10. For the full text, see www.cyprus-conflict.net/TC-reaction-1930.htm.

11. Katsiaounis, *Labor, Society and Politics,* 75–76.

12. Nancy Crawshaw, *The Cyprus Revolt: An Account of the Struggle for Union with Greece* (London: Allen and Unwin, 1978), 404.

13. Colin Thubron, *Journey into Cyprus* (London: William Heinemann, 1975), 98.

14. Crawshaw, *The Cyprus Revolt,* 405.

15. Thubron, *Journey into Cyprus,* 37–38.

16. Crawshaw, *The Cyprus Revolt,* 287.

17. Ibid., 293.

18. Patrick, *Political Geography,* 8.

19. See Arend Lijphart, *Democracy in Plural Societies: A Comparative Exploration* (New Haven: Yale University Press, 1977), and Arend Lijphart, *Democracies: Patterns of Majoritarian and Consensus Government in Twenty-one Countries* (New Haven: Yale University Press, 1984).

20. See Sumantra Bose, *Bosnia after Dayton: Nationalist Partition and International Intervention* (New York: Oxford University Press, 2002), chaps. 2 and 5; and Brendan O'Leary, "The Nature of the British-Irish Agreement," *New Left Review* 233 (Jan.–Feb. 1999): 66–96.

21. See Diana Markides, "The Issue of Separate Municipalities in Cyprus, 1957–63," *Journal of Mediterranean Studies* 8, 2 (1998): 177–203.

22. Michael Attalides, *Cyprus: Nationalism and International Politics* (New York: St. Martin's Press, 1979), 50–51.

23. Patrick, *Political Geography,* 35.

24. Ibid., 40.

25. Ibid., 8.

26. See Michael Cox, Adrian Guelke, and Fiona Stephen, eds., *A Farewell to Arms? Beyond the Good Friday Agreement* (Manchester: Manchester University Press, 2006).
27. See Bose, *Bosnia after Dayton.*
28. Peter Loizos, *The Heart Grown Bitter: A Chronicle of Cypriot War Refugees* (Cambridge: Cambridge University Press, 1981), 43.
29. Patrick, *Political Geography,* 63.
30. Thubron, *Journey into Cyprus,* 72–73.
31. Ibid., 36.
32. Patrick, *Political Geography,* 62.
33. Loizos published his findings in his *The Greek Gift: Politics in a Cypriot Village* (Oxford: Basil Blackwell, 1975).
34. Patrick, *Political Geography,* 28.
35. Loizos, *The Heart Grown Bitter,* 55–61.
36. Mehmet Ali Birand, *30 Hot Days* (Nicosia: Rustem Kitabevi, 1985), 81.
37. Loizos, *The Heart Grown Bitter,* 79.
38. Ibid., 89–90.
39. Ibid., 97–98.
40. David Hannay, *Cyprus: The Search for a Solution* (London: Tauris, 2005), 8.
41. See Lellos Demetriades, "The Nicosia Master Plan," *Journal of Mediterranean Studies* 8, 2 (1998): 169–176. Demetriades was the mayor of Greek Cypriot Nicosia.
42. Hannay, *Cyprus,* 13–14.
43. Interview given to Greek daily *Elefterotipia,* reprinted in Greek Cypriot daily *Alithia* and in the TRNC press and information office daily briefing, 18 July 2005.
44. Hannay, *Cyprus,* 19.
45. Ibid., 172.
46. Ibid., 195.
47. Ibid., 181.
48. Ibid., 223.
49. "Report of the Secretary-General on His Mission of Good Offices in Cyprus," S/2004/437 (28 May 2004), 16.
50. Hannay, *Cyprus,* 245.
51. The actual number of Turks who settled in northern Cyprus after 1974 is disputed. They include very poor families arrived from Turkey, but also Turks, including soldiers of the 1974 invasion force, who have married Turkish Cypriot women. Some settlers are resented by "native" Turkish Cypriots, who regard them as uneducated and overly religious.
52. "Report of the Secretary-General," 25.

53. "The Comprehensive Settlement of the Cyprus Problem," 31 Mar. 2004, mimeo. The Foundation Agreement, which summarizes the key provisions of the plan, consists of the preamble and fourteen articles.

54. "Report of the Secretary-General," 20.

55. Andreas Theophanous, "The Accession of the Republic of Cyprus to the EU: The Annan Plan and the Solution of the Cyprus Problem" (discussion paper, Inter-college, Nicosia, Jan. 2003); and Andreas Theophanous, "The Republic of Cyprus as a Member State of the EU and the Solution of the Cyprus Problem" (discussion paper, Inter-college, Nicosia, May 2004).

56. Peter Loizos, "In Denial: The Greek Cypriot Rejection of the Annan Plan" (discussion paper, London School of Economics, 2004).

57. Hannay, *Cyprus,* 246.

Chapter 3 • Bosnia

1. A fine illustrated history is *Mostar: From Its Beginnings to 1992* (Mostar: Mutevelic, 2004), a reprint of an edition published by the municipality of Mostar in 1982.

2. Misha Glenny, *The Fall of Yugoslavia* (London: Penguin, 1996), 160.

3. See Sumantra Bose, *Bosnia after Dayton: Nationalist Partition and International Intervention* (New York: Oxford University Press, 2002), chap. 3.

4. "Mostar: The Bridge over the Neretva," *Transitions Online,* 26 July 2004.

5. Susan Woodward, "Transitional Elections and the Dilemmas of International Assistance to Bosnia & Herzegovina," in Susan Riskin, ed., *Three Dimensions of Peace-Building in Bosnia* (Washington, DC: U.S. Institute of Peace, 1999), 5–6.

6. Fitzroy Maclean, *Eastern Approaches* (London: Jonathan Cape, 1949), 337–338.

7. Clinton reportedly read Robert Kaplan's 1993 book *Balkan Ghosts.*

8. Maria Todorova, *Imagining the Balkans* (New York: Oxford University Press, 1997), 188.

9. Chuck Sudetic, *Blood and Vengeance: One Family's Story of the War in Bosnia* (New York: Norton, 1998). The town of Visegrad, located on the natural border demarcated by the Drina River between Bosnia and Serbia, is home to another famous Ottoman bridge. This bridge is the reference point of the Yugoslav Nobel laureate Ivo Andric's best-known novel, *The Bridge on the Drina* (London: Allen and Unwin, 1959). Andric, an ethnic Croat born in Travnik, a town in the hills of central Bosnia that was once the seat of Bosnia's Ottoman authorities, identified as a Yugoslav throughout his adult life.

10. Glenny, *The Fall of Yugoslavia,* 162.

11. Xavier Bougarel, "Bosnia & Herzegovina: State and Communitarianism,"

in David Dyker and Ivan Vejvoda, eds., *Yugoslavia and After* (New York: Addison-Wesley Longman, 1996), 87.

12. Robert Donia, *Sarajevo: A Biography* (London: Hurst and Co., 2006), 101–106, 112–114.

13. Susan Woodward, *Balkan Tragedy: Chaos and Dissolution after the Cold War* (Washington, DC: Brookings Institution, 1995), 33.

14. Michael Ignatieff, *Blood and Belonging: Journeys into the New Nationalism* (New York: Farrar, Straus and Giroux, 1994), 21.

15. See Woodward, *Balkan Tragedy*, chaps. 2 and 4. A study of the crisis of communist power in Bosnia during Yugoslavia's last years is Neven Andjelic, *Bosnia-Herzegovina: The End of a Legacy* (London: Frank Cass, 2003).

16. Tone Bringa, *Being Muslim the Bosnian Way: Identity and Community in a Central Bosnian Village* (Princeton: Princeton University Press, 1995).

17. See Semezdin Mehmedinovic, *Sarajevo Blues* (San Francisco: City Lights Books, 1998), 14–23.

18. Woodward, *Balkan Tragedy*, 122.

19. An account of these sessions can be found in Robert Hayden, *Blueprints for a House Divided: The Constitutional Logic of the Yugoslav Conflicts* (Ann Arbor: University of Michigan Press, 1999), 92–97.

20. David Owen, *Balkan Odyssey* (London: Indigo, 1996), 34.

21. Hayden, *Blueprints*, chap. 5; Peter Radan, "The Badinter Arbitration Commission and the Partition of Yugoslavia," *Nationalities Papers* 25 (1997): 537–557; and Peter Radan, "Yugoslavia's Internal Borders as International Borders: A Question of Appropriateness," *East European Quarterly* 33, 2 (June 1999): 137–155.

22. The acute practical difficulties of "drawing a better line" in inflamed sovereignty disputes are exposed in American legal scholar Steven Ratner's unconvincing attempt to come up with a viable alternative to the *uti possidetis* formula. See Steven Ratner, "Drawing a Better Line: Uti Possidetis and the Borders of New States," *American Journal of International Law* 90 (1996): 590–624. Ratner's ideas are critiqued with reference to the Yugoslav case in Bose, *Bosnia after Dayton*, 49–51.

23. David Butler and Austin Ranney, *Referendums: A Comparative Study of Practice and Theory* (Washington, DC: American Enterprise Institute, 1978), 36.

24. Frederick Whelan, "Democratic Theory and the Boundary Problem," in J. Roland Pennock and John Chapman, eds., *Liberal Democracy, NOMOS XXV* (New York: New York University Press, 1983), 13–47; Robert Dahl, *Democracy and Its Critics* (New Haven: Yale University Press, 1989), 207.

25. John McGarry, "Orphans of Secession: National Pluralism in Secessionist Regions and Post-Secession States," in Margaret Moore, ed., *National Self-*

Determination and Secession (New York: Oxford University Press, 1998), 215–232.

26. The most substantive account of the war is Steven Burg and Paul Shoup, *The War in Bosnia-Herzegovina: Ethnic Conflict and International Intervention* (Armonk, NY: ME Sharpe, 1999).

27. Quoted in Bose, *Bosnia after Dayton,* 169.

28. Richard Holbrooke, *To End a War* (New York: Random House, 1998), 168.

29. Detailed accounts of the Dayton talks can be found in Laura Silber and Allan Little, *Yugoslavia: Death of a Nation* (New York: Penguin, 1997), chaps. 29 and 30; and in Holbrooke, *To End a War.*

30. Carl Bildt, *Peace Journey: The Struggle for Peace in Bosnia* (London: Weidenfeld and Nicholson, 1998), 392.

31. See Bose, *Bosnia after Dayton,* chaps. 2 and 5.

32. Dahl, *Democracy and Its Critics,* 207.

33. Robert Dahl, *Democracy, Liberty and Equality* (Oslo: Norwegian University Press, 1986), 124–125.

34. Ivo Andric, "A Letter from 1920," in Andric, *The Damned Yard and Other Stories* (Belgrade: Dereta, 2000), 107–119.

35. Quoted in Sumantra Bose, "The Bosnian State a Decade after Dayton," *International Peacekeeping* 12, 3 (Autumn 2005): 325.

36. It should be noted, however, that the Northern Ireland settlement has a very important *external* confederal dimension, which establishes institutions of cross-border cooperation between Northern Ireland and the Republic of Ireland, and that Lebanon's ethnoconfessional communities are to a considerable degree demographically territorialized, as are Catholics and Protestants in Northern Ireland.

37. See Samir Khalaf, *Civil and Uncivil Violence in Lebanon: A History of the Internationalization of Communal Conflict* (New York: Columbia University Press, 2002), chaps. 9 and 10.

38. See John McGarry and Brendan O'Leary, *The Northern Ireland Conflict: Consociational Engagements* (Oxford: Oxford University Press, 2004).

39. See Gerald Knaus and Felix Martin, "Travails of the European Raj: Lessons from Bosnia & Herzegovina," *Journal of Democracy* 14, 3 (July 2003): 60–74.

40. Statistics at www.unhcr.ba accessed on 29 August 2005. These statistics somewhat inflate the real extent of minority returns, since a proportion of returnees sell their property and go back to places dominated by their own community. Minority returnees also tend to be disproportionately elderly, rather than young people or families with children. But despite these caveats it remains true that there has been substantial minority return in Bosnia.

41. David Hannay, *Cyprus: The Search for a Solution* (London: Tauris, 2005), 139.

42. On this issue see Michael Fischbach, *Records of Dispossession: Palestinian Refu-*

gee Property and the Arab-Israeli Conflict (New York: Columbia University Press, 2003); and Nur Masalha, *The Politics of Denial: Israel and the Palestinian Refugee Problem* (London: Pluto Press, 2003).

43. European Stability Initiative, "Making Federalism Work: A Radical Proposal for Practical Reform" (discussion paper, ESI, 2004).

44. "100,000 Bosnians Have Left the Country since War," Reuters (Sarajevo), 10 Nov. 2000.

45. Roland Paris, "Peace-Building and the Limits of Liberal Internationalism," *International Security* 22, 2 (1997): 63, 78.

46. *Mostar: From its Beginnings to 1992, 66.*

47. "Reconstruction of Bosnia's Famous Bridge Begins," Reuters (Mostar), 8 June 2001.

Chapter 4 • Kashmir

1. Agha Shahid Ali, "Farewell," in *The Country without a Post Office: Poems, 1991– 1995* (Delhi: Ravi Dayal, 2000), 7–9.

2. Another 198 kilometers of heavily militarized border south of the LOC separate the southwestern parts of Indian-controlled Kashmir's Jammu region from Pakistan's Punjab province. The Indians regard this stretch as essentially a part of the international border between India and Pakistan, while the Pakistanis prefer to call it a "working boundary."

3. Muzamil Jaleel, "At the LOC, Two Armies Try to Bridge an Old Divide," *Indian Express,* 9 Mar. 2005.

4. "Spirit Willing, the Dream Lives On," *Indian Express,* 16 Mar. 2005.

5. "Kashmir Bus Sparks Fears of Property Wrangles," *Indian Express,* 13 May 2005.

6. "Text of Musharraf-Singh Joint Statement," *Indian Express,* 18 Apr. 2005.

7. "US Says It Is Impressed with India-Pakistan Peace Moves," *Indian Express,* 17 Apr. 2005.

8. "India Races to Fix Kashmir Fence Damage, Stop Militants," *Indian Express,* 10 Apr. 2005.

9. Bernard Wasserstein, *Israel and Palestine: Why They Fight and Can They Stop?* (London: Profile Books, 2004), 147–152.

10. "Race against Time, Nature to Shut Out Militants," *Indian Express,* 1 Aug. 2005.

11. See Mushirul Hasan, ed., *India's Partition: Process, Strategy and Mobilization* (Delhi: Oxford University Press, 1993).

12. C. E. Tyndale Biscoe, *Kashmir in Sunlight and Shade* (London: Seeley, Service and Co., 1922), 77.

13. Quoted in Sumantra Bose, *Kashmir: Roots of Conflict, Paths to Peace* (Cambridge, MA: Harvard University Press, 2003), 36, 38, 74.

14. Quoted in ibid., 59.

15. Quoted in ibid., 61.

16. Josef Korbel, *Danger in Kashmir* (Princeton: Princeton University Press, 1954), 246.

17. Jyoti Bhushan Dasgupta, *Jammu and Kashmir* (The Hague: Martinus Nijhoff, 1968), 212.

18. Ibid., 227.

19. Quoted in Bose, *Kashmir,* 78.

20. Shaheen Akhtar, "Elections in Indian-Held Kashmir," *Regional Studies* 18, 3 (2000): 38–39.

21. See Sumantra Bose, *The Challenge in Kashmir: Democracy, Self-Determination and a Just Peace* (Thousand Oaks: Sage, 1997), 67–71.

22. A. G. Noorani, *The Kashmir Question* (Bombay: Manaktalas, 1964), 61.

23. Dasgupta, *Jammu and Kashmir,* 223–224.

24. R. K. Jain, ed., *Soviet-South Asian Relations, 1947–1978* (Atlantic Highlands, NJ: Humanities Press, 1979), 15–20.

25. Noorani, *The Kashmir Question,* 73.

26. The population of Indian-controlled Kashmir is two-thirds Muslim, while Muslims constitute only 13 percent of the total population of India. The population of Pakistani-controlled Kashmir is almost entirely Muslim.

27. Quoted in M. J. Akbar, *India, the Siege Within: Challenges to a Nation's Unity* (Harmondsworth: Penguin, 1985), 267.

28. Prem Nath Bazaz, *Kashmir in Crucible* (New Delhi: Pamposh, 1967), 99–100.

29. *Speeches and Interviews of Sher-e-Kashmir Sheikh Mohammad Abdullah* (Srinagar: Jammu and Kashmir Plebiscite Front, 1968), 2:13, 1:15–16.

30. For an exhaustive account, see Bose, *Kashmir,* chap. 3.

31. "16,000 Terrorists Killed over Thirteen Years," *Kashmir Times,* 5 Dec. 2002.

32. Amanullah Khan, *Free Kashmir* (Karachi: Central Printing Press, 1970), 139–149.

33. Mass conversions to Islam in Kashmir were inspired during the fourteenth century by wandering Sufi mystics, who are venerated as saints. See Muhammad Ishaq Khan, *Kashmir's Transition to Islam: The Role of Muslim Rishis* (New Delhi: Manohar, 1994).

34. "The Blessed Word: A Prologue," in Ali, *Country without a Post Office,* 3–5.

35. Quoted in Bose, *Kashmir,* 14.

36. "A Pastoral," in Ali, *Country without a Post Office,* 23–24.

37. For the full text, see P. R. Chari and Pervaiz Iqbal Cheema, *The Simla Agreement, 1972: Its Wasted Promise* (New Delhi: Manohar, 2001), 204–206.

38. See Neville Maxwell, *India's China War* (London: Jonathan Cape, 1970). The Indians were severely defeated in this conflict, and Indo-Chinese relations did not recover until the 1990s.

39. For the full text, see www.indianembassy.org/South_Asia/Pakistan/ lahoredeclaration.html. SAARC has seven member-states: India, Pakistan, Bangladesh, Sri Lanka, Nepal, Bhutan, and the Maldives.

40. See Sankarshan Thakur et al., *Guns and Yellow Roses: Essays on the Kargil War* (New Delhi: Viking, 1999).

41. See Strobe Talbott, *Engaging India: Diplomacy, Democracy, and the Bomb* (Washington, DC: Brookings Institution Press, 2004).

42. On the principle of self-determination in theory and practice, see Donald Horowitz, "Self-Determination: Politics, Philosophy and Law," in Margaret Moore, ed., *National Self-Determination and Secession* (New York: Oxford University Press, 1998); and Ved P. Nanda, "Self-Determination and Secession under International Law," *Denver Journal of International Law and Policy* 29, 4 (2001): 305–326.

43. On this period, see Mridu Rai, *Hindu Rulers, Muslim Subjects: Islam, Rights and the History of Kashmir* (Princeton: Princeton University Press, 2004).

44. JKLF declaration issued in the "Azad Kashmir" town of Mirpur on 5 January 1995, quoted in Bose, *Kashmir*, 169.

45. See, for example, Khan, *Free Kashmir,* 139–149; and Balraj Puri, *Simmering Volcano: A Study of Jammu's Relations with Kashmir* (Delhi: Sterling, 1983). Puri first presented his ideas in the late 1960s; Khan's book was published in 1970.

46. Strobe Talbott, "Self-Determination in an Inter-Dependent World," *Foreign Policy* 118 (2000): 152–163.

47. On the relevance of the framework of the Good Friday Agreement to the conceptualization and construction of the institutional architecture of peace in Kashmir, see Bose, *Kashmir,* chap. 5.

48. The UN's only presence is a tiny military observer mission of forty-five personnel on the LOC.

49. "India-Pakistan Peace Talks Seek Way Off Siachen Glacier," *Indian Express,* 23 May 2005; "India, Pakistan Fail to Break Dam on Baglihar Project," *Indian Express,* 7 Jan. 2005.

Chapter 5 • Israel and Palestine

1. Nir Hasson, "Thousands Mark Last Independence Day in Gush Katif," *Haaretz,* 13 May 2005.

2. Gideon Levy, "The IDF Is Investigating," *Haaretz Magazine,* 14 Jan. 2005, 11.

3. Zeev Schiff and Ehud Yaari, *Intifada: The Palestinian Uprising, Israel's Third Front* (New York: Simon and Schuster, 1990), 87–90.

4. Dennis Ross, *The Missing Peace: The Inside Story of the Fight for Middle East Peace* (New York: Farrar, Straus and Giroux, 2004), 102; Jack Khoury and Yoav Stern, "PM: Gaza Pullout Meant to Strengthen Galilee, Negev, Jerusalem," *Haaretz,* 16 June 2005.

5. "UN Envoy: Gaza Pullout Encouraging, but Road-Map the Only Way Forward," Associated Press (New York), 24 Sept. 2005; Zvi Barel, "Of Course, Egypt Is to Blame," *Haaretz,* 18 Sept. 2005; Megan K. Stack, "Arab World Sees Gaza as a Frustratingly Small Step," *Los Angeles Times,* 22 Aug. 2005.

6. "A Poorly Timed Provocation," *Haaretz,* editorial, 27 Aug. 2005.

7. Daniel Seidemann, "Friends Don't Let Friends Drive Drunk," *Washington Post,* op-ed, 26 Aug. 2004.

8. Ephraim Yaar and Tamar Hermann, "Jewish Public Split on Second Settlement Evacuation," *Haaretz,* 7 Sept. 2005.

9. Walter Laqueur, *A History of Zionism* (London: Tauris Parke Paperbacks, 2003), 590.

10. Avi Shlaim, *The Iron Wall: Israel and the Arab World* (London: Penguin, 2001), 3.

11. Laqueur, *A History of Zionism,* 591; Shlaim, *The Iron Wall,* 597, 3.

12. Edward Said, *The Question of Palestine* (London: Routledge and Kegan Paul, 1980), 56–114; Laqueur, *A History of Zionism,* 590, 596; Edward Said, *The Politics of Dispossession: The Struggle for Palestinian Self-Determination, 1969–1994* (London: Chatto and Windus, 1994), 167, 171; Laqueur, *A History of Zionism,* 595–596; Said, *The Politics of Dispossession,* 168.

13. Laqueur, *A History of Zionism,* 589.

14. Said, *The Politics of Dispossession,* 164–165.

15. Michael Tarazi, "Two Peoples, One State," *New York Times,* op-ed, 4 Oct. 2004; Jacqueline Rose, *The Question of Zion* (Princeton: Princeton University Press, 2005), 28, 115–116.

16. See Muhammad Y. Muslih, *The Origins of Palestinian Nationalism* (New York: Columbia University Press, 1988), 69–87.

17. Mark Tessler, *A History of the Israeli-Palestinian Conflict* (Bloomington: Indiana University Press, 1994), 170, 148.

18. Shlaim, *The Iron Wall,* 5.

19. Tessler, *Israeli-Palestinian Conflict,* 148–150.

20. Tom Segev, *One Palestine, Complete: Jews and Arabs under the British Mandate* (London: Abacus, 2001), 327. For a detailed account of the dispute, see Philip Mattar, *The Mufti of Jerusalem: Al-Hajj Amin Al-Husayni and the Palestinian National Movement* (New York: Columbia University Press, 1988), 33–49. For a graphic account of the Hebron killings, see Segev, *One Palestine, Complete,* 314–327.

21. Mattar, *The Mufti of Jerusalem,* 67–68; Tessler, *Israeli-Palestinian Conflict,* 231.

22. Quoted in Mattar, *The Mufti of Jerusalem,* 73.

23. Bernard Wasserstein, *Israel and Palestine: Why They Fight and Can They Stop?* (London: Profile Books, 2004), 109.

24. Mattar, *The Mufti of Jerusalem,* 81; Tessler, *Israeli-Palestinian Conflict,* 242; Walid

Khalidi, ed., *Before Their Diaspora: A Photographic History of the Palestinians, 1876–1948* (Washington, DC: Institute for Palestine Studies, 1984), 193.

25. Yehoshua Porath, *The Palestine Arab National Movement: From Riots to Rebellion* (London: Frank Cass, 1977), 260.

26. Mattar, *The Mufti of Jerusalem,* 83; Khalidi, *Before Their Diaspora,* 224.

27. Tessler, *Israeli-Palestinian Conflict,* 246; Segev, *One Palestine, Complete,* 440.

28. Wasserstein, *Israel and Palestine,* 118; Tessler, *Israeli-Palestinian Conflict,* 259.

29. On 31 December 1946, Palestine's Arab and Jewish populations were calculated by the Mandate authorities to total 1,972,559 persons—1,364,332 Arabs and 608,227 Jews; Khalidi, *Before Their Diaspora,* 239.

30. Shlaim, *The Iron Wall,* 13–14.

31. Laqueur, *A History of Zionism,* 596.

32. Quoted in Nahum Goldmann, *The Jewish Paradox* (New York: Grosset and Dunlap, 1978), 99.

33. Meron Benvenisti, *Sacred Landscape: The Buried History of the Holy Land since 1948* (Berkeley: University of California Press, 2000), 121.

34. Quoted in Rashid Khalidi, *Resurrecting Empire: Western Footprints and America's Perilous Path in the Middle East* (London: Tauris, 2004), 121.

35. Walid Khalidi, *All That Remains: The Palestinian Villages Occupied and Depopulated by Israel in 1948* (Washington, DC: Institute for Palestine Studies, 1992), xv–xvi; Khalidi, *Before Their Diaspora,* 306; Benvenisti, *Sacred Landscape,* 121, 71.

36. Benvenisti, *Sacred Landscape,* 110.

37. Benny Morris, *The Birth of the Palestinian Refugee Problem Revisited* (Cambridge: Cambridge University Press, 2004), 588–597, emphasis added; Benvenisti, *Sacred Landscape,* 122; Walid Khalidi, "Why Did the Palestinians Leave, Revisited," *Journal of Palestine Studies* 34, 2 (Winter 2005): 42–54 (originally published in 1959).

38. Benvenisti, *Sacred Landscape,* 116; Elias Srouji, "The Fall of a Galilee Village during the 1948 War," *Journal of Palestine Studies* 33, 2 (Winter 2004): 71–80.

39. Benvenisti, *Sacred Landscape,* 130, 153, 116–117.

40. Zachary Lockman, *Comrades and Enemies: Arab and Jewish Workers in Palestine, 1906–1948* (Berkeley: University of California Press, 1996), 355; Julie Peteet, "Words as Interventions: Naming in the Palestine-Israel Conflict," *Third World Quarterly* 26, 1 (2005): 158; Benvenisti, *Sacred Landscape,* 14; Nur Masalha, *The Politics of Denial: Israel and the Palestinian Refugee Problem* (London: Pluto Press, 2003), 178; *Haaretz,* 4 Apr. 1969.

41. Walid Khalidi, "Thinking the Unthinkable: A Sovereign Palestinian State," *Foreign Affairs* 56 (1978): 695–713.

42. Shlaim, *The Iron Wall,* 598; Peteet, "Words as Interventions," 161. For an Israeli perspective on the war, see Michael B. Oren, *Six Days of War: June 1967*

and the Making of the Modern Middle East (New York: Ballantine Books, 2003); on the IDF, see Martin van Creveld, *The Sword and the Olive: A Critical History of the Israel Defense Force* (New York: Public Affairs, 1998). On the PLO, see Yezid Sayigh, *Armed Struggle and the Search for State: The Palestinian National Movement, 1949–1993* (Oxford: Oxford University Press, 1997); Helena Cobban, *The Palestinian Liberation Organization* (Cambridge: Cambridge University Press, 1984); and William Quandt, Fuad Jabber, and Ann Mosely Lesch, *The Politics of Palestinian Nationalism* (Berkeley: University of California Press, 1973).

43. Meron Benvenisti et al., *The West Bank Handbook: A Political Lexicon* (Jerusalem: Jerusalem Post, 1986), 17–18. For an account of the October 1973 war based mainly on Israeli sources, see Abraham Rabinovich, *The Yom Kippur War: The Epic Encounter That Transformed the Middle East* (New York: Schocken Books, 2004). On the cost of the Israeli invasion, see Zeev Schiff and Ehud Yaari, *Israel's Lebanon War* (London: Allen and Unwin, 1984), and Robert Fisk, *Pity the Nation: Lebanon at War* (London: Deutsch, 1990). On the Hezbollah movement, see Hala Jaber, *Hezbollah: Born with a Vengeance* (New York: Columbia University Press, 1997).

44. Marwan Darweish, "The Intifada and Social Change," *Race and Class* 31, 2 (Oct. 1989): 47; Said, *The Politics of Dispossession,* 160. On the first intifada, see Schiff and Yaari, *Intifada,* and Zachary Lockman and Joel Beinin, eds., *Intifada: The Palestinian Uprising against Israeli Occupation* (Toronto: Between The Lines, 1989). On the long-term legacies of the first intifada for its participants and for Palestinian society at large, see John Collins, *Occupied by Memory: The Intifada Generation and the Palestinian State of Emergency* (New York: New York University Press, 2004). Collins's work is based on a study of the Balata refugee camp near Nablus.

45. Ian Lustick, "Reinventing Jerusalem," *Foreign Policy* 93 (Winter 1993–1994): 41–59.

46. On the Gush Emunim, see Israel Shahak and Norton Mezvinsky, *Jewish Fundamentalism in Israel* (London: Pluto Press, 2004).

47. Said, *The Politics of Dispossession,* 173.

48. "Looking Back, Looking Forward," Haidar Abd al-Shafi interviewed by Rashid Khalidi in the *Journal of Palestine Studies* 32, 1 (Autumn 2002): 28–35.

49. Khalidi, *Resurrecting Empire,* 135.

50. See Ahmed Qurei, *From Oslo to Jerusalem: The Palestinian Story of the Secret Negotiations* (London: Tauris, 2006).

51. For the full text, see *Journal of Palestine Studies* 23, 1 (Autumn 1993): 116–121.

52. Ibid., 115; William B. Quandt, "Clinton and the Arab-Israeli Conflict: The Limits of Incrementalism," *Journal of Palestine Studies* 30, 2 (Winter 2001): 26–27.

53. Ross, *The Missing Peace*, 188–189, 123.

54. Wasserstein, *Israel and Palestine*, 128, quoting the Israeli scholar David Newman's phrase; Hussein Agha and Robert Malley, "The Lost Palestinians," *New York Review of Books*, 9 June 2005; Edward Said, *The End of the Peace Process: Oslo and After* (London: Granta Books, 2002), 14, 138.

55. Ron Pundak, "From Oslo to Taba: What Went Wrong?" *Survival* 43, 3 (Autumn 2001): 32–35.

56. Rashid Khalidi, "Towards a Clear Palestinian Strategy," *Journal of Palestine Studies* 31, 4 (Summer 2002): 5.

57. Ross, *The Missing Peace*, 199, 338; Shlaim, *The Iron Wall*, 601; Pundak, "From Oslo to Taba," 33, 33–34.

58. Ross, *The Missing Peace*, 339.

59. Ibid., 207.

60. Said, *End of the Peace Process*, 132; Michael Dumper, *The Politics of Sacred Space: The Old City of Jerusalem in the Middle East Conflict* (Boulder: Lynne Rienner, 2002), 147; Gideon Levy, "The Real Uprooting Is Taking Place in Hebron," *Haaretz*, 12 Sept. 2005. Settler abuse of Palestinians in Hebron has also been documented by the Israeli human rights organization B'Tselem.

61. Ross, *The Missing Peace*, 467.

62. Ibid., 597.

63. Ibid., 502; Pundak, "From Oslo to Taba," 37, 38; Ross, *The Missing Peace*, 593; Yaar and Hermann, "Jewish Public Split."

64. Khalidi, *Resurrecting Empire*, 141.

65. Hussein Agha and Robert Malley, "Camp David: The Tragedy of Errors," *New York Review of Books*, 9 Aug. 2001.

66. Ross, *The Missing Peace*, 690.

67. Pundak, "From Oslo To Taba," 40.

68. Ross, *The Missing Peace*, 758; "Looking Back, Looking Forward," 30; Dahlan quoted in Ahron Bregman, *The Elusive Peace: How the Holy Land Defeated America* (London: Penguin, 2005), 249; Ross, *The Missing Peace*, 592.

69. Ross, *The Missing Peace*, 261.

70. Ibid., 770; David Makovsky, *A Defensible Fence: Fighting Terror and Enabling a Two-State Solution* (Washington, DC: Washington Institute for Near East Policy, Apr. 2004), 4; Ariel Sharon, "The Silliness of Separation," *Jerusalem Post*, 27 Jan. 1995; Gideon Levy, "The Rabin State," *Haaretz*, 2 Oct. 2005; Janet Aviad, quoted in Daniel Ben-Simon, "What's the Story with This Arik?" *Haaretz*, 5 Oct. 2005. A fine account of the meaning of the barrier for Israelis and Palestinians, and its implications for the conflict, can be found in Isabel Kershner, *Barrier: The Seam of the Israeli-Palestinian Conflict* (New York: Palgrave Macmillan, 2005). On the hardships experienced by West Bank and Jerusalem Palestinians because of the barrier, see, for example, Ada Ushpiz,

"Fenced Out," *Haaretz*, 16 Sept. 2005 (on the consequences of the barrier for Palestinians in the northern West Bank, focusing on the village of Jayyus near Qalqiliya); Meron Rapoport, "Symbol of Struggle," *Haaretz*, 10 Sept. 2005 (on its consequences in the central West Bank, focusing on the village of Bilin near the Jewish settlement of Upper Modin); and Menachem Klein, "Old and New Walls in Jerusalem," *Political Geography* 24, 1 (Jan. 2005): 53–76.

71. Shlaim, *The Iron Wall*, 603; Pundak, "From Oslo to Taba," 45.

72. Michele K. Esposito, "The al-Aqsa Intifada: Military Operations, Suicide Attacks, Assassinations and Losses in the First Four Years," *Journal of Palestine Studies* 34, 2 (Winter 2005): 103–104. On Hamas's strategic dilemma resulting from the peace process, see Shaul Mishal and Avraham Sela, *The Palestinian Hamas: Vision, Violence and Co-existence* (New York: Columbia University Press, 2000), esp. chap. 5; see also the Hamas covenant reproduced as Appendix II on 175–199.

73. Agha and Malley, "Camp David"; Shlaim, *The Iron Wall*, 603; Pundak, "From Oslo to Taba," 40; Agha and Malley, "Camp David."

74. Khalidi, "Thinking the Unthinkable," 708; "Looking Back, Looking Forward," 32; Pundak, "From Oslo to Taba," 31, 44.

75. Ross, *The Missing Peace*, 768–769, 770–771; Pundak, "From Oslo to Taba," 33, 40–41; Quandt, "Clinton and the Arab-Israeli Conflict," 34; Agha and Malley, "Camp David"; Dennis Ross's response to Agha and Malley in the *New York Review of Books*, 20 Sept. 2001.

76. Ross, *The Missing Peace*, 116, 764.

77. See ibid., 801–805, for the full text of the parameters reproduced as an appendix.

78. Lustick, "Reinventing Jerusalem," 59; Meron Benvenisti, *City of Stone: The Hidden History of Jerusalem* (Berkeley: University of California Press, 1996), 224–225; Lustick, "Reinventing Jerusalem," 59; Klein, "Old and New Walls," 66; Dumper, *Politics of Sacred Space*, 163; Benvenisti, *City of Stone*, 126. On the two parallel societies in Jerusalem, see Amir Cheshin et al., *Separate and Unequal: The Inside Story of Israeli Rule in East Jerusalem* (Cambridge, MA: Harvard University Press, 1999); Michael Romann and Alex Weingrod, *Living Together Separately: Arabs and Jews in Contemporary Jerusalem* (Princeton: Princeton University Press, 1991); Marshall Breger and Ora Ahimeir, eds., *Jerusalem: A City and Its Future* (Syracuse: Syracuse University Press, 2002); and Bernard Wasserstein, *Divided Jerusalem: The Struggle for the Holy City* (London: Profile Books, 2001).

79. Nadav Shragai, "Out of Jerusalem," *Haaretz*, 28 Sept. 2005; in June 2005, Israeli municipal authorities announced their intention to demolish eighty-eight Palestinian houses in Silwan to build "an archeological park devoted to

Jewish history and . . . the biblical King David"—see Laura King, "Jerusalem
Park Imperils Arab Homes," *Los Angeles Times,* 7 June 2005; Wasserstein, *Divided Jerusalem,* 351.

80. Khalidi, *Resurrecting Empire,* 151, 126. An explanation of why the Israeli tail
wags the American dog so effectively is offered in John Mearsheimer and
Stephen Walt, "The Israel Lobby," *London Review of Books,* 23 Mar. 2006, 3–
12. They emphasize the influence wielded by organized pro-Israel groups on
U.S. political institutions and policymaking structures.

81. "Looking Back, Looking Forward," 32–33.

82. See Josef Joffe, "A World without Israel," *Foreign Policy* 146 (Jan.–Feb. 2005):
36–42; Michael Scott Doran, "Palestine, Iraq, and American Strategy," *Foreign
Affairs* 82, 1 (Jan.–Feb. 2003): 19–33.

83. Ross, *The Missing Peace,* 783.

84. Quoted in Stack, "Frustratingly Small Step."

85. See, for example, Wasserstein, *Israel and Palestine;* Makovsky, "A Defensible
Fence," 19; and Arnon Soffer, *Israel Demography* 2020 (Haifa: University of
Haifa, Mar. 2005).

86. See Makovsky, "A Defensible Fence," 6.

87. Rose, *The Question of Zion,* 48.

88. Beverley Milton-Edwards and Alastair Crooke, "Elusive Ingredient: Hamas
and the Peace Process," *Journal of Palestine Studies* 33, 4 (Summer 2004): 43–44;
Agha and Malley, "The Lost Palestinians"; Laura King, "Abbas for Hamas
Men in Cabinet," *Los Angeles Times,* 2 July 2005; on Hamas's established position, see Agha and Malley, "The Lost Palestinians"; Milton-Edwards and
Crooke, "Elusive Ingredient"; Jonathan Steele, "Ostracizing Hamas Will Not
Help in the Search for Peace," *Guardian,* 15 July 2005. For an astute analysis
published in the aftermath of the Hamas victory, see Hussein Agha and Robert Malley, "Hamas: The Perils of Power," *New York Review of Books,* 9 Mar.
2006, 22–24.

89. Articles 11 and 13 of Chapter III of the Hamas covenant. See Mishal and Sela,
The Palestinian Hamas, 181, 183; on the willingness to abide by *hudna,* see
Agha and Malley, "The Lost Palestinians," and Milton-Edwards and Crooke,
"Elusive Ingredient," 45; Danny Rubinstein, "Haniyeh: Withdrawal to 1967
Borders Will Lead to Peace," *Haaretz,* 23 May 2006; "Former Mossad Chief
Calls for Long-Term Deal with Hamas," *Haaretz,* 27 May 2006.

90. Article 27 of Chapter IV of the Hamas covenant. See Mishal and Sela, *The
Palestinian Hamas,* 192–193; Steele, "Ostracizing Hamas."

91. Arnon Regular, "Hamas Leader Says Charter not Koran," *Haaretz,* 22 Sept.
2005; Chris McGreal, "Ceasefire Will End if Israelis Block Elections, Says
Hamas," *Guardian,* 22 Sept. 2005.

92. Milton-Edwards and Crooke, "Elusive Ingredient," 51.

93. Meron Benvenisti, "What Kind of Bi-national State?" *Haaretz*, 20 Nov. 2003; Said, *End of the Peace Process*, 112; Khalidi, *Resurrecting Empire*, 151.

94. Laqueur, *A History of Zionism*, 595; Meron Benvenisti, *Intimate Enemies: Jews and Arabs in a Shared Land* (Berkeley: University of California Press, 1995), 233. On the apparent posturing in favor of the binational idea, see, for example, Tarazi, "Two Peoples, One State."

95. Tarazi, "Two Peoples, One State"; Benvenisti, *Intimate Enemies*, 234, 232. On Peres's view, see Shimon Peres, *The New Middle East* (New York: Henry Holt, 1993).

96. Stanley Fischer, "Building Palestinian Prosperity," *Foreign Policy* 93 (Winter 1993–1994): 60–75; Barak interview in *Haaretz*, 18 June 1999.

97. Wasserstein, *Israel and Palestine*, 150–152. On the discrimination experienced by Arab minorities in the Jewish state, see Elia Zureik, *The Palestinians in Israel: A Study in Internal Colonialism* (London: Routledge and Kegan Paul, 1979); David Grossman, *Sleeping on a Wire: Conversations with Palestinians in Israel* (New York: Picador, 2003); and Yoav Peled, "Ethnic Democracy and the Legal Construction of Citizenship: Arab Citizens of the Jewish State," *American Political Science Review* 86, 2 (June 1992): 432–443. On the involvement of some Palestinian citizens of Israel in the first intifada, see Schiff and Yaari, *Intifada*, chap. 6.

98. Benvenisti, *Intimate Enemies*, 234.

Conclusion

1. I. William Zartman, "Dynamics and Constraints in Negotiations in Internal Conflicts," in Zartman, ed., *Elusive Peace: Negotiating an End to Civil Wars* (Washington, DC: Brookings Institution Press, 1995), 20–21.

Acknowledgments

This book draws on numerous trips to contested lands between 1991 and 2005. While it is not feasible to name the very many people and organizations who have helped me to learn over the years, I would like to mention Aida Velic-Hotic in Bosnia, Ved Bhasin in Kashmir, Peter Loizos in Cyprus, the peace secretariat of the Liberation Tigers of Tamil Eelam in Sri Lanka, and the Ben-Gurion University of the Negev in Israel. Among friends in London, Zhand Shakibi, Nebojsa Vladisavljevic, and Tamara Kummer took a particular interest in the writing of this book. I would like to thank Kathleen McDermott, my commissioning editor at Harvard University Press, for her support of this project, the second book we have worked on together in the space of just three years. Thanks are also due to the Board of Syndics of Harvard University Press, three anonymous reviewers for the Press, and cartographer Philip Schwartzberg. My mother, Krishna Bose, and brother, Sugata Bose, have always been deeply supportive. I miss the calm and loving presence of my father, Sisir K. Bose, who passed away in the autumn of 2000, but his memory is a powerful inspiration.

The Bosnia map is based on information from the Office of the United Nations High Commissioner for Refugees. The maps of Jammu and Kashmir and the Kashmir Valley originally appeared in my book *Kashmir: Roots of Conflict, Paths to Peace* (Harvard University Press). The following maps are based on material from the Palestinian Academic Society for the Study of International Affairs: the Gaza Strip (Jan de Jong); the West Bank; Hebron; Jerusalem and its environs; the Old City of Jerusalem (Jan de Jong).

Index